Working with
the under-threes:
training and
professional
development

EARLY INTERACTIONS

Working with the under-threes: training and professional development

Edited by
Lesley Abbott and
Helen Moylett

OPEN UNIVERSITY PRESS
Buckingham · Philadelphia

Open University Press
Celtic Court
22 Ballmoor
Buckingham
MK18 1XW

email: enquiries@openup.co.uk
world wide web: www.openup.co.uk

and
325 Chestnut Street
Philadelphia, PA 19106, USA

First published 1997
Reprinted 2002

A catalogue record of this book is available from the British Library

ISBN   0 335 19837 6 (pb)   0 335 19838 4 (hb)

A catalog record for this book is available from the Library of Congress

Copy-edited and typeset by The Running Head Limited, London and Cambridge
Printed in Great Britain by Biddles Ltd, www.biddles.co.uk

To Connor, Evie and Kathleen and all the under-threes
from whom we learned so much

Contents

Contributors   ix
Acknowledgements   xii
Abbreviations   xiii

Series introduction – why focus on the under-threes?   1

Introduction   7

1 'I know I can do it' – training to work with the under-threes   13
   Lesley Abbott

2 'Have experience: want to learn' – creating a new pathway to
   professionalism with a little European money and a lot of hard
   work from our friends   35
   Anne-Marie Graham

3 'I'm not working with the under-threes!' – the need for continuing
   professional development within an early years team   51
   Jean Coward

4 'Buildings as well as systems can appear as negative to males in
   early years settings' – exploring the role and status of the
   male educarer working with the under-threes   60
   Terry Gould

5 'We need to know' – identifying and supporting very young
   children with special educational needs   78
   Sylvia Phillips

6 'I'm like a friend, someone to chat to . . . but a professional friend'
   – how educators develop positive relationships with parents
   and children   95
   Chris Marsh

7 'There are lots of activities for him to do and plenty
   of help and care from the educarers' – supporting
   under-threes and their parents in a parent-toddler group   107
   Jenny Lively and Karen McMahon

8 'Who is listening?' – protecting young children from abuse   129
   John Powell

9 'Our very best show' – registration and inspection,
   implications for work with under-threes   141
   Rosemary Rodger and Shirley Barnes

   Concluding thoughts – drawing the threads together   162
   Lesley Abbott

Index   168

Contributors

Lesley Abbott is Professor of Early Childhood Education at the Manchester Metropolitan University where she leads the Early Years team. She is responsible for early years training and development at pre-service and in-service levels for teachers and other early years professionals. She has successfully introduced one of the first multi-professional degrees in the country – the BA (Hons) in Early Childhood Studies – and is involved in a range of projects designed to increase training opportunities for all early years professionals. She was a member of the Council for the Accreditation of Teacher Education (CATE), the Rumbold Committee and the steering group for the RSA Early Learning Project. She has contributed nationally and internationally to the development of early years work and is Director of the research project 'Shaping the Future – Educare for the Under Threes'. She has written a number of books on play in the early years and on training and has recently co-edited the successful *Quality Education in the Early Years*.

Helen Moylett is a Senior Lecturer in Education Studies at the Manchester Metropolitan University. She has worked in several inner-city Manchester primary schools in both early and later years settings, both as a class teacher and as an advisory teacher. She was a home–school liaison teacher for four years and continues to pursue her interest in home–school issues through her research and work with students. She is particularly interested in the ways in which practitioners can reflect upon and research their practice with a view to improving it.

Anne-Marie Graham is Childcare Development Officer with the Kirklees Early Years Service. She gained a BA in 1965 at the University of Wales, a Diploma in Education in 1966 at the University of Durham and worked as a teacher in adult and further education both full- and part-time for many years. She has three grown-up children. As a playgroup worker she became involved in many campaigns for more and better childcare provision. For the last five years she has worked as a local authority early years development worker (first with Calderdale, now with Kirklees) involved with a variety of partnerships aimed at increasing the quality, quantity and accessibility of early years provision.

Jean Coward is Coordinator of Bradshaw Community Nursery Centre with Salford Social Services and Education Department. She has a range of experiences in early years education including nursery classes and schools, special schools and community nursery centres. While being involved for four years with Salford's Oracy Project, she developed an interest in the different ways adults talk and listen to young children. On her recent completion of a BEd (Hons) at the Manchester Metropolitan University she became involved in work with children under three years of age and the adults who work with them.

Terry Gould is currently a nursery teacher at a community nursery centre jointly funded by the local education authority and social services. Terry came into teaching as a mature student, gaining a first class honours BEd degree; he has recently been awarded an MA in teaching. He has chosen to work with nursery-aged children because of his belief in the importance of this period of a child's learning, believing that it substantially underpins much of a child's future achievements. He believes that nursery children benefit from having opportunities to develop relationships with both male and female educarers and speaks positively on his experiences of working with under-fives. He advocates that all male teachers should give serious consideration to spending some time working with this age group.

Sylvia Phillips is Principal Lecturer at Didsbury School of Education, the Manchester Metropolitan University, where she leads the Special Educational Needs team. She has responsibility for coordinating the special educational needs (SEN) component of initial teacher education courses and the development and organization of specialist in-service courses in SEN, many of which emphasize a multi-professional approach. Currently, she is involved in a European project on 'Teacher Education for Inclusive Education' and is co-director of a research project investigating the experiences of children with epilepsy and their parents during events leading up to diagnosis and assessment. She has a particular interest in SEN in the early years and works closely with the Early Years team.

Chris Marsh is a Senior Lecturer at the Manchester Metropolitan University where she teaches on the BEd, PGCE Primary and BA Early Childhood Studies courses and provides in-service work for local authorities. She has taught nursery- and primary-aged children. Her major research interests include the relationships between educators, parents and children in the early years. She was involved in the partnership research project 'Quality Education for the Under Fives' (Salford/the Manchester Metropolitan University 1994) and is currently involved in the 'Educare for the Under Threes' research project funded by the Esmée Fairbairn Charitable Trust. She has published in the field of early interactions.

Jenny Lively is a Senior Educarer and team member in a large, multi-professional team in a combined nursery centre which feeds over 40 schools. She is
responsible for extended day provision and liaison with other professionals.
She has worked in the centre for 27 years and has seen the changes and positive developments in the move from social service provision to joint
LEA–social services funding. Her development from nursery nurse to Senior
Educarer via post-qualifying study has reinforced her commitment to the
under-threes and their families and to the concept of 'educare'.

Karen McMahon is Deputy Head of Care in a large nursery centre. She completed her nursery nurse training in 1971 and since then has had a range of
experience in day nurseries, nursery classes and infant schools. In 1991 she
completed the Diploma in Post Qualifying Studies and undertook a number
of courses arranged by social services. Her community role involves liaison
with health visitors, social and family resource workers. In addition to her
role in the nursery centre she is responsible, with Jenny Lively, for organizing and running a thriving toddler group.

John Powell is a Senior Lecturer at the Manchester Metropolitan University
and is responsible for the development of the multi-professional Centre for
Early Childhood Studies. Having gained the CQSW at Manchester Poly-
technic in 1980, he was a practising social worker and worked in a team
dealing with families and young children in north Manchester. In 1988 he
began working for the South Manchester College as a lecturer teaching social
studies to NNEB and BTEC Diploma students, as well as the DPQS. In 1992 he
gained an MA in teaching at the Manchester Metropolitan University. He is
currently engaged in PhD research in the area of equal opportunities. He is
course leader of the interdisciplinary BA (Hons) Early Childhood Studies
degree and director of a number of innovative projects in early years training.

Shirley Barnes is a local authority inspection and registration officer and has a
particular research interest in provision for the under-threes. She is one of
the first students to embark on the multi-professional BA (Hons) in Early
Childhood Studies and will graduate in 1997. She has undertaken a special
study in provision for under-threes as part of her degree course.

Rosemary Rodger is Senior Lecturer in the School of Education at the Manchester Metropolitan University and a member of the Early Years team. She
was coordinator of a joint local authority and university project, the aim of
which was to identify quality factors in provision for the under-fives. She is a
registered Ofsted inspector and trainer and is co-editor with Lesley Abbott of
Quality Education in the Early Years.

Acknowledgements

As the series title suggests, this book is about interactions. These have taken place in a variety of contexts and with many people of very different ages. Without these interactions this book would not have been possible.

As editors our first debt of gratitude is to all the contributors who have provided a broad spectrum of experiences and perspectives on their work with the under-threes. They have allowed us to share their enthusiasm, concerns, successes and hopes – but above all, their commitment to young children.

We are grateful to all those under-threes who have allowed us to share their experiences and to eavesdrop on some of their 'early interactions'.

We are particularly indebted to the Esmée Fairbairn Charitable Trust who, with the Manchester Metropolitan University, have jointly funded the research project on which some of these chapters are based. We acknowledge their commitment to funding in this important field. We are very grateful to the administrative staff of the Research Base in the School of Education at the Manchester Metropolitan University, in particular Jean Davidson for her tireless and good humoured support, together with Trish Gladdis and Barbara Ashcroft; also to Julia Gillen for her advice, support, professionalism and dedication in helping us with the difficult and demanding task of editing all the contributions. Special thanks are also due to Mags Stopford and her family and to Jo Mathieson for allowing us to use their words and experience as childminders.

Tribute is also paid to the local authorities and centres on which we have relied, in particular, Stockport, Salford, Manchester and Rochdale LEAs; Bradshaw Community Nursery Centre (Salford), Briercliffe Nursery (Burnley), Charnwood Nursery (Stockport), Higher Downs Nursery (Trafford), Hilary's Nursery (Mold, Clwyd), Hollywood Park Nursery Centre (Stockport), Ladywell Community Nursery Centre (Salford), Mosside Children's Centre (Manchester), Old Moat Children's Centre (Manchester), Princess Christian Nursery (Manchester), Sparrow Hill Community School (Rochdale) and Family Day Care Centres in Western Australia.

Without all these people this series would never have been written.

Abbreviations

ADCE	Advanced Diploma in Child Care and Education
BTEC	Business and Technology Education Council
CACHE	Council for Awards in Children's Care and Education
CATs	Credit Accumulation and Transfer points
CQSW	Certificate of Qualification in Social Work
DES	Department of Education and Science
DfE	Department for Education
DfEE	Department for Education and Employment
DoH	Department of Health
DPQS	Diploma in Post-Qualifying Studies
GNVQ	General National Vocational Qualification
HE	higher education
HMI	Her Majesty's Inspectorate of Schools
HND	Higher National Diploma
LEA	local education authority
NCMA	National Childminding Association
NNEB	Certificate or Diploma of the Nursery Nurse Examining Board
NVQ	National Vocational Qualification
Ofsted	Office for Standards in Education
OND	Ordinary National Diploma
PGCE	Postgraduate Certficate in Education
RSA	Royal Society for the Encouragement of the Arts, Manufacture and Commerce
SCAA	School Curriculum and Assessment Authority
SEN	special educational needs
STAC	Specialist Teaching Assistant Certificate
SVQ	Scottish Vocational Qualification

Series introduction – why focus on the under-threes?

The Carnegie Task Force report on meeting the needs of young children (1994: 4) points to the 'critical importance of the first three years as being a crucial "starting point" on the child's educational journey'.

The series 'Early interactions' consists of two books, *Working with the Under-threes: Training and Professional Development* and *Working with the Under-threes: Responding to Children's Needs*. These two books aim to address some of the key issues surrounding the young child and the family as the first steps are taken on this all-important educational journey. They are intended to complement each other but are capable of standing alone.

Working with the Under-threes: Training and Professional Development both offers information on, and raises questions about, the kinds of training and professional development and support available to the wide range of adults who work with young children. It is written by a range of people with different experiences and perspectives on early education and care. Both trainers and practitioners share their experiences and raise questions which, it is hoped, will both challenge and encourage those with responsibility for children at this critical stage in their learning.

Working with the Under-threes: Responding to Children's Needs focuses upon ways in which researchers, parents and practitioners seek to meet the diverse needs of young children in specific ways. Important questions are raised with regard to children's rights and entitlement, and ways in which early interactions with people, environment, culture, curriculum and context help to shape the educational lives of children under 3.

The focus of both books is clearly on those adults responsible for the care and education of the youngest children in our society. Their experiences, views, roles and responsibilities are shared and examined from both theoretical and practical standpoints. Acknowledgement is made of the holistic nature of early learning, in which care and education are viewed as complementary and inseparable.

Writing an introduction to any new book inevitably makes the editors reflect on how far our original vision has been realized, and on what has emerged in the process. The 'intended outcomes', as anyone involved in course planning knows, whether at the level of a curriculum for children under 3 in the nursery, or the implementation of a new honours degree in a university, are those things which give the writers a real buzz of excitement and achievement, or a real headache, as they recognize just how much more there is to be written!

So guarding against the danger of writing a concluding rather than an introductory chapter, we outline some of the key aims in putting together this book.

The main aim, we both admit unashamedly, is a selfish one. At the time of writing we are both totally involved in the lives of children under 3. As Director of a two-year research project looking at 'Educare for the Under Threes', funded by the Esmée Fairbairn Charitable Trust and the Manchester Metropolitan University (1995–7), Lesley is working closely with the Early Years team at the university and with parents and practitioners in the UK and other European countries in the identification of key factors in the provision of quality out-of-home experiences for children under 3.

Helen is even more involved and has a very real vested interest in 'early interactions' as an initiator and responder to the needs and demands of her own lively under-three! Her experiences and those of Connor are discussed in Chapter 1 of *Working with the Under-threes: Responding to Children's Needs*, in which some very real dilemmas facing parents and professionals at this crucial stage in both adults' and children's lives are addressed.

Both of us have had many years' experience working with children of all ages and in planning and providing training and support for all the professionals responsible for them. We share a strong commitment to the principle of 'educare', i.e. that care and education are inseparable and that anyone who is responsible for young children is an 'educarer'.

Our work over many years with students training to teach young children, and our partnerships with schools and other early years establishments whose staff are on our in-service programme, working at diploma, degree or masters level, has convinced us of the importance of interdisciplinary involvement in the lives of young children.

Helen's work in the early 1980s as a home–school liaison teacher helped her to understand the difficult relationship parents often have with educational establishments. On the one hand, though they have love, commitment and a deep knowledge about their child, on the other, they may be swiftly deskilled by 'the experts'. She is convinced that if parents and educarers are to work together effectively throughout a child's educational career, they have to respect each other's roles and expertise and start communicating as soon as they meet – usually long before the age of compulsory schooling. Lesley's work with early years professionals in schools and centres convinced her long before 'official recommendations' were made that multiprofessional training and teamwork were the answer to shared understanding and continuity in children's learning.

As a contributor to the Rumbold Report (DES 1990), *Start Right* (the RSA Early Learning Report) (Ball 1994) and the Report of the Early Years Training Group (Pugh 1996), she became increasingly aware of the need for training and support for the vast number of early years educators currently working with children under 3, issues which are addressed in Chapter 1.

A number of factors influenced our decision to use the series title 'Early interactions'. The first is our belief, borne out by research (Trevarthen 1992; Selleck and Goldschmied 1996) that from birth, babies are effective initiators of early interactions.

Second, the power of early interactions in shaping future attitudes and dispositions is reinforced by research findings and our own experience. New research demonstrates young children's amazing capacity for learning in their earliest years (Trevarthen 1992; Gardner 1993; Goleman 1996); many of the chapters reflect this capacity and describe ways in which parents and educators harness and develop the skills, enthusiasm, curiosity and motivation which young children bring to every experience.

Our third reason for choosing 'Early interactions' as a series title is because this was exactly the process through which we went. As editors we engaged in early interactions in talking about why we considered a book like this was needed, what our aims were and who the contributors would be; we also realized that, because of our work in which we are in constant dialogue with a whole range of professionals, many of whom work with children under 3, we had access to a group of people with a vast range of knowledge, understanding, skill and commitment. Why not provide a much needed forum in which dialogue and interactions could begin to take place?

We are in the privileged position of having known the authors of the chapters for many years in different capacities: as colleagues within the university or local authorities in which we work, as former in-service students or ex-students, or as parents, childminders and managers of services across different sectors and departments. It was *our* 'early interactions' with these colleagues which resulted in both books.

The many issues addressed are intended to provide information and provoke further discussion. Each contributor has written from their own perspective and experience; there are still many other points of view which we have not had space to represent. Some chapters are based on research findings, particularly from the 'Educare for the Under Threes' project (Manchester Metropolitan University 1996); others reflect the day-to-day experiences of particular practitioners and the under-threes with whom they spend their time.

Key themes include the identification of, and provision for, children with special educational needs, relationships between practitioners and parents, children's rights, new training opportunities and initiatives, equality of opportunity and child protection.

It is timely, at a stage where the future of early education and care is on the political agenda, that those issues which most affect the youngest children and their educarers are acknowledged and discussed.

Issues are raised throughout concerning quality – a much defined yet still elusive concept (Abbott and Rodger 1994; Moss and Pence 1994). Questions are asked about quality interactions, care, education, training, childminding, parenting, play, programmes and support.

In the introduction to his excellent report for the Bernard Van Leer Foundation on pathways to quality, Woodhead (1996) states:

> Our perception of 'quality' in early childhood programmes can be likened to our perception of the rainbow composed as it is of sunshine and rain, it changes with every shift in perspective. And just as people have searched for the illusory crock of gold at the rainbow's end, so development experts search for universal definitions and standards of quality. But quality is contextual . . . Sensitivity to diversity and to one's own preconceptions should be key elements informing all early childhood work.

Because of the diversity of roles and experience of the writers of these chapters it is inevitable that a range of contexts and perspectives are represented. We hope that readers will recognize and welcome these diversities.

While we agree with Woodhead that 'quality is contextual' we also consider that there are certain underlying principles which should underpin any educare service, programme or interaction, irrespective of context. These are to do with the rights and entitlements of children however young they might be.

Cathy Nutbrown (1996) in the title of her book encompasses children's right to 'respectful educators' and to become 'capable learners'. She quotes the four goals for a policy on children held by the Children's Welfare Commission in Denmark (Vilien 1993):

- to respect the child as an individual in the family and in society;
- to give the child a central position in the life of grown-ups;
- to promote – in a wider sense – the physical conditions in which children grow up;
- to promote equal opportunities in the conditions of life of children, both in a material and in a cultural sense.

While we are aware that in Denmark national policy ensures that young children are valued and those who work with them are respected, surely these aims should hold for all young children in all societies and cultures.

Siraj-Blatchford (1996: 23) also emphasizes the need for 'promoting respect for all groups and individuals regardless of "difference"'. She points out that

> Despite the calm and friendly appearance that most early childcare and education settings display there may be a great deal of inequality in for instance, the interactions, displays, policies or curriculum that staff offer. These are important issues to be considered because they concern the early socialisation of both the oppressed and the oppressors. In other words, here we have a real concern for people with, and without, power to affect one another's behaviour, their actions, intentions and beliefs.

Goldschmied and Jackson (1994) talk about 'people under three', not babies, toddlers, or even children, but people with rights which include being treated with dignity and respect.

Article 2 (1) of the UN Convention on the Rights of the Child (UNICEF 1989) states:

1. The States Parties to the present Convention shall respect and ensure the rights set forth in the Convention to each child within their jurisdiction without discrimination of any kind, irrespective of the child's or his or her parents' or legal guardian's race, colour, sex, language, religion, political or other opinion, national, ethnic or social origin, property, disability, birth or other status.

2. States Parties shall take all appropriate measures to ensure that the child is protected against all forms of discrimination or punishment on the basis of the status, activities, expressed opinions, or beliefs of the child's parents, legal guardians or family members.

Throughout both books in this series the writers have focused on specific aspects of 'educare' with the intention of addressing both the needs and rights of young children. We recognize the need for children under 3 to be nurtured in a safe, supportive environment in which they are given appropriate experiences which provide them with opportunities to learn and grow. *Working with the Under-threes: Training and Professional Development* focuses on the training and professional development needs of the adults who work with under-threes in out-of-home settings. Children have the right to positive relationships with adults who will foster their self-concept and develop their self-esteem, will value their home language and provide opportunities to acquire basic literacy and oracy skills. We recognize young children's entitlement to be treated as 'special' and for their needs to be properly met in an environment which supports and fosters their growing independence. *Working with the Under-threes: Responding to Children's Needs* also relates to these entitlements but concentrates on particular adults responding to children's needs.

To the 'educarer', whether as parent, childminder, nursery officer, teacher or playgroup leader, is given the responsibility for providing the kinds of quality experiences which are instrumental in bringing about appropriate *early interactions*.

References

Abbott, L. and Rodger, R. (eds) (1994) *Quality Education in the Early Years*. Buckingham: Open University Press.

Ball, C. (1994) *Start Right: The Importance of Early Learning*. London: Royal Society for the Encouragement of the Arts, Manufacture and Commerce.

Carnegie Task Force (1994) *Starting Points – Meeting the Needs of Our Youngest Children*. New York: Carnegie Corporation.

Department of Education and Science [DES] (1990) *Starting with Quality, the Report of the Committee of Inquiry into the Quality of Educational Experience Offered to 3 and 4-year-olds*. London: HMSO.

Gardner, H. (1993) *Multiple Intelligences: The Theory in Practice*. New York: Basic Books.

Goldschmied, E. and Jackson, S. (1994) *People Under Three*. London: Routledge.

Goleman, D. (1996) *Emotional Intelligence – Why it Can Matter more than IQ*. London: Bloomsbury.

Moss, P. and Pence, A. (1994) *Valuing Quality in Early childhood Services*. London: Paul Chapman.

Nutbrown, C. (ed.) (1996) *Respectful Educators – Capable Learners, Children's Rights and Early Education*. London: Paul Chapman.

Pugh, G. (ed.) (1996) *Training for Work in the Early Years*, Report of the Early Years Training Group. London: National Children's Bureau.

Selleck, D. and Goldschmied, E. (1996) Communication between babies – video resource pack. London: National Children's Bureau.

Siraj-Blatchford, I. (1996) Language, culture and difference: challenging inequality and promoting respect, in C. Nutbrown (ed.) *Respectful Educators – Capable Learners, Children's Rights and Early Education*. London: Paul Chapman.

Trevarthen, C. (1992) An infant's motives for speaking and thinking in the culture, in A. H. Wold (ed.) *The Dialogue Alternative*. Oxford: Oxford University Press.

UNICEF (1989) *Convention on the Rights of the Child*. New York: United Nations.

Vilien, K. (1993) Pre-school education in Denmark, in T. David (ed.) *Educational Provision for our Youngest Children: European Perspectives*. London: Paul Chapman.

Woodhead, M. (1996) In search of the rainbow, *Early Child Development Practice and Reflections*, 10. The Hague: Bernard Van Leer Foundation.

Introduction

Each of the writers in this book recognizes with Nutbrown (1996) the right of every child to a 'respectful educator', whether that educator has the title of parent, carer, nursery nurse, childminder, teacher, nursery coordinator, special needs assistant, toddler group leader, social worker or inspector.

The following chapters are each written from one of these perspectives. Chapter 1 raises important questions about training to work with the under-threes, including those concerning availability, access, funding and appropriateness of early childhood training programmes and opportunities. It details the range of courses available and points to the importance of multi-professional training, which, in response to recent recommendations (DES 1990; National Commission 1993; Ball 1994) is now available in some, but not enough, areas of the country.

'I know I can do it' is a statement made by a student on one of the new interdisciplinary degrees (such as the BA (Hons) in Early Childhood Studies) offered on both a full- and part-time basis at the Manchester Metropolitan University and others such as Bristol, North London, Belfast and Canterbury.

The following comments sum up some of the feelings of students for whom access to this kind of training has previously been denied:

The exchange of ideas and information between the different professions represented has helped me to take a critical look at my workplace setting.

One of the main issues for me is that I have realized my potential and that I am as capable as the next person.

The idea of a multidisciplinary group of tutors, teaching students with a divergence of experience appealed to me. The focus of 'educare' fired me with enthusiasm.

Since commencing this course I feel that I am in a better position, not only to ensure that the minimum standards in childcare are maintained, but also to offer advice which will improve the services of those offering a good standard of care but wanting to improve it.

I undertook this course partly for my own professional development and job satisfaction, not with the idea of looking for promotion.

The student voice can also be heard in Chapter 2, in which Anne-Marie Graham reports on a European-funded project which provides a unique opportunity for women with minimal qualifications to be assessed for NVQ level 3, to gain an Advanced Diploma in Childcare and Education or to gain access to level 1 of the BA in Early Childhood Studies. In providing new opportunities in early years training, this partnership project between a local authority and institute of higher education offers a model for the future. It also raises the important question regarding funding for early years training and the need for government recognition of this area as a national priority. The Early Childhood Forum's draft discussion document (1995) recognized the contrast between the UK and European commitment to this important area: 'Most of our partner countries in the European Community and beyond have recognized the vital nature of national investment in provision which is staffed by people with appropriate, initial and continuing professional education and training.'

The need for continuing professional development is addressed by Jean Coward in Chapter 3. As coordinator of a community nursery centre she deals specifically with the ways in which staff development and support is handled in relation to in-house training and support. She writes honestly about the process necessary to bring about change in terms of both attitude and practice.

'I'm not working with the under-threes' is an understandable point of view particularly when staff feel that their initial training has not equipped them either to recognize the importance of this age group or to understand their needs and to respond appropriately. This chapter is a story of developing professionals and highlights the need for availability of a variety of training opportunities and providers in order to meet the diverse needs of a large staff in a community nursery centre.

In Chapter 4, Terry Gould – as one of that rare breed, the male educarer – examines the role of the male working with the under-threes. Drawing on his experience as a male and a teacher in a female, nursery-nurse-dominated, inner-city community nursery centre, he raises issues concerning the importance for young children of a male role model in a childcare setting. He also identifies ways in which relationships between parents and a male educarer can serve the needs of the family, particularly in the lives of children where mum is the lone 'caretaker'. His views may challenge both traditional and feminist ideas about women's roles in educare.

By means of case studies he discusses ways in which children's lives have been influenced by his presence. Some of the difficulties of being the only male are also recounted as he argues that 'buildings as well as systems can appear as negative to males in early years settings'.

Equality of opportunity is a key strand which permeates 'Early inter-actions'. Sylvia Phillips in Chapter 5 provides valuable insights into ways in which educarers can identify and support very young children with special educational needs. The crucial role of the adult working with children under 3 is highlighted, and by means of case studies she examines ways in which support can be offered, not only to the child, but to her family.

Quality interactions, examining ways in which educarers develop rela-tionships with parents and children, feature strongly in all chapters. In Chapter 6 Chris Marsh draws on the interim findings of a research project in which she is involved. *Educare for the Under Threes – Identifying Need and Opportunity* (Manchester Metropolitan University 1996) focuses on a number of key issues in the lives of young children. One of these is the concept of the 'key worker' and how this operates in two different nursery centres. This chapter highlights some of the advantages experienced by staff, parents and children of being able to identify a 'special' adult with whom relationships are forged.

The recognition that families and children require contact with the wider world of educare prior to the more formal signing on at the nursery at the age of 3, led Jenny Lively and Karen McMahon to start a toddler group. The group serves a wide area and offers quality educare experiences to children from birth to 2½ years and to their parents and carers, extended family, other groups, professionals, researchers and students. It is a lively ever-changing world of children and adults in which everyone is made to feel wel-come and valued. In Chapter 7 Jenny and Karen trace the development of the group as it grows and expands, so much so that a larger room is needed. They include comments from users and include examples of newsletters, events and comments which ensure that the group is constantly developing and responding to the needs of the community and of the nursery.

The UNICEF (1989) statement on children's rights and international pro-tection emphasizes the importance of ensuring the survival and develop-ment of children in all parts of the world, and the need to protect them from harm and exploitation, thus enabling them to participate in decisions directly affecting their lives.

John Powell in Chapter 8 shares his experience both as a social worker, and now as a trainer of early years professionals, and offers support in the important area of protecting young children from abuse. He offers practical support while drawing on the theoretical perspectives which underpin his work. By means of case studies he allows the reader to share in his work and offers further advice and resources for all those who have the lives of young children in their hands.

Ensing, a former HMI with particular responsibility for the early years, holds the view that 'Inspection, done properly, matters because its goal is to improve' (1996: 11). A BA Early Childhood Studies student who happens to be an inspection and registration officer with a local authority social services department also writes about the importance of the inspection process in her evaluation of the course:

I have been forced to take a closer look at my status as an Inspection Officer. I have never seen myself as being in a controlling role but I realize that the very words inspector and inspection conjure up the epitome of control. I prefer to see myself as a developer and supporter but I cannot avoid my statutory obligations to inspect. Realistically speaking you cannot have one without the other, I just need to get the balance right.

(Burgess 1995)

Getting the balance right particularly for the under-threes is the focus of Chapter 9, in which Rosemary Rodger and Shirley Barnes examine the role of the inspector and the inspection process as a professional development exercise. As social services and Ofsted inspectors respectively, they are involved in making judgements about appropriateness and quality in relation to provision for young children. Both are registered nursery inspectors and are involved in training as well as inspection. They raise important questions about the need for continuing professional development and support for all educare staff and see the inspection process as an important framework for ensuring that the issues of quality and appropriateness are addressed.

Woodhead (1996: 89) makes the important point that whatever age group we are working with,

Setting standards, assessing standards, measuring indicators – these are all key stages of quality development – with a number of provisos. If the aim is enhancing quality in context-relevant ways, they are best seen as: formative not evaluative; practical not bureaucratic; participatory not prescribed; offering guidelines not regulations, in a way that is dynamic and not fixed.

The aim of this book, then, is to provide a forum in which the support and training needs and experiences of early years professionals are identified and shared.

It is intended that the different perspectives, life experiences and degrees of expertise offered will provide not only a focus on 'early interactions' but also issues for discussion and staff development, thus leading to those all important *later interactions* too!

References

Ball, C. (1994) *Start Right: The Importance of Early Learning*. London: Royal Society for the Encouragement of the Arts, Manufacture and Commerce.

Burgess, G. (1995) Evaluation of first year of BA Early Childhood Studies degree, unpublished study, the Manchester Metropolitan University.

Department of Education and Science [DES] (1990) *Starting with Quality, the Report of the Committee of Inquiry into the Quality of Educational Experience Offered to 3 and 4-year-olds*. London: HMSO.

Ensing, J. (1996) Inspection of early years in schools, in C. Nutbrown (ed.) *Respectful Educators – Capable Learners, Children's Rights and Early Education*. London: Paul Chapman.

Goldschmied, E. and Jackson, S. (1994) *People Under Three*. London: Routledge.

Manchester Metropolitan University (1996) *Educare for the Under Threes – Identifying Need and Opportunity*, Interim Report. Manchester: The Manchester Metropolitan University.

National Commission on Education (1993) *Learning to Succeed: Report of the Paul Hamlyn Foundation, National Commission on Education*. London: Heinemann.

Nutbrown, C. (ed.) (1996) *Respectful Educators – Capable Learners, Children's Rights and Early Education*. London: Paul Chapman.

UNICEF (1989) *Convention on the Rights of the Child*. New York: United Nations.

Woodhead, M. (1996) In search of the rainbow, *Early Child Development Practice and Reflections*, 10. The Hague: Bernard Van Leer Foundation.

1 | 'I know I can do it' – training to work with the under-threes

Lesley Abbott

> One of the most significant factors in providing quality care and education for our youngest children is the appropriateness of the training received by the adults responsible for them.
>
> (Manchester Metropolitan University 1994: 1)

I have long been involved in the training and professional development of people working with young children or intending to enter that field. Most of them have been teachers.

My own experience in school had been in primary education – gradually working my way up (I prefer to call it 'up' rather than 'down') from teaching the junior age range to what I now know to be the most rewarding and the most important stage, the early years.

Moving into teacher training in the 1970s, life was fairly uncomplicated. The main qualification for the majority of teachers was the Teaching Certificate, gained after three years in a college of education or one year in a college or university department following a first degree.

Students usually specialized within the primary age range in either infants or juniors. The infant course, if you were lucky enough to be in a college in an area with a strong nursery tradition, combined nursery/infant training with requirements that teaching practice should be undertaken in both nursery and infant schools and classes. Many courses started at 5 (the compulsory school starting age) giving the strong message – which unfortunately is still around – that what happens earlier is not as important.

My work in teacher training for the early years, then defined as 3- to 7-year-olds, took me into a range of establishments including separate nursery schools, nursery classes attached to primary schools, and infant schools; in some there were nursery classes, in others children arrived aged 4 or 5 from a vast array of other types of provision, for example playgroup, crèche, childminder or straight from home. For the first time I encountered the combined nursery centre, jointly funded by social services and the education authority. This establishment provided combined care and education for children from birth to 5. Although the age of admission has since been revised and very young babies are more likely to be in the care of a sponsored childminder, nevertheless this seemed to me at the time to be the ideal kind of provision to meet the needs of babies, young children and working parents. I was in the fortunate position of working with an authority with a long history of good nursery provision, who, in reviewing their policy and realizing that care and education were falsely separated, decided that the combined nursery centre would be the way forward for their authority.

It was about this time that the nursery nurse – or NNEB as they were (and still are) fondly called – became significant in my life. I got to know many of them in their workplace. I had met many nursery nurses in my visits to students and teachers in schools. In the combined centres I was outnumbered by them! The long hours in which the centres were open, early morning until early evening, 51 weeks of the year, meant that a shift system had to operate. Although ostensibly my visit was to see the teacher or teacher training student, I was invariably involved in discussion with the nursery nurses who were working closely in the centre with students in training or with their teachers who may have been working for an in-service award.

All this seems a long time ago, but looking back it was this experience which sowed the seed for the kinds of training opportunities to which I am committed and for which I have worked over the years.

The close involvement of the nursery nurse and teacher in planning for, supporting and assessing the needs of the young children for whom they were responsible meant that, in order to do this effectively, they needed to have a shared understanding of underlying principles relating to their work. Unfortunately most courses available for teachers were not open to the nursery nurse or classroom assistants. So much for collaboration, coordination and communication – the three important Cs on which good team work relies! Access and funding were the main barriers, and for many early years educators nothing has changed.

In an effort to redress this balance I encouraged early years teachers to bring along their nursery nurse to in-service courses, but whereas teachers were able to gain a certificate or diploma, non-teaching staff were unable to gain accreditation even for course attendance.

The publication of the Rumbold Report *Starting with Quality* (DES 1990) reflected the concerns of the multi-professional, interdisciplinary, cross-sector committee of which I was proud to be a member. One of the major concerns was that the barriers which prevented the provision of opportunities for joint training should be removed and that access to appropriate and continuing professional development should be available for all early years workers.

For someone whose background had been mainly concerned with teacher education, in researching training opportunities for other staff it came as a surprise to realize just how many different roles there are within the early years field.

My involvement in the research project which aimed to identify quality factors in the care and education of the under-fives (Manchester Metropolitan University 1994) and more recently in research into provision for the under-threes (Abbott *et al.* 1996) strengthened my commitment to wider training opportunities for all early years staff.

Figure 1.1 identifies some of the questions raised in a consideration of issues relating to training for work with the under-threes. There are many more, and the reader will no doubt be able to add considerably to the information under each heading.

Moss and Penn (1996) identify the six most commonly employed workers as being teachers (7,000 excluding reception), nursery nurses (education – 7,000), nursery nurses (social services – 7,500), playgroup workers (40,000), childminders (100,000) and private day nursery nurses (25,000). Supporting

---

Who works with the under-threes?

Parents, childminders, nursery nurses, teachers, playgroup leaders, family centre workers, day nursery staff, paediatric nurses, ancillary staff, play workers, non-teaching assistants, social services staff, voluntary workers, private nursery staff, community workers, special needs staff.

Where do they work?

Private nurseries, social services day nurseries, combined centres, parent-toddler groups, pre-school playgroups, community nursery centres, workplace nurseries, crèches, hospitals' assessment units, family centres, nursery schools (LEA), voluntary sector provision.

Where and how are they trained?

(It is not always possible to match the type and level of training with the worker. In the case of teachers this is fairly straightforward – although course content varies – but the range of qualifications of those working in other forms of provision is often extremely wide ranging)

Parenting classes, NVQ level 2–3, childminding, NCMA training, Early Learning Alliance, Montessori training, social work, nursing, in-house training, local authority training, special needs training, FE college, HE (university or college), distance learning, workplace training, assessment centre.

What qualifications do they gain? Examples include:

Montessori diploma
NVQ level 2–3
BTEC ⎤   Child care,
OND ⎟   nursery nursing
HND ⎦   qualifications
Advanced Diploma in Child
  Care and Education (ADCE)
BEd degree
BA Early Childhood Studies
  degree
Postgraduate Certificate of
  Education (PGCE)
Childminding qualification.

Figure 1.1 Training for work with the under-threes

this finding, Curtis and Hevey (1996), in their review of training for early years workers, point out that it sometimes comes as a surprise to find that the majority of day care and pre-school education services in the UK are not staffed by teachers but by

> a largely unqualified army of more than 200,000 childcare and education workers. In England and Wales alone there are roughly 100,000 self-employed childminders and at least 50,000 playgroup leaders and assistants in some 20,000 playgroups. Workers with young children and their families are also found in day nurseries, nursery and primary schools, crèches, parent and toddler groups, family centres, parent support and home visiting schemes, toy libraries, play buses and many other types of provision.
>
> (Pugh 1996a: 212)

The Early Childhood Forum, representing 36 different early years organizations, makes the point that

> Those who work with our youngest children, right from birth, need a range of underpinning knowledge and relevant experience with babies, young children, their families and other workers, in order to be considered fit to have the privilege of fostering the talents of our most precious national resource.
>
> (Early Childhood Forum 1995: 1)

As a member of the Early Learning Inquiry undertaken by the Royal Society for the Arts, I was encouraged by the concern expressed for an increase in training opportunities.

'Working with young children is a complex and demanding task' as the Start Right Report recognized (Ball 1994). The complexities (in terms of roles and qualifications, services and training opportunities) were identified by Hevey and Windle (1990) in their occupational mapping survey of ten local authority areas in which they identified some 85 distinct job roles of early years workers. Because roles are so diverse (depending upon the employing service, sector or department) it is not possible, except perhaps in the case of teaching, to equate a particular type of training or qualification with a specific role.

In Figure 1.2 (pp. 18–19) Moss and Penn (1996: 100) identify the range of staff and complexities of training in the early years field.

As far back as 1975 Mia Kellmer Pringle in her book *The Needs of Children* (1975: 148) made the important point that 'A willingness to devote adequate resources to the care and education of children is the hallmark of a civilized society as well as an investment in our future.'

One of the most important resources is an appropriately trained adult. A number of influential reports, published in recent years, have focused upon the need for training opportunities to meet the needs of the wide range of adults presently employed in work with the under-threes.

Reference has already been made to the publication of the *Report of the Committee of Inquiry into the Quality of Education Offered to 3 and 4-year-olds*

(DES 1990) which led to discussions regarding possibilities for joint training and cooperation between departments and sectors. The Committee stated:

> We see as essential needs: a closer linkage between the three strands of health, care and education in initial and in-service training. A pattern of vocational training and qualifications for child care workers which will bridge the gap between the vocational and academic qualifications, safeguarding both the rigour and relevance of initial training for teachers of the under fives; and affording improved opportunities of in-service training for childcare workers in education settings.
>
> (DES 1990: 27)

One of the most significant developments in which I have been involved in an effort to improve opportunities for high level interdisciplinary training was the introduction of the BA (Hons) Early Childhood Studies degree.

In recent years a number of integrated degree courses such as the multidisciplinary BA (Hons) Early Childhood Studies degree have been developed in a number of universities and colleges. In 1993 support for these new developments came from the National Commission on Education:

> We place particular emphasis on appropriate training. Whether in day-care facilities, playgroups, nursery schools and classes and in primary school infant classes, the education of children under school age shows the responsibility of staff with an appropriate early years educational qualification. Teaching very young children is a complex task, demanding a high level of skill and understanding. The Commission supports graduate level training. We welcome the efforts now being made to establish a variety of routes to qualification, including higher level NVQs and modular degrees specialising in early childhood study, which might be combined with teacher training. Consideration should also be given to incorporating a multi-professional dimension in training so that both child care and education are covered.
>
> (National Commission on Education 1993: 132)

The Audit Commission's (1996) inspection of over 50 early years settings found strengths and weaknesses in all types, but two features emerged as being common to all the highest graded settings. These were: 'staff trained specifically for working with young children and the planning of work appropriate to children's needs' (p. 7).

The 'educare' concept

The Commission also noted (p. 7) that:

> All services for young children contribute to both education and care . . . some nurseries and playgroups explicitly combine education and care in their aims. In some countries the connection between care and education is recognized in national policy. For example, Spain passed a law in 1990 which seeks to guarantee the right to education for children

Type of provision	Number of children	Hours	Ages	Cost to parents (approx.)
Day care	% of 0–4			
Childminders	9%	All day	0–4	£1.50/hour £50/week
Local authority day nurseries/family centres	<1%	Some all day, some sessional	0–4 (but few under 2)	Means tested
Private day nurseries, partnership and workplace nurseries	3.5%	All day	0–4	£55–£160/week depending on age of child and avail-ability of subsidy
Education and play	% of 3–4			
LEA nursery schools and classes	27%	Term time: usually 2½ hrs/day	3–4	Free
Infant classes	24%	Term time: 9 a.m.–3.30 p.m.	mainly 4	Free
Playgroups	60% (1.8 children/ place)	2½ hours for 2–3 days a week, some all day	2½–4	£2.00 for a 2½ hour session
Private nursery and other schools	3.5%	9 a.m.–3.30 p.m.	2½–4	Various fees

Services on which there are no national statistics

Combined nursery centres – about 100 centres	All day	0–4	Education free; day care means-tested
Family centres (may include some local authority day nurseries) – about 500 members of Family Centre Network (1994)	Usually all day	Vary	Vary
Out of school/holiday clubs – 1,700 clubs (December 1994)	Before/after school and in holidays	Vary	Vary

Figure 1.2 Day care and pre-school education, provision and costs in Great Britain (1994)

Provided by	Staffing	Training	Ratios
Private arrangement	Registered childminders	Variable, no UK requirements NVQ level 2/3	1:3 for children 0–5 1:6 for children 5–7
Local authority social services	Mainly nursery nurses	BTEC/NVQ level 2/3 NNEB/DPQS	1:3 for children 0–2 1:4 for children 2–3 1:8 for children 3–5
Employers, private organizations and individuals	Nursery nurses, some untrained staff	At least 50% staff must be trained as above	1:3 for children 0–2 1:4 for children 2–3 1:8 for children 3–4
LEA	Nursery teachers	Degree and PGCE/BEd	1 (teacher): 23 1 (all staff): 10/13
LEA	Primary teachers, teaching assistant or nursery nurse recommended	Degree – PGCE/BEd NNEB/NVQ level 3	1:30/40 (better ratios if nursery nurse is employed)
Parents and voluntary groups	Playgroup leader	Foundation course/ diploma in play-groups practice, NNEB/NVQ level 2/3	1:8 for children 3–5
Private individuals and organizations	Not specified: often teacher or nursery nurse	Unknown	1:8 for children 0–4 1:20/30 for children age 5–7
LEA, social services, also health and voluntary sector	Nursery teachers, nursery nurses	As for nursery schools/classes and day nurseries	As for nursery school/classes and day nurseries
Local authority, health authorities, voluntary sector	Nursery nurses, social workers, range of staff	Variable	Depends on nature of centre
Schools, leisure departments, voluntary sector	Play leaders, community workers, volunteers	Variable, no UK requirements, some NVQ level 2/3	1:8 for children 5–7

Source: Devised by the Early Childhood Unit, National Children's Bureau, drawing on government statistics and information from voluntary organizations. From Moss and Penn (1996).

between the ages of 0–18. For the 0–6 age group, care services are integrated under the education umbrella. Denmark has a network of daycare, financed by local government which has both developmental and educational aims.

(Audit Commission 1996: 7)

In this country the educare principle, i.e. that in quality provision for young children care and education are inseparable, is far from universally accepted. In those authorities where it has been adopted the departmental barriers to collaboration have been removed and all services for young children are the responsibility of one department. However, it does not automatically follow that joint training is equally available for all those employed within that service, although there are examples of positive development in this field.

In 1992 Curtis and Hevey claimed that training for childcare and education workers was at a crossroads. Since then a number of significant developments have taken place, but their original concerns remain that 'decisions and events in the next few years are likely to have a profound effect on the nature of the early childhood professional for many years to come' (Curtis and Hevey 1996: 211).

They also point to the tension between existing notions of what a professional is and what this implies about other types of workers. They question whether the advent of National Vocational Qualifications can bring a new style of professionalism to all childcare workers.

In an attempt to identify the links between formal education and workplace-based routes, Hevey (1995) developed the model shown in Figure 1.3 (pp. 22–3). Others have developed similar models (for example Calder 1996) in an effort to explore and develop flexible training routes for all early years workers.

In an answer to the question posed by Curtis and Hevey, Moss and Penn (1996: 4) in their book *Transforming Nursery Education* put forward a model of a trained workforce to match their vision of a comprehensive, integrated and coherent early childhood service:

> In a nutshell, we would replace nursery teachers and many other workers by early childhood teachers trained to graduate level to be able to work in a multi-functional and flexible service: they would be supported by less trained workers, able, however, to acquire extra qualifications, as and when they choose, including early childhood teacher status.

Even if this vision is some time in the future many would agree that the compartmentalized training which has characterized previous early years provision no longer meets current needs in early years settings nor the adults who staff them. But in suggesting one kind of training for all early childhood staff, are Moss and Penn denying the range of skills, attitudes and areas of knowledge which workers in many different kinds of settings require or already possess? Should we be providing the same level of training for all those working with young children across all services and sectors? In answer to these questions the Rumbold Report states:

The extent to which adults working with the under fives and their families possess different areas of knowledge and understanding, skills and attitudes will vary according to the role of the workers and the training they have received. Given the differences in type, quality, level and aims of training courses, those working with under threes may be well-qualified in certain aspects but less familiar with others. The Report provides a set of summary statements outlining attributes which a group of adults working in an educational setting between them should possess in order to provide a high quality educational experience.

(DES 1990: 47)

They include:

Knowledge and understanding
- understanding of the way young children learn;
- understanding the range and importance of play in the education of the young child;
- understanding of the way children acquire language;
- understanding of what is necessary to ensure the provision of *quality* experiences;
- understanding of the varying roles of adults working with young children and the crucial nature of the role of parents as first educators;
- understanding of factors affecting ease of transition and continuity of experience and ability to employ strategies to avoid discontinuity;
- knowledge of the range of provision, services and contexts in which under-fives may be educated;
- knowledge and understanding of the needs and characteristics of young children;
- knowledge of the earlier experiences of children, their home circumstances and any special educational needs;
- curriculum knowledge and understanding of appropriate experience for under-fives and ability to relate this to National Curriculum requirements; knowledge of recent research and understanding of its implications in relation to the provision of quality experiences for young children.

Skills
- the development of particular skills, interest and expertise in a subject or curriculum area and awareness of appropriate strategies for work with young children;
- skill in planning and implementing the curriculum in order to ensure breadth, balance and continuity with the National Curriculum;
- organizational skills and strategies for effective learning;
- observational skills and effective recording, monitoring and assessment of the curriculum;
- interactive and communication skills – child/child, child/adult;
- management and leadership skills;
- skills in collaborative working, including working with parents and with other professionals;

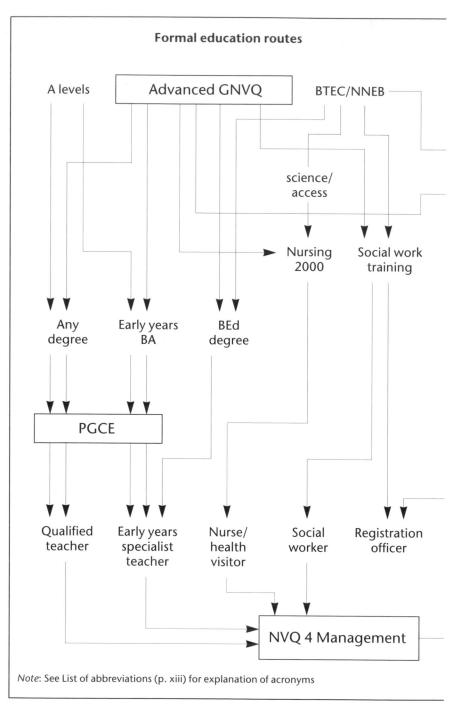

Figure 1.3 Emerging models of training for early years workers

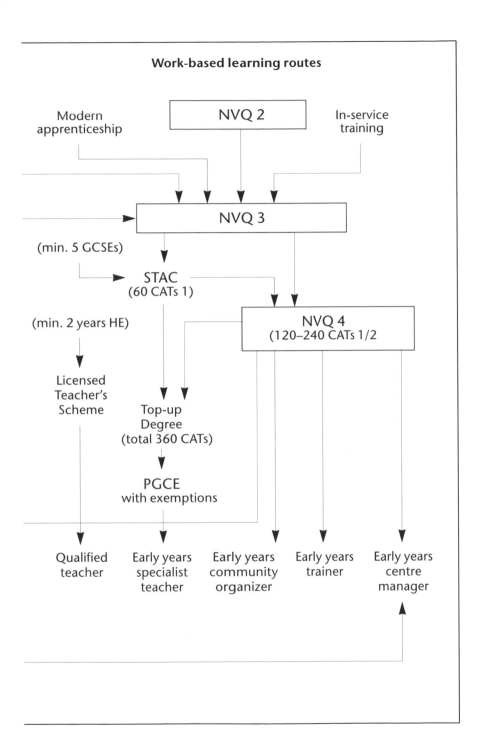

Work-based learning routes

Modern
apprenticeship

NVQ 2

In-service
training

NVQ 3

(min. 5 GCSEs)

STAC
(60 CATs 1)

NVQ 4
(120–240 CATs 1/2

(min. 2 years HE)

Licensed
Teacher's
Scheme

Top-up
Degree
(total 360 CATs)

PGCE
with exemptions

Qualified
teacher

Early years
specialist
teacher

Early years
community
organizer

Early years
trainer

Early years
centre
manager

- skill and ability to provide, or facilitate the provision of, equal opportunities for all under-fives notwithstanding differences of race, gender and educational need.

Attitudes
- high expectations of children and self;
- genuine liking for, and sensitivity towards, children and readiness to value them as people in their own right;
- respect for, and appreciation of, the contribution of other adults – parents, colleagues and other professionals;
- a commitment to develop a partnership with parents – with a shared sense of purpose, mutual respect and a willingness to negotiate.

This daunting list of areas of knowledge, range of skills and necessary attitudes raised the important question concerning the degree to which it is possible for all early years staff to acquire them. The need for differentiated training is discussed in the Report of the RSA Early Learning Inquiry. Ball (1994: 58) suggests that the availability of differentiated training means that

> professionals should be able to progress at their own pace, as they acquire further levels of skill, competence and understanding. The idea of a professional continuum is not only of benefit to children, but is also a way of ensuring that adults with high potential to develop professionally are not frustrated or turned away from work with children.

Work with young children is characterized by diversity, different sectors, departments, services and spheres of activity – each have their own differentiated and distinct training. Yet if the coordination and collaboration argued for by the Rumbold Committee is to be effective, professionals must be prepared to break down barriers and to share skills and knowledge, at the same time recognizing that there will be times when their distinct contribution will be necessary. The move towards the development of interdisciplinary training is an important breakthrough in this respect, although as the Early Childhood Forum (1995) argues, 'this does not preclude the idea of role-specific training either at pre-service levels e.g. Early Childhood Studies degrees as routes into different professions or as Continuous Professional Development opportunities'. Joint training is an important part of sharing knowledge and expertise, but while some workers may prefer to continue to deepen their understanding of a particular role, others may wish to move on to courses of study and experience which will carry 'higher level' qualifications. In this respect the links between workplace assessment and further and higher education must continue to be strengthened. At the Manchester Metropolitan University, the appointment of multi-professional tutors with backgrounds in social work and further education provides support for students along the professional continuum and is leading to innovative developments.

In 1986 Hevey talked about the 'muddle' that existed in terms of training for work with young children. There is still some way to go in developing the 'ladder of progression' or 'continuum of learning' on a nationwide basis. Indeed, many would question whether it should be seen as a ladder or more as a climbing frame with appropriate access and stopping-off points. The opportunity to pause and start again is necessary in appealing to many early years workers juggling family and finances. There are some interesting and encouraging initiatives which go some way towards the provision of an appropriate climbing frame, with exit and take-up at appropriate points. As Ball (1994) suggests, 'some of these rungs are already in place'. The ten years following Hevey's expression of concern have seen a range of far-reaching training initiatives, the most influential being the development of National Vocational Qualifications.

National Vocational Qualifications

The National Council for Vocational Qualifications was established in 1986 with a remit to reform and rationalize the whole pattern of vocational qualifications across all occupational sectors within a single comprehensive, progressive framework. Some ten years on Hevey (1995) firmly believes that the development of NVQs is helping to unravel the 'muddle'. The aim is to provide a guarantee of competence to do a job, based on nationally agreed standards of competence and assessed primarily in the workplace. They were designed to break down barriers to qualifications through abolishing time-serving or formal educational requirements, and to give credit for knowledge and competence, however they had been achieved. The first NVQs in Child Care and Education at levels 2 and 3 were launched in 1991, but level 4, equalling a National Diploma – thus completing the route into higher education – has yet to be developed. One of the main barriers to taking up NVQs is funding. Assessment is expensive, and since most candidates work in small, private nurseries, community-based playgroups or as self-employed low-paid childminders, this is a major problem. However, NVQs have the potential to offer early years workers real opportunities to gain credit for the skills and knowledge they already have, and to extend them by giving the necessary underpinning knowledge and skills via some of the new initiatives which provide access into further and higher education.

In recent years other training schemes have been developed or reorganized in order to make explicit their links to underpinning knowledge and understanding for NVQ and SVQ (Scottish Vocational Qualifications). These include:

- awards offered by CACHE – the Council for Awards in Children's Education;
- Certificate in Child Care and Education (CCE), a one-year course;
- Diploma in Nursery Nursing (DNN), a two-year modular course;
- Advanced Diploma in Child Care and Education (ADCE), a six-module course for those who have been working with children for some time. The ADCE attracts Credit Accumulation and Transfer points (120 CATs points) and is therefore advantageous to those wishing to progress to higher education;
- BTEC has similar courses designed to meet the needs of career entrants;

- the Pre-school Learning Alliance (formerly PPA) develops courses nationally to meet local need. A wide range of courses, taught by registered trained tutors, is provided, though not all areas have all types of courses at any one time;
- the Diploma in Pre-School Practice (DPP) provides underpinning knowledge for Child Care and Education NVQ/SVQ level 3. The course covers a wide range of key training issues such as equal opportunities, child development, observation, curriculum planning, business and administration, children with special needs, care and education of the under-twos. It is also offered in distance learning format.

In Wales the PPA Diploma in Playground Practice is a one-year, 200-hour course accredited through the Open College Network leading to eight credits which facilitate access to further education.

In Scotland, locally based training courses are very practical in nature and are part of a condition of employment for all playgroup workers. The New Basic Training Playwork Self-Study Pack is intended as a starting point for developing knowledge and understanding about working with young children. It includes child development, play and early years curriculum and observation.

In Northern Ireland the Pre-school Playgroups Association offers a two-year combined early years certificate and diploma course together with a wide range of short courses including child development, observation, assessment and record-keeping, special needs, child protection, partnership with parents and HighScope approach.

Childminders

The National Childminding Association (NCMA) has developed a model of training for and throughout a childminding career. This consists of:

- preparation courses for childminders in the process of registration;
- follow-on courses within the first year of childminding;
- in-service training throughout time spent as a childminder.

NCMA has also published training materials, including 'The Key to Quality', to enable the planning and delivery of courses. In Scotland SCMA works in collaboration with local authorities and lobbies for training as an integral part of the registration process.

In Northern Ireland training for childminders is provided through health and social services boards responsible for registration of childminders.

Montessori training

Montessori Education UK was formed in 1993 to raise educational standards in Montessori practice and training. It has laid down minimum standards and criteria for courses offering Montessori training in the UK leading to a recognized Montessori diploma. Diploma courses aim to develop in students a thorough understanding of:

- Montessori philosophy, that education is a preparation for life, that its purpose is to facilitate the development of each individual's potential to the full, and that through education will come improvements in society and protection of the natural environment;
- Montessori theory and approach to education as developmentally-based, so course curricula cover all aspects of child development, with a strong emphasis on observation;
- Montessori materials, which are developmental and provide the concrete basis from which learning of abstract concepts develops. The approach to the different subject areas in the Montessori curricula is holistic and integrated, so there is emphasis on the development of transferable skills through use of materials within the broader context of life skills development which they are designed to promote.

These courses provide underpinning knowledge for NVQ/SVQ Child Care and Education level 3. Courses are taken by full- or part-time study, or by distance learning.

HighScope training

The HighScope Institute (UK) opened in 1991 in response to growing interest in the HighScope approach within the United Kingdom and Ireland. It offers a range of training opportunities for all those involved with the care and education of young children. It enables them to:

- become familiar with the HighScope approach and the research principles which underpin it;
- train to use the approach in their own setting;
- become an endorsed HighScope trainer.

Training involves:

- awareness raising or planning meetings;
- workshops to introduce the HighScope approach. These two-day events present an overview of the curriculum and introduce such topics as active learning, room arrangements, daily routine, key experiences and record keeping;
- a Curriculum Implementation Course (CIC) designed for those wishing to become fully accredited HighScope practitioners. It consists of 12 sessions delivered over a period of weeks to enable trainees to introduce incrementally the approach in their settings. Trainees complete assignments and a journal and are visited in their setting by the trainer. Ongoing support is available for students completing the initial training.

Other training providers

Useful information with regard to a wide range of available training opportunities has been compiled by Griffin (1996). As Training Officer with the

National Childminding Association she is aware of the many schemes which have been developed and rearranged in order to make explicit their links to underpinning knowledge and understanding for NVQ/SVQ. This information is available in Pugh (1996).

Other providers include:

- Kids Club Network, which offers a range of training packages including a Playwork Foundation Course and Investing in Playwork linked to NVQ levels 2 and 3. A wide range of further courses are offered and a distance/flexible learning programme is being developed.
- National Toy and Leisure Libraries, which provides information and training on working with families. Courses include: evaluating your toy library; learning through play; learning to share (based on a video). Courses are linked to RSA Advanced Diploma and NVQ levels 2 and 3 Child Care and Education and Play Work.
- National Play Bus Association, which has a history of producing innovative training for workers involved in mobile projects who take on the role of play and care worker. Courses contribute to underpinning knowledge for some units within NVQs in Child Care and Education and Play Work. There is an emphasis on equal opportunity and anti-discriminatory practice.
- Home Start UK, which has produced a handbook for staff who deliver training. Each Home Start scheme is independent and trains its own volunteers. New organizers are offered a comprehensive induction programme and staff are encouraged to plan their own professional development.
- Other organizations such as Community Insight, Early Years Trainers Anti-Racist Network and Save The Children Fund, which offer training courses and workshops on a range of issues which include equal opportunities, children's behaviour and children with disabilities.

Key issues

All of the above training opportunities provide rungs on the 'ladder' or points on the training 'climbing frame' which allow students to plan their own professional development and to recognize that learning is a continuous process. It is my view that the word 'development' is preferable to 'training', which suggests something being done to the student in order to change practice or behaviour rather than personal involvement and response. Students at all levels of training should be encouraged to analyse their practice.

The reflective-practitioner model of professional development is an important one and underpins the new multidisciplinary degrees and teacher education courses in which self-assessment is fundamental, and where students are required to keep a personal/professional development portfolio in which they monitor their own progress and recognize the competences which they are acquiring. This is a particular requirement of all students on teacher training courses, particularly for early years students as they come to terms with the complexities of provision.

Teacher education

Although an increasing number of teachers work with children under 3 in combined provision, nursery schools, children's centres and in a range of private and voluntary provision, there is little recognition of this in teacher training courses. In fact, early years specialists still fight hard to gain adequate recognition for the 3–5 age group, and the lack of child development courses for all age groups has long been a concern to practitioners and trainers. This view is now supported by several reports, such as DES (1990), Ball (1994) and Early Childhood Forum (1995).

Teacher education courses must meet the demands of Government Circular 14/93, with its heavy emphasis on National Curriculum subject and professional competence. In many training institutions this results in limited opportunities for the study of early years specific issues, in particular the needs of children under 3 and the knowledge and skill required to teach them.

One of the main concerns is that practical experience in most courses is undertaken in schools, and for early years students this is mainly in nursery schools or classes and reception classes, working with 3- to 5-year-olds. Visits may be arranged to other settings where under-threes are found, but it is unusual for a teacher training student to spend any length of time predominantly with this age group. It can be argued that the skills needed to work in settings other than schools are quite different, and these must form an important part of any early years teacher training course if students are to be appropriately trained to work in these contexts.

On a more optimistic note, there is evidence that more BEd courses are providing opportunities for early childhood to be studied as a main subject. Child development is also becoming more apparent on course outlines, but until the stranglehold of the main subject is released, sufficient time for in-depth study will always be a problem. While this is a concern, it is nevertheless important that students do have a specialism and expertise which they are able to share with even the youngest children. A clear need for new courses targeted at the very early stages of educare is already identified. The variety of routes into teaching – which include the BEd degree or other degrees such as BA or BSc with qualified teacher status and part-time or shortened courses for students with prior learning and full-time and part-time PGCE courses – must in future offer opportunities for age-related studies to include the 0–3 age range in order to staff the new multi-professional centres in which it is planned that teachers will be involved. PGCE courses provide the ideal opportunity for students who want to teach and graduate from the part-time, multidisciplinary degrees such as the BA (Hons) in Early Childhood Studies at the Manchester Metropolitan University. Although now offered as both full- and part-time courses (which target very different client groups), the part-time course attracts mature students already working in the educare field who wish to remain in-post while training. For these students a part-time postgraduate course is essential, providing that practical experience is offered in as wide a range of early years contexts as possible.

As the Rumbold Report (DES 1990) states, 'the rigour and relevance of early years teacher training must be safeguarded'. Entry to teacher training courses requires passes in mathematics, English language and science at GCSE grade C and above, and further passes in a range of other GCSE subjects. In addition, two A levels are the normal entry requirement, although mature entry may be via access courses or other advanced study and may include accreditation for prior learning and/or experience (APL/APEL).

Interdisciplinary/multi-professional degrees

Many consider the introduction of interdisciplinary degrees to be one of the most exciting developments in the move towards the provision of a professional framework for early years workers. A number of colleges and universities have developed such degrees, which are all based on the premise that child development is a central area of study for all educarers. They usually contain a core of compulsory modules on child development, health issues, family policy, child protection and welfare issues and the law as it relates to children and the family. Elective modules provide opportunities for students to follow up or develop a specialism. Students graduating with a degree in Early Childhood Studies may then take a further qualification in teaching, social work or in the health-related field. Others may choose nursery management or inspection, but many will simply want the degree as recognition for what they are already doing. Courses are offered on a full- and part-time basis; the workplace or practice element, in a wide range of early years contexts, is considered as central to the course. On part-time courses the range of knowledge, skill and experience which the students bring to the course provides a powerful resource on which the course builds and, as new generations of graduates emerge, employers will recognize it as being a very real strength in providing collaborative networks.

Continuing professional development

It is recognized that continuing support and opportunities for updating and refreshment, retraining and attainment of further qualifications is an important consideration in developing the professional continuum. Part-time, distance learning and updating skills opportunities are important for all early years professionals. An encouraging development is the provision of masters level study for early years professionals, either by research or by course attendance. Course attendance on a flexible modular programme allows students to build on existing qualifications and gain accreditation in a variety of ways for previous study and to target specific areas of interest. A masters degree in Early Childhood Studies is now possible in a number of universities; a recent development is an MA in Multi-professional Studies in Early Childhood offered by the Manchester Metropolitan University.

Access and funding

One of the main barriers to professional development and training at all levels is funding. Access to appropriate training is denied to many because of a lack of financial support. Many educare workers are in low-paid jobs and are not supported by their employers in terms of training. There is evidence that many people fund themselves, but training is costly. NVQ assessment is particularly expensive and there is no national policy of support. Funding for in-service training for teachers, if and when it is available, often denies access to nursery nurses and other educare workers, thus creating unnecessary divisions at a time when these should be abolished. Many in-service students, particularly on award bearing courses, continue to fund themselves. The National Commission on Education (1993) called for national criteria to cover 'the training and continuing professional development of education and care workers'. A key issue for lobby groups is the provision of financial support for all early years staff in order to provide a high quality, appropriately trained workforce.

In her vision for the future presented at the National Commission Early Years Seminar, Pugh (1993) highlights key issues with regard to training. These include:

- a well-trained workforce is the key to quality;
- teachers need to spend time during their training with children under 3;
- all heads and managers of centres should be trained to degree level;
- all workers should have NVQ level training – but there is still a lack of clarity between NVQ levels;
- there is a lack of funding for childminder training – this must be addressed;
- all staff need time for reflection and analysis;
- a lack of funding of early years training has led to the loss of support previously given by early years advisers. Ring-fenced funding is required for the early years;
- we must build on diversity but not at the expense of quality;
- training and support structures are required to make the difference.

Appropriate training is therefore crucial. It is clear that the present system does not meet the needs of a changing early years society, although encouraging developments are taking place.

Hevey (1995) asked the question 'so is there light at the end of the tunnel?' In answering she said:

> One has to be optimistic and assume [so]. Surely no government can continue to ignore the development work that has been done or the potential of the NVQ framework – not only to make sense of the muddle, but to

provide access to appropriate training and qualifications to thousands of people who work with young children and their families to whom it has been denied. All this talk of raising standards in education is a non-sense unless the standards of workers are addressed. The climbing-frame must be completed if early years practitioners are ever to gain the recog-nition they deserve and find their way to the top.

(Hevey 1995: 11)

Opportunities for early years practitioners to access a variety of training options, particularly those which focus on the under-threes, must continue to be a priority for providers and for funding agencies.

As long ago as 1972, at a time of promised expansion of nursery provision, Lesley Webb wrote: 'The education of young children is an essential under-pinning of all future education; without that education all subsequent efforts may be useless.' In a rallying cry which we failed to heed then she claimed that:

In the last analysis it will not be government policy – which is ephem-eral, purpose-built schools or even money which will dictate whether children are indoctrinated into conformity, given simple custodial care, or receive a liberal education. It will be the quality of the educators which will be absolutely decisive!

(Webb 1972: 182)

Useful contacts

BTEC (British Training and Enterprise Council), Central House, Upper Woburn Place, London WC1H 0HH (Tel: 0171 413 8400).
CACHE (Council for Awards in Children's Care and Education), 8 Chequer Street, St Albans, Hertfordshire AL1 3XZ (Tel: 01727 847636).
GTTR (Graduate Teacher Training Registry) [for PGCE], Fulton House, Jessop Avenue, Cheltenham, Gloucestershire GL50 3SH (Tel: 01242 225868).
HighScope Institute UK, Copperfield House, 190–192 Maple Road, London SE20 8HT (Tel: 0181 676 0220).
Home Start UK, 2 Salisbury Road, Leicester LE1 7QR (Tel: 0116 238 9955).
Kids Club Network, Bellerive House, 3 Muirfield Crescent, London E14 9SZ (Tel: 0171 512 2112).
Montessori Education (UK) Ltd, 21 Vineyard Hill, London SW19 7JL (Tel: 0171 433 1548).
National Childminding Association, 8 Masons Hill, Bromley, Kent BR2 9EY (Tel: 0181 464 6164).
National Children's Bureau, 8 Wakley Street, London EC1V 7QE (Tel: 0171 843 6000).
National Toy and Leisure Libraries Association, 68 Churchway, London NW1 1LT (Tel: 0171 387 9592).
Northern Ireland Childminding Association, 17a Court Street, Newtonards, County Down BT23 5NX (Tel: 01247 811015).
Northern Ireland Pre-school Playgroup Association, Enterprise House, Boucher Crescent, Boucher Road, Belfast BT12 6HU (Tel: 01232 662825).

Pre-school Learning Alliance, 69 Kings Cross Road, London WC1X 9LL (Tel: 0171 833 0991).
Scottish Childminding Association, Stirling Business Centre, Wellgreen, Stirling FK8 2DZ (Tel: 01786 445377).
Scottish Pre-school Playgroup Association, 14 Elliot Place, Glasgow G3 8EP (Tel: 0141 221 4148).
UCAS (University Council for the Admission of Students) [entry/clearing house for BEd/BA degrees], PO Box 67, Cheltenham, Gloucestershire GL50 3SF (Tel: 01242 227788).
Wales Pre-school Playgroup Association, 2a Chester Street, Wrexham, Clwyd LL13 8BD (Tel: 01978 358195).

References

Abbott, L., Ackers, J., Griffin, B. and Marsh, C. (1996) *Educare for the Under Threes, Research Project.* The Manchester Metropolitan University.
Audit Commission (1996) *Counting to Five, Education of Children Under Five.* London: HMSO.
Ball, C. (1994) *Start Right: The Importance of Early Learning.* London: Royal Society for the Encouragement of the Arts, Manufacture and Commerce.
Calder, P. (1996) Early childhood studies degrees, in G. Pugh (ed.) *Education and Training for Work in the Early Years.* London: National Children's Bureau.
Curtis, A. and Hevey, D. (1992) Training to work in the early years, in G. Pugh (ed.) *Contemporary Issues in the Early Years – Working Collaboratively for Children.* London: Paul Chapman Press/National Children's Bureau.
Curtis, A. and Hevey, D. (1996) Training to work in the early years, in G. Pugh (ed.) *Contemporary Issues in the Early Years – Working Collaboratively for Children* (second edition). London: Paul Chapman Press/National Children's Bureau.
Department of Education and Science [DES] (1990) *Starting with Quality, the Report of the Committee of Inquiry into the Quality of Educational Experience Offered to 3 and 4-year-olds.* London: HMSO.
Early Childhood Forum (1995) *Draft Document on Provision for Children aged from Birth to Five: The Education and Training of Early Years Workers,* October 1995. London: National Children's Bureau.
Griffin, S. (1996) Vocational training in childcare and education: a richly diverse pattern, in D. Hevey (ed.) (1986) *The Continuing Under Fives Training Muddle.* London: Volcuf.
Hevey, D. (1995) *Still in a Muddle about Early Years Training* – Coordinate Supplement. London: Volcuf.
Hevey, D. and Windle, K. (1990) Unpublished report of working with under sevens, Occupational Mapping Survey.
Manchester Metropolitan University (1994) *An Identification of Factors Contributing to Quality Educare for Children Under Five,* Research Report. Manchester: The Manchester Metropolitan University.
Manchester Metropolitan University (1996) *Educare for the Under Threes – Identifying Need and Opportunity,* Interim Research Report. Manchester: The Manchester Metropolitan University.
Moss, P. and Penn. H. (1996) *Transforming Nursery Education.* London: Paul Chapman.
National Children's Bureau (1996) *Training in the Early Years – a Discussion Paper.* London: National Children's Bureau.

National Commission on Education (1993) *Learning to Succeed*. London: Heine-mann.

Pringle, M. K. (1975) *The Needs of Children*. London: Hutchinson.

Pugh, G. (1993) 'Early childhood – a vision for the future', paper presented at the National Commission on Education Seminar, London (February).

Pugh, G. (ed.) (1996a) *Education and Training for Work in the Early Years*. London: National Children's Bureau.

Pugh, G. (1996b) Policy questions in a British context, in *Pre-school Education in France and Britain*, Summer Report. London: Franco-British Council.

Webb, L. (1972) *Purpose and Practice in Nursery Education*. Oxford: Blackwell.

2 | 'Have experience: want to learn' – creating a new pathway to professionalism with a little European money and a lot of hard work from our friends

Anne-Marie Graham

Is experience enough?

When my first child was born many years ago, I thought his happy contentment was largely down to my effective management ably supported by Dr Spock. Listening to other parents' tales of sleepless nights, tantrums and tears I found it difficult to resist an inner smugness resting on an untested assumption that they (unlike me) just weren't doing 'it' right.

My next child, inevitably (and perhaps I should be grateful to her), challenged all my theories. Neither Spock nor Jolly cut much ice with her. Despite a birth a New Ager would have been proud of, in her mother's bed with only a rotund local midwife and her father to welcome her into the world, she quickly established a pattern of midnight waking, followed by four-hour wailing sessions which resisted all comfort and quickly wore away much more than just my smugness!

I gained a great deal of experience from bringing up these two children in their early years, some of it valuable. It stood me in good stead when my third child was born, for by then I had learned to make better use of the theories and could recognize each child as a complete individual. I was a little more sure-footed about trusting my own judgement.

Like a child myself I learned, sometimes painfully, from first-hand experience, gradually growing in confidence as I acquired more skills. And most importantly, I'd been able to draw on the experience offered by friends and professionals, either passed on by word of mouth or gleaned from books. I was able to accept my failures and give credence to others' advice where it seemed appropriate.

Thank God for that, otherwise I'd have had to give birth to a football team before my own childrearing capabilities could anything like meet the task in hand! And of course by that time their broader life experience might well have been such that I wouldn't wish to answer for what might have become of my brood.

My experience is not unique: many other parents and educarers have trodden a similar path, yet we still find some rather glib assumptions about knowledge and experience being made about parents and professionals. Theory is a thin gruel without experience, but equally experience is not always enlightening. Both parents and professionals need to remind themselves of the vast variety of expertise required in working with and caring for young children, and that parents and carers, just like their children, need to grow their own self-assurance in order to be able to distil their experience, reflect on and learn from it.

Life is surely too short to oversee the full range of experience we would require to become an expert from personal observation alone. Yet the view persists that working with the under-threes is simply an extension of motherhood, as well as the view that parenthood itself is instinctive. The latter makes something of a nonsense of the current near-paranoia about parental responsibility. If so many parents, as so many politicians would have us believe, are, in fact, so bad at this 'instinctive' job of parenting, how can we persist in undervaluing the education and training of those who educate and care for very young children?

The huge learning curve that under-threes are working on is now readily acknowledged. Parents are recognized as their children's first and most significant educators. The statistics reveal the upward trend in the number of children under 5 whose care is shared with a childminder or day nursery for long hours while parents are at work. We have ample evidence of the effect of a high quality, warm and stimulating early years experience on children's later development, on their ability to make use of later educational opportunities and on their life chances. We have evidence of the negative effects of a poor experience. We have a broadening knowledge of what constitutes a 'high quality' early years experience.

Yet such subjects as child development lie well outside the National Curriculum; our young adults are not offered any systematic training in parenthood, and legislation only requires half of those who work with young children in a group day care setting to have any qualification at all. A childminder is not required to be trained, and though many are, they have often acquired such training in their own time and at their own expense, because there is no national investment whatsoever in this field.

Can you imagine a situation where only half of those who taught on degree level courses in our universities were required to have some sort of qualification relevant to their work? We'd get pretty annoyed if our 15-year-old preparing for GCSEs was offered unqualified teachers for five hours a day, yet it's OK for a 2-year-old to spend as much as ten hours a day with an unqualified carer to guide her through the biggest intellectual strides she'll ever take! She may be lucky enough have a good one-to-one relationship with an excellent childminder, but as a national strategy, it's just not good enough.

As the training of teachers has become increasingly subject-orientated, the vital understandings about how children learn (which one might expect to be explored during child development studies) have been squeezed into near non-existence. And though most teachers will work with children of at least

4 years of age and older, it is hardly helpful to imagine that they sprang from the womb, fully uniformed and clutching their pencil cases, into the school reception class.

Conversely, the commonest qualification in what we in the UK call 'child-care' is the NNEB, the Certificate or Diploma of the Nursery Nurse Examining Board, which suggests that young children need to be cared for by a 'nurse'. Despite the changes in the NNEB course in recent years, it is still firmly rooted in the vocational field with strong historical connections to health. Now that we recognize a child's need for care and education and play, and that these are bound up together, we seem to be making heavy weather of addressing these needs with a professional training for the many 'edu-carers' who are so often faced with learning on the job as the only route on offer!

The Early Childhood Studies degrees which have recently emerged at a number of higher education institutions aim to fill this gap. What is particularly interesting and useful is that, at their core, these degrees bring together the knowledge and understanding which would surely underpin any useful training for those who come into contact with young children and their families in nurseries, family centres, crèches, playgroups or at home. In other words the heart of the subject matter can be made appropriate for work with childminders, day nursery workers, family support workers, teachers, parents and so on.

The idea of the multi-professional approach, so valuable at the higher education stage, is particularly useful at a local, practitioner level. Bringing together childminders, parents, nursery workers, health visitors, teachers, playgroup and crèche workers makes for a tough tutor assignment, but the synthesis of experience and the challenge of alternative disciplines, if well handled and led, can encourage insight and rigour. This can more than compensate for the organizational difficulties. Such opportunities for reflecting on one's own and others' experience, for articulating and defending or amending one's ideas, for appreciating the how and the what and the why of work in other settings – these should not be denied to any student or worker, if we are to develop the expertise required to do justice to the potential of our youngest children.

But to most it *is* denied. Each educarer comes via their own route. Even the new National Vocational Qualification (NVQ) in Child Care and Education, while recognizing the fullness and variety of the work and its disciplines, may deny another generation these opportunities unless both the training and the assessment process is properly funded by government. It needs to be developed with the support of both professionals and providers, and to aim for quality rather than whatever profits can be made out of paper-qualified trainees.

The attraction of the NVQ system is obvious for those who have experience but little opportunity to take significant time out to study. But the evidence of those trying to implement the NVQ system is showing up the inadequacies of an assessment-based system which has abandoned responsibility for the training. Consequently there is a vast diversity, not only in the nature and length of training associated with NVQ but, inevitably in these circumstances, in the quality of the qualification.

What we need at the centre of the early years training field is a single, rigorous, well-respected, professional training route which can be built on to encompass a variety of specialisms and with stopping-off points at several levels. When we have a common core at the heart of work with young children across all disciplines, professionals will understand one another better. A common approach among managers and workers at different levels will strengthen professionalism and allow for improved multi-agency work. Greater coherence will lead to a stronger voice being heard on behalf of young children.

Pathway to professionalism

This is the story of one attempt to build such a system in microcosm in Kirklees. In one course we wanted to combine a delivery and programme of study which could support a group of students, most of whom had no previous qualifications and whose abilities covered a fair range, in achieving the highest level of skill and understanding possible over the two-year period of the initial funding. Along the way we could offer them assessment at NVQ level 3 in Child Care and Education, the Advanced Diploma in Child Care and Education (ADCE) and a number of Early Childhood Studies degree level modules accredited through the Manchester Metropolitan University leading into the second year of a three-year degree course. We called it Pathways to Professionalism in Early Childhood Educare, but it quickly became known as the NOW course, after its funder, the European-funded Employment Community Initiative, NOW (New Opportunities for Women).

Kirklees Early Years Service (KEYS), newly set up as an integrated local authority service in 1993, had already given high priority to offering training opportunities both to its own staff – early years workers across all settings – and to parents. In its first year of existence, KEYS set up a training programme of short courses offered in the day time, in the evenings and sometimes at weekends, to anyone working with or caring for young children. Teachers in nursery and infant school classes could access the training through their INSET systems, while special rates were negotiated for playgroup and day nursery staff, in both the local authority and independent sectors, and childminders. The sessions ranged through the principles and practice of nursery education, music in the early years, fostering early literacy and numeracy skills, parental partnerships and so on. As it moved into its second and third years of operation, it featured areas of practice targeted by the inspection process, or by the development plans of individual settings.

Tutors sometimes struggled with the different attitudes and expectations that participants brought into the sessions. Organizers struggled with the problems of access – venues, times, teaching styles and so on. Of course it might have been easier to put on the sessions on the principles and practice of nursery education for teachers alone, but it is just as appropriate for playgroups and day nurseries, and the mix of experience generally provides enrichment. Given our anxiety to assure participants of the ability of young children to learn from each other in a well-planned setting, we had to understand the importance of early years workers doing just that!

At the same time as the integrated training course was establishing itself in Kirklees, other work was uncovering the demand for training from parents. A project aimed at developing innovative strategies for supporting early literacy showed how confidence-building work with parents opened up many further training opportunities. As parents acquired new skills in a variety of areas, their parenting abilities broadened and increased. And for some the motivation to learn more about early childhood took them further into training for working with young children.

To build on these developments, KEYS managed to obtain European Social Fund resources to set up a series of basic courses in childcare and education based around the NVQ standards. They were well attended and, of course, produced a demand for more training and, in particular, for the opportunity for progression in this field if we could maintain a similar approach in terms of cost, accessibility and support.

I had previously been involved in a project funded through the first round of NOW and was therefore well aware of the requirements for innovation at home, for partners abroad and, above all, of the necessity for public acknowledgement of the EU funding.

For the second NOW course there was funding for just over two years by the time we were given the go-ahead. We recruited a group of 26 women, mostly unemployed, with varying amounts and types of experience and knowledge. Six of them were already working in the field and were to be trained as trainers. They were generally uncertain about their prospects, hungry for knowledge, unused to the academic process and impatient of its complexity and tendency towards contemplation. They wanted to dive straight in, but at the same time showed the need for much confidence building and reassurance. In short, they demanded expert pastoral as well as academic support.

We have been able to deliver on these requirements through establishing a partnership with the Early Years Centre at the Manchester Metropolitan University's Department of Educational Studies. It is here that a new multiprofessional BA (Hons) degree in Early Childhood Studies has been developed and offered as both a full- and part-time course. This is one of the first degree-level courses in this field in the UK and is leading the way in the development of professionalism in educare.

One of the main avenues of access to an in-depth study programme in our setting was a high level of support from staff leading to the establishment of a study community. This is not normally available in institutions of higher education. Without the sense of belonging to a group, the individual support given by the programme managers, the approach and style of the course tutors, and the arrangement of the course to encourage the building of a self-help structure, it is clear that many of the students would have given up before they reached first base. But strong initial input from the staff paid enormous dividends. The students quickly bonded themselves into a mutually supportive group, giving each other the practical help they needed in everyday situations to combine family and course commitments. They also developed an ability to work together and to learn from each other, which required both trust and confidence. This was particularly important in allowing them to deepen their thoughtful and reflective approach to the curriculum.

We also made childcare provision an integral feature of the programme. Students worked intensively in the classroom for two days a week, and in a variety of settings for young children for a further two sessions. Provision during this time was made for their own children: making sure that this was suitable and fitted the families' needs was one of the major headaches in setting up the programme and an essential feature of its success. Very few of the participants could have considered the course without this.

The programme was not without its difficulties, and students voiced some criticism. This was generally concerned with uncertainty in the early days of the course about what was expected of them and what qualifications they might obtain. As part of an innovative programme, students had to learn to accept that some questions have to wait for an answer! And innovation is what such European programmes are all about. This meant that it was not easy to be clear, at the beginning of the course, about the exact outcome possibilities for each student.

Given the limited timescale of the funding and the diversity of the group, one of the main challenges facing the course organizers was to make sure that the participants were able to access a meaningful qualification within the programme, as well as build accreditation towards the Early Childhood Studies degree *and* find a way of continuing this to fruition. This meant building other forms of assessment around the core of a degree module and gnawing away at the differences of approach and expression to create a seamless programme for our guinea pig students. Not an easy job. But the students played an integral part in shaping this process. It was their needs and their perceptions which eventually wore away the difficulties and set up our new 'pathway'.

The course was organized on a modular basis with work experience at its core. There were taught modules which help students to develop the skills of reflection, analysis and research, forming a link between skills-based training and academic learning. The aims, objectives and outcomes are given in an Appendix to this chapter.

In order to cover the course requirements to enable students to have the opportunity to access the Manchester Metropolitan University (MMU) BA degree and at the same time qualify for the Advanced Diploma in Child Care and Education, particular modules were selected. This Early Childhood Studies course was also designed to provide underpinning knowledge required for the NVQ level 3 in Child Care and Education. In addition to the assessment process required for the academic qualifications, students who wished to obtain an NVQ also had to demonstrate their ability to translate their knowledge into professional practice in work with young children. The modules and units of this two-year package are listed in the Appendix.

A Council for Awards in Children's Care and Education (CACHE) approved centre for the assessment of NVQ levels 2 and 3 in Child Care and Education had already been established by a consortium of early years organizations including Kirklees Early Years Service. We successfully applied to CACHE to include assessment of the ADCE for the students undertaking this course. The major part of the teaching was delivered by staff from the MMU's Multi-professional Centre, and assessment of the degree level modules was approved by the MMU. Although these developments can be described with ease, this simplicity conceals the difficulties involved in overcoming a lot of hurdles very successfully. This was achieved with much tenacity on the part of project managers and sympathetic support from CACHE and the university.

Out of all the lessons we learned from getting this far, the most important must be that, if it appears to be in the interests of improving quality for young children and if it is what is required to meet the needs of those who will be providing for those children, then it can be done. Even when you're told it can't!

We held on to the belief that what is good for children must underpin any training for those who seek to support and encourage them. That means that what we teach comes from the same core of thinking about young children and their development; it does not change whether the student finishes up working in a nursery school, as a health visitor, as a childminder or is the owner of a chain of nurseries.

Some personal experiences

One way of judging our success in these aims is to look at the programme through the eyes of course participants.

Sadja

Sadja came to England from Pakistan in 1962 when she was 4 years old. She remembers her first days in a nursery class in Huddersfield, isolated in her difference and unable to communicate with other children or staff. Her first year must have been very hard as she faced the stares and taunts of other children as they poked fun at her trousers and pierced nose. In fact, it has taken her until very recently to put back the traditional nose piercing which she shied away from as a child as a result of local incomprehension and ridicule. But when she made friends with a part-Asian girl she began to feel more secure and began to pick up English quickly.

She left secondary school with seven CSEs and followed her older sister into the sixth form college to study GCE O levels. During this period a marriage was arranged for her to which she agreed. She was engaged to be married while her fiancé applied for entry to the UK. It was 18 months before her future husband was allowed to join her in this country. Although she had five science O levels and was very keen to train to become a teacher, she needed to show the immigration authorities that she could support her husband if they allowed him entry to the UK, so she got herself a part-time job in Tesco.

A year later she gave up her job to have the first of her four children. By the time her second son was 3 she became aware of his learning difficulties. His disability sometimes leads to behaviour problems creating difficulties for his schooling and for his family. He has been educated in a special school locally and also in a residential school where he was very unhappy. He faced the same isolation, as the only Asian child, that Sadja herself faced when she started school in England back in the early 1960s.

Despite these difficulties and the full-time job of bringing up three boys, caring for her husband and running a home, Sadja was always seeking to increase her skills and knowledge. She did various courses in business administration and typing but found that what she enjoyed most was her work as a bilingual assistant in primary schools. She also developed her skills in working with children with special needs when she began learning signing while working with hearing-impaired children.

When she became pregnant again she gave up work reluctantly. After a long spell in hospital and with so many domestic duties she was unable to return. But she was always planning to continue to develop her skills and knowledge, so when she saw a local course in childcare and education advertised with crèche facilities available she signed up straight away. It was a very basic course but Sadja enjoyed the company and was soon using her bilingual skills to help some of the other course participants. The course was one of a number funded through the European Social Fund and delivered by the Kirklees Early Years Service. When an interpreter was needed Sadja was quickly taken on in this role.

When the BA course in Early Childhood Studies was advertised Sadja was immediately interested. Encouraged by her earlier course tutor, she applied, went through the interview process and was taken on the course. Then, you could say, the struggle began. She is balancing the demands of the course which she is enjoying immensely with her love for and commitment to her family; the needs of her teenage son put a great strain on the family, Sadja in particular.

The hard work has its compensations. Sadja's youngest child has been involved with her mother in the training from her earliest days, in the crèche, acting out with her mother the practical applications from the course and benefiting from her mother's new approach. Sadja reckons that at 3 1/2 her daughter's language skills are far more advanced than those of her sons when they were the same age. Her wider family have recognized this too, even though they did not always encourage her involvement in the course, seeing it as something which would take her away from her family work. But Sadja puts in an almost superhuman effort to ensure that both her work on the course, and with her family, is of the best.

She is well aware of the ways in which the course has changed her thinking. Interaction with her children is much better, she says, and she is trying out lots of ideas she is developing through her studies. Her increased knowledge has given her the self-confidence to participate more fully in decisions being made about the education of her children. In particular she has been able to intervene in the debate about the welfare and education of her son with learning difficulties.

Sadja has the intelligence, sensitivity and experience which will enable her to become an enormous asset to any service operating in the area of support for children and families in difficulty. She has the knowledge and commitment. But the existence of the right kind of opportunities has been an essential factor in allowing her to bring out these skills and develop them. First there was the 'doorstep' opportunity, the short, basic course, friendly and informal with crèche on hand. Then there was the recognition and encouragement of her skills in helping others through interpreting, followed up by the possibility of much more in-depth study, but still in an environment which was supportive and enabled her to maintain full commitment to her family responsibilities.

The availability of these opportunities has ensured that her unique combination of skills and experience will be used to give Sadja increased personal fulfilment, her children a more knowledgeable and confident parent, while at the same time putting an enormous contribution back into society.

As I write, Sadja is about to set off on a student work practice visit to the project's transnational partner in Aarhus, Denmark. I am sure that the new experiences of the college and childcare centres there will provide a stimulating contribution to her developing knowledge and opinions. I look forward to the discussions to follow.

Marie

Throughout her school days no one seemed to notice that Marie was a bright child who had somehow failed to learn to read. An art teacher did recognize her creativity and encouraged her to go to art college, but her parents couldn't afford for her to do that. So she took a succession of dead-end jobs, which hid her lack of literacy.

Her parents separated when she was young and Marie lived with her mother and stepfather while she was in school in West Yorkshire. After she left school she went to live in Wales with her father for a while. During that period she did some voluntary work at a residential centre for people with learning difficulties and realized how much she enjoyed helping and supporting people, especially those facing difficulties.

But Marie had no qualifications and suffered from epilepsy; with little literacy, access to training was difficult. She clearly had lots of ability and could usually find some work but not the kind that would make use of her intelligence and develop her confidence. It was not until she married and had her first child that she began to face up to and come to terms with the abuse she faced in her childhood, and all the consequences.

It is a sad and disappointing fact that the underlying causes of Marie's lack of achievement in school were never discovered. Her creativity, intelligence and empathy are now so apparent it is hard to believe that her underachievement in earlier days failed to shine sufficiently brightly to come to the attention of those who may have been able to help her.

Despite the problems she faced, Marie had attended some adult literacy classes and successfully completed a counselling course. She was increasingly aware of her desire to work with people in an area where she could use her experience to support others through difficulties. However, after her son was born she became very protective and almost imprisoned herself in her own home. As a parent she found it very difficult to let him out into the world or to recognize and meet her own needs.

With her son, James, she came to the playgroup at a local nursery run by the Social Services Department. Through involvement with the nursery, Marie started to share James with a wider world, to allow his development and her own. When the Bright Sparks project, a partnership between the Daycare Trust and Kirklees Early Years Service, set up a base in the nursery Marie was one of the pioneer parents helping it to get off the ground.

Bright Sparks is an early literacy and numeracy project working with parents, carers and staff in one neighbourhood. It is based in a nursery school, the social services nursery, a workplace nursery, a playgroup and a childminding group. Parents began to meet informally and moved on into groups working with and for their children on developing their language skills from the earliest stages and learning about interaction with their children in a variety of ways. Out of this parents themselves were able to grow in confidence and skill; a number of them took on other responsibilities. Marie became a co-opted member of the council's Early Years Sub-Committee as a parent representative.

Gradually she learned to let her son grow at his natural pace into a sturdier independence. She had a little girl, and though initially she clearly went through a period of sadness and fear as she recollected her own childhood, she has been able to avoid the overprotective compulsion which she went through with her first child. She is recognizing her own needs and finding ways of meeting them. Not only has she developed her own literacy skills from very limited beginnings but she has been able to take on the NOW programme and approach a degree level course with a thoughtful and increasingly confident approach.

The support of staff both on the course and at her child's nursery have been particularly important in nurturing Marie's talent. Fulfilment of the expectation that there would be help with producing written work and someone to approach in confidence when she experienced difficulties has been very important, as is the support of her husband. Her children have clearly gained from her opportunity and personal development. I spoke to her on the day before her son started school, and though this was going to be a difficult experience for both of them, they were showing an excitement about the future which was positive and infectious.

Marie has always known she wanted to work with families. Through her own struggles to overcome personal difficulties she has developed an empathy which will be invaluable in such work. Her academic work is of use to her in providing underpinning knowledge and encouraging her own growth as a reflective practitioner. This is an essential part of training for the kind of work she would like to do.

Like her fellow students, Marie needed this particular opportunity. For her it began with contact with the nursery and its supportive work with parents, developed through the literacy project, and is coming into fruition in the NOW programme. But it was essential that the study opportunity was in a place she could reach easily, in an environment in which she felt secure, and with staff who recognized her abilities and the importance of ensuring she could combine the course with the best possible care of her children.

Marie had very particular difficulties to overcome, but the needs she has in being able to attempt this programme are very similar to those of hundreds of other women with talent and experience who want the opportunity to develop those assets through study in a non-threatening environment. It can be done!

Into Europe

When the European Community initiatives first began, the requirement to work in partnership with at least two other projects from different European Union countries was sometimes seen (dare I say it?) as yet another hoop to jump through in order to access funding. However, working Europe-wide in the early years field has a lot of advantages. For one, most of Europe has a far greater amount of publicly-funded provision than we have in the UK, so there is a lot to see and learn about. But, more important still, there is so much to learn about how they do it, what they provide and how we all think about the early years.

At the outset, this project was very positive about European cooperation; we chose our partners carefully and visited before the funding application was made. The Kirklees Early Years Service had already forged links with the Education Institute in Barcelona and taken part in a study visit where the plans for development of under-threes provision from within the Education Department of the regional Catalonian government had been discussed with interest. Here was an educare approach going through the process of activating change, from which we could learn.

We also visited Aarhus in Denmark and established a partnership with the Jydsk Paedagog-Seminarium, the Jutland College for Social Care and Education. Here students who have already gained experience in the field undergo a three-and-a-half-year training to equip them to work as teachers in nurseries, kindergartens, recreation centres and centres for those with disabilities. Visits to the many kindergarten and school-aged childcare centres (some of them age-integrated) were often challenging and always useful to our thinking on early years. The idea of the pedagogue or 'social educator' as a highly trained professional educating children outside of the school system is one which interested us and fitted closely with our educare philosophy.

A further partnership was created through the help of the Irish Council for the Status of Women, who put us in touch with a project being developed by the Ronanstown Women's Group based in Clondalkin on the outskirts of Dublin. This is a voluntary organization developing training opportunities for women on a very large estate with high levels of deprivation. They have secured funding to set up a new childcare and training centre on the estate, and they are particularly interested in working with us on planning new early years provision and in ways of providing school-aged childcare. One of their concerns was that the women they worked with, many of them parents and with considerable experience of working with children, should have the opportunity to build on this experience by being able to access the kind of training which would qualify them to work in the new centre they are trying to establish. We felt that each of our projects had something of value to offer the other.

Thorough preparation does not, unfortunately, defend you against the mysteries of European bureaucracy. This means that partners have to be identified prior to funding being agreed and then each country makes its project selection individually. So Ireland and our own project were funded; Denmark and Spain were not! Denmark agreed to continue to work with us despite the lack of funding for their project. This was very important for us: their long experience in this field, and the breadth and quality of their provision have helped to inform and stimulate the Kirklees project. Sadly, Spain was not able to stay involved with the partnership.

Our visits and discussions with our two partners are developing a true element of transnationality. Discussion and observation in these two other countries is forcing students, tutors and managers alike to set provision for children in their early years in a cultural and historical context and review their own thinking as a result. As well as being able to learn directly from each other, members of this transnational partnership are finding their ideas and practice challenged by this wider experience.

An interesting evaluation is taking place around student perceptions, expectations and outcomes in the partner organizations. As I write, student study visits to Denmark and Ireland are yet to be completed. We feel confident that these events will feed back into the programme here in Kirklees in ways which can enrich the quality of provision for young children in this area.

An enhancement to our European programme has been achieved through the Manchester Metropolitan University's involvement in an Erasmus early years network which is working with a wider European group including our Danish partner. This connection has led to a bid to the European Leonardo programme for further funding for a research project involving our transnational partnership.

The intention is to monitor and evaluate the experiences and responses of students, tutors and employers involved in the NOW project and develop from this data a statement of core competence in terms of knowledge, skills, understandings and attitudes required by all educare workers with young children. Moving outwards from this core, a framework within which other competences specific to the country or region of origin will be developed, and the appropriate training identified. It will then be possible to consider the critical issues arising from a celebration of the differences between the philosophies and practices of educare within the European Union which should encourage a greater flexibility of thinking about current practice.

This ever-widening international experience is being directly input into the Kirklees course through MMU's Young Europeans Module, which is composed of contributions from seven EU countries. Each session takes a particular aspect of early years work in relation to theory and practice associated with provision in one country or region. The module is becoming an effective way of encouraging students to reflect on the dilemmas implicit in all early years work and to be open to a wider range of philosophies and practices. We are expecting to host a seminar towards the end of the project in which the UK students will be involved. We shall look for a synthesis of the ideas and practices of the educare approach as they have been distilled through our partnership.

Where to from here?

The achievement of the process of setting up this course, involving the bringing together of the academic and vocational routes and providing a delivery which is accessible in every way, is a considerable one. The challenge now is to embed this 'pathway to professionalism' into the Kirklees setting permanently.

One aspect of this is to ensure that the degree modules achieved can be continued after the end of the programme, through both the Manchester Metropolitan University and other higher education institutions.

A more complex procedure is underway as regards training delivery: integrating the attainment of these modules into our regular training programme and maintaining them alongside the delivery of underpinning knowledge for other qualifications such as ADCE and NVQ. This involves matching every short course we present to parts of the requirements for these qualifications and building them into modules which do not lose sight of the whole through compartmentalization.

Success in this work would suggest we are well on the way to achieving our overall objective of bringing together the theory and the practice for *all* our trainees. To continue this process we now need the funding to ensure that the expertise already acquired can be extended. There also needs to be national recognition that the child's needs for play, care and education make demands on the education and training of the adults working with them; these demands at present are not being met adequately. There are programmes like the one described here which show ways of meeting these needs. Will government at local, national and European level see fit to promote them?

Appendix: pathways to professionalism in early childhood educare – aims and objectives of the project

Aims of the course

- to meet local needs for highly trained professionals in childcare;
- to provide a structure which is flexible to meet students' needs, but also provides a degree of coherence that supports and gives the group identity;
- to meet the needs of local women who wish to undertake a course leading to a higher education qualification in the child educare field with a view to future employment working with young children;
- to provide underpinning knowledge for students to be assessed for National Vocational Qualifications at level 3;

- to build on the variety of expertise, knowledge and skills course members will bring as a valuable resource to the course, and recognize this formally by accrediting prior learning (APL);
- to strengthen the links between theory and practice and, through work experience, develop and provide opportunities for reflection and analysis of practice.

Objectives

- to provide core modules which all students will take and which will enable students to understand the issues central to working with young children in a variety of contexts;
- to employ a range of teaching methods, including lectures, seminars, projects, discussion, video, visits, research, distance learning and practice placements so as to give students a stimulating learning experience which will develop their analytical, oral and written skills;
- to use a personal tutor system to support students in achieving the aims of the course;
- to use the student group to act as a support network and provide mutual constructive feedback;
- to meet the specialist needs of students;
- to encourage the reflection and recording of the students' professional development by compiling a 'Personal/Professional Development Portfolio' enabling students to be self-critical and reflective;
- to value the practical experiences and professional roles of course members, linking assessment to the workplace and placements, giving credit for the application of knowledge and the demonstration of their competence in professional settings;
- to promote the concept of equal opportunities both among the course participants and in all work settings, and to ensure there are no unnecessary barriers.

Outcomes of the course

On fulfilment of the course the student:

- will have a broad understanding of key issues and influences affecting the lives of young children;
- will be aware of the importance of communication and of ways of achieving this between professionals;
- will have developed skills of analysis and communication;
- will have developed a group identity thereby fostering their own and each other's development;
- will have undergone an individual programme of study built upon their own initial experience, shared professional experiences and particular areas of special interest;
- will have reflected critically upon their practice and will have modified it in the light of their increased understanding;
- will have gained confidence in their professional competence and will have developed a holistic view of education;
- will be sensitive to issues of equal opportunities and be able to relate these to their professional activities.

Module details

The following modules were selected for study over a two-year (part-time) period. The course is designed to enable students to access into the second year of the three-year degree in Early Childhood Studies at the Manchester Metropolitan University and to enable the student to qualify simultaneously for the Advanced Diploma in Child Care and Education.

Child development 1
Legal issues and agency coordination
Child development 2
Organizational structures
Verbal presentations
Working with parents and carers
Play, language and learning
Raising awareness in equal opportunities issues
The 3 to 5 curriculum
Child protection
Issues in the early years
Multi-professional links and coordination of services
Play in the primary years
Young Europeans – young children learning and growing in the European Community

The parts of the Advanced Diploma in Child Care and Education covered in the above modules are as follows:

ADCE M1   How children learn
ADCE M4   Work with children from birth to 3
ADCE M6   Early years curriculum
ADCE M17   Child protection
ADCE M18   Social and legal content of services
ADCE M21   Dissertation (linked to Child development 1 and 2 course modules)

NVQ

The 'Pathways to Professionalism – Early Childhood Studies' course provides underpinning knowledge which is required for NVQ level 3 in Childcare and Education. As with other NVQs, this qualification is based on assessment of competence in the workplace. Competence is assessed against National Occupational Standards which describe the level and quality of practical skills that are required, including the principles that underpin good child educare practice. Students will thus have to demonstrate their ability to translate the underpinning knowledge into professional practical skills working with children.

To obtain the NVQ level 3 in Child Care and Education the student will have to be assessed as competent in all of the core units and in all of the units in one endorsement.

Core units

C2   Care for children's physical needs
C3   Promote the physical development of young children

C5   Promote children's social and emotional development
C7   Provide for the management of children's behaviour
C10   Promote children's sensory and intellectual development
C11   Promote the development of children's language and communication skills
C15   Contribute to the protection of children from abuse
C16   Observe and assess the development and behaviour of children
E1   Maintain a child-oriented environment
E2   Maintain the safety of children
P2   Establish and maintain relationships with parents of young children

Endorsement

This relates to the work situation. At NVQ level 3 the choices are:

• Group care and education
• Family day care
• Pre-school provision
• Family support
• Special needs

Source

'Pathways to Professionalism – Early Childhood Studies Course – Student Handbook 1995–1997' Kirklees Early Years Service and the Manchester Metropolitan University, Didsbury School of Education, supported by the European Social Fund.

3 | 'I'm not working with the under-threes!' – the need for continuing professional development within an early years team

Jean Coward

When I first heard the declaration 'I'm not working with the under-threes!' in 1991, it was often supplemented by such phrases as 'they don't do anything', 'they don't talk to you', and 'there's not much display work'. I was at the time a senior nursery officer in a community nursery centre (Nursery A) during a challenging time of transition in our internal structures and ways of working. When I changed my role to coordinator of a different community nursery centre (Nursery B) in 1994 I wasn't too surprised to hear similar comments about the under-threes, but this time I had the experience of my previous nursery to support me. The effect of change on the first staff team had been very difficult so at least I was aware of some of the problems ahead. During my time at both centres, I have carried out research both in order to investigate the qualifications and attitudes of those working successfully with under-threes and also to investigate learning in that age group, with the practical aim of making our curricula and practices work for the children's optimum benefit. In this chapter I will discuss aspects of my research and some of the changes in which I have been involved.

In both nurseries, before we began any changes in the organization of the day, we began to re-examine the way young children learn and to consider ways in which we could offer quality educare, a concept to which both nurseries were committed. This was also something which our political managers prioritized. At the time I began the role of coordinator in Nursery B, the Social Services and Education Departments jointly produced the statement shown in Figure 3.1 defining their approach to educare. Changes in both establishments meant looking at similar areas: to operate a key worker system, to ensure that all the children had access to a quality curriculum, to support the staff in acquiring the knowledge and skills needed to understand and respond to the needs of very young children. These were not always easy tasks!

In 1991 we decided to divide Nursery A into two areas where two teams of staff, each individual with a key worker role, would be working with two groups of children of mixed ages. This system had been implemented for a year when we identified areas of concern for the under-threes. The needs of the older children seemed to be taking precedence over the needs of the youngest age group.

It was then decided to operate two different groups, these would become the over-threes and the under-threes. Staff responded in different ways to this suggestion, but as senior nursery officer I had concerns about the high number of staff who preferred to work with the older group. Only a minority of staff did not have a preference at all.

This is where my research began. I began to examine staff qualities, knowledge, qualifications and experiences to try to discover the attributes of an

---

- Parents play the first key role in developing their child's emotional, social and intellectual abilities and are their prime educators. They provide the foundations on which children can build their knowledge.
- Children go on from their families to learn from a multitude of experiences, from contact with other adults and children in a variety of settings. Play and interaction with adults is therefore a very important element of early learning, providing opportunities for emotional, social, intellectual and physical development.
- Educare is a term which has been developed nationally and internationally to describe provision for young children where programmes combine education and care elements. The term reflects the fact that for very young children, care and education are inseparable and children learn through all early experiences. Emotional and social development have a crucial influence on intellectual development; the two are interdependent.
- Community nursery centres exist to work in partnership with parents and to provide additional learning experiences to complement those provided in the home. Educare in the centres draws on the skills of both nursery officers and teachers to provide a rich educational experience and care environment.
- Salford has a commitment to nursery education and most children are offered a school place by the age of 3 1/2 years. The community nursery centres' particular role is therefore to provide a supportive environment in which children from 2 to 5 years old can begin to develop the foundation life skills through an all embracing planned 'Educare' programme.
- To enable this to happen, all staff in the centres, as educarers, will provide planned programmes to meet children's individual needs combining opportunities for the emotional, social, intellectual and physical development of children. Within this, the teacher's role in term time will be to provide the foundation and pattern for the next stage of schooling and prepare children for that.

Figure 3.1 City of Salford Social Services and Education Departments' (1993) definition of educare

adult who provides quality educare for the under-threes. This project formed the basis of a special study for my in-service degree. Having clarified my own views as to how very young children learn, and realizing that some staff members had difficulty in responding to their needs, dealing with this issue became a clear focus for my research and for staff development within the centre.

As part of my study I used questionnaires. The first questionnaire was to gain straightforward information. My intention was to examine the initial qualifications of the staff; I also needed to know of any further training and qualifications undertaken by staff which had relevance for their jobs. The reason for seeking this information was to see how far my own establishment matched Andersson's (1990) finding that where educarers have more and better quality education and training themselves, they seem to provide better quality educare for young children.

Of the 13 people who completed the questionnaire, all held a qualification in early years, either BEd or NNEB. Seven staff had undertaken further long-term training following their original qualification and held a Certificate in Post-Qualifying Studies. Various in-service training courses had been completed mainly covering curriculum areas.

I was surprised to discover that a high proportion of staff had completed a counselling course and had gained a Certificate in Counselling. Of the seven staff with this certificate five showed a particular interest in working with the under-threes. I felt very positive about this finding and wondered whether, in addition to the skills which Pugh (1992) considers could be developed with sensitive training, counselling should be included in any in-service course for educarers.

A second questionnaire was developed to examine the more personal feelings of the staff and their attitudes and responses towards working with the under-threes. The following selected responses, based on a section relating to creative activities, illustrate the range of feelings about, and understanding of, the needs of these very young children:

• Creative activities provide stimulation and help children to socialize.
• Creative activities are not as important for the under-threes as they are for a 4-year-old: the older children enjoy an end product, the little ones don't make anything anyway.
• Creative activities for very young children helps them to make sense of their world, they need to experience the glueness of glue and the paintness of paint before they appreciate what an end product is.
• The trouble with little ones is that they don't do any work.

The results of asking the staff for their responses to the under-threes helped to find a baseline for the provision of support and training. In 1991 there was not much in-service training on offer within the authority that was aimed at the under-threes, so we began to use our own development time to look at issues.

The management team in 1991 consisted of a head teacher, a head of care, a teacher and a senior nursery officer (myself). It was the role of the teacher and the senior nursery officer to lead the staff teams for planning:

the teacher worked with the over-threes and I worked with the under-threes. As middle managers we had a responsibility for liaising in order to ensure that all the children had access to a quality curriculum. As part of my own professional development in working towards a BEd I had become interested in the concept of a child-centred approach; this seemed to be a way of offering a quality curriculum to all children, including those under 3. The teacher and the rest of the management team shared this commitment and we were able to work together to overcome many problems. One of the most well-thumbed books in the nursery at this time was *Time to Play in Early Childhood* by Tina Bruce (1991), which was a great support to us.

We also found the statements shown in Figure 3.2, by the Early Years Curriculum Group (1989), supported the way which we wanted the nursery to operate. Consideration of these statements and those of Tina Bruce helped us to change our approach to young children's learning. We had teamwork problems to overcome, especially from the staff who felt that being child-centred meant never saying 'no' to children and that children were 'having all their own way'. These comments taken together with the comments about not working with the under-threes illustrate the amount of support and training that some members of the team needed.

The Manchester Metropolitan University's modular in-service programme meant that we could dip into whatever we felt would support our needs. The first module, which three staff attended, was 'Quality in the Early Years'. The involvement in this training meant that the three staff had to involve the rest of the nursery as part of their studies. This proved to be invaluable: a power of three has more impact than a power of one, especially when they had to feed back in our staff development meetings.

Early childhood is valid in itself, and is part of life, not simply a preparation for work or for the next stage of education.

The whole child is considered to be important, social, emotional, physical, intellectual and moral development are interrelated.

Learning is holistic, and for the young child is not compartmentalised under subject headings.

Autonomy and self-discipline are emphasised.

In the early years children learn best through first-hand experience.

What children can do, not what they cannot do, is the starting point in children's education.

There is potential in all children which emerges powerfully under favourable conditions.

The adults and children to whom the child relates are of central importance.

The child's education is seen as an interaction between the child and the environment, which includes people as well as materials and knowledge.

Figure 3.2 Underlying principles
Source: Early Years Curriculum Group (1989: 3).

With the support of this training the staff began to examine ways in which resources were being offered to the children. Autonomy and self-discipline became significant issues for us. How for instance could young children develop autonomy if there were insufficient resources to allow children to acquire the necessary skills? This initial training had a direct effect on organization and planning.

The Community Nursery Centre worked towards its own philosophy statement in 1991 and this then formed the basis for our consideration of ways in which the needs of the children could be met: 'We believe that children learn best when they are motivated, and that they are best motivated when they have set the task for themselves. That they are capable of working purposefully and directing their own learning when given the opportunity. This is a child-centred approach to education.'

Once we had written this statement as a staff team we were able to begin to offer opportunities for children to learn in a very different way. I carried out more research. We learned a lot from the children, and change, although at times difficult and painful for some staff, took place and was maintained. I could write much more about this but I want to turn now to my next post. This is where I still work and am still involved in researching my own and others' practice and in bringing about change for the benefit of the children.

When I began to work at Nursery B similar issues needed to be looked at and worked upon. We began first by looking at how young children learn; we asked ourselves if we were offering the right environment for this learning to take place. It was interesting that the team at both nurseries tackled the issues in the same way. I did not explicitly influence the ways in which the team in either nursery tackled the problem of how to make the changes happen, but they both wanted to attack it head-on! In both places training and support were offered as a first step, which enabled staff to develop their own ideas and work confidently as a team to make the changes happen. I have been in my present role for two-and-a-half years now. Our nursery now has a staff development time when we can plan for children, have development meetings which offer support for children's learning, invite other professionals in to discuss child-related issues, and plan our own ways forward. We feel this development time is vital for the support we require in meeting children's needs. If we are to follow the authority's educare policy we recognize that time to plan and discuss is a vital part of our role.

One of the most effective training courses which staff in my current workplace have attended was provided as a partnership between the LEA and the Early Years team at the Manchester Metropolitan University. This course was entitled 'Children Under Three and Their Learning' and was attended by the majority of staff.

The information and direction the staff received from this training had a definite effect upon the current practice in our nursery. Staff were asked to examine what they were providing for the under-threes and to ask themselves why they were providing it. Children's needs were explored in an attempt to find out how we could meet them. Audits of the environment were undertaken which examined not only the curriculum, but also the way it was offered. Staff were asked to look at the nursery through the eyes of an under-3-year-old child. Pretending to be 2 years old had some hilarious moments: staff could regularly be observed sitting on the floor looking at their surroundings. It may be of interest to note some of the observations made: for example, if you sat in a particular place in the under-threes area there was a huge draught whistling through whenever the front door was opened which an adult couldn't feel standing up. While sitting on the floor near the bathroom and toilets there was a very definite 'whiff' – this was easily cured by changing our cleaning materials. The staff also developed stiff necks by having to look upwards at some of the displays. This was rather a frustrating discovery for the staff, with no easy solutions. When the nursery was built we presume the architects had forgotten the sizes of the under-threes – most of the lower spaces were taken up by radiators, windows, doors or furniture!

Maybe readers could do this simple exercise in their own environment and make some interesting discoveries previously unnoticed by adults.

The key worker system

I would now like to discuss two of the most significant changes we have made. We have moved to a key worker system and a child-centred approach based on schema spotting. I do not pretend to offer a detailed analysis of either approach, but I hope readers will appreciate how fundamental we have found them to be in meeting the needs of the under-threes in our care. Both the key worker system and our work on schemas have arisen from, and contributed to, staff development and training. They continue to play an important role in our professional development.

The key worker system happened as a direct result of staff having concerns about the under-threes and their need for security. It was also felt that many parents had similar needs as this was often the first time their child had been left in a strange environment with adults whom they did not know. It was felt that a parent might be less threatened in a strange environment if there was at least one designated person to whom they related.

Goldschmied and Jackson (1994: 50) discuss the importance of developing intimate relationships in order to support children's development and happiness. They suggest that the key worker system is a form of organization which allows warm attachments to develop in a group care setting. Once the system is established, the key person takes on many important functions, such as managing the child's settling in, relating to parents and carers, easing separation, fostering language and cognitive development, organizing assessment and record keeping, and liaising with outside specialists and agencies.

Even prior to starting at the nursery, the parent, child and key worker are introduced and the key worker explains how the child's introductory visits will begin. Once these visits are under way the key worker completes a book with the parents which is called 'All About Me'. That is what the book is all about: the child. This book forms the beginning of a profile which the child will keep throughout their stay at the nursery. The key worker has a responsibility for information being put into the book, so beginning a record for the child and parent to have when the child leaves.

Because we are in a group day care setting, the key worker works with all the other children as well as their own key worker group. We have also looked at as many different ways as possible to enhance what we consider to be the important role of the adult. As each child enters the nursery in the morning or afternoon they are received into their own room where their own key worker is based. At the end of the session the child will go back to their room for their meal which is a family-type service where each child sits at the table with their key worker. By developing an under-threes area and having a staff team based in this area we hope to offer as much continuity as possible in what is really a very busy place. As with any system we encounter problems such as staff holidays, sickness and training, but we try to overcome these as much as possible by constantly examining our organization of rotas. It is made slightly easier by having two nursery officers based in one room so that there is always one person who knows the child. Outside each room is a board which displays the photographs of the children and their key worker; this is to help the children and parents develop a sense of ownership. When we work with other agencies it is of great importance that there is good communication, and the key worker undertakes the responsibility for this. The job is a demanding one but we feel that the individual involvement with the child and parent is more beneficial than a constantly changing role. Comments from the parents reassure us that this is a good system to have in operation. Parents have shared with us how they have felt when they have had to leave their child, and how it makes it easier when they know the key worker. We have parents who come in very upset over personal issues which in turn have an effect upon the child; the key worker has often been known to 'put the kettle on'.

A child-centred approach

We have been influenced by the work of Athey (1990), who suggests that the nursery curriculum would be more appropriate to children's needs if it was based on recognition and observation of their recurring patterns of behaviour and thought rather than on more arbitrary content.

With the under-threes age group we have considered various ways of recording and assessing their achievement. We needed some way of finding out how a child was doing things: did they persevere, was it easy, was there a pattern of learning or schema?

Athey maintains that when she focused on how 2- to 5-year-old children work on particular patterns of behaviour then each of these patterns is a recalculated schema. She defines a schema as 'A pattern of repeatable behaviour into which experiences are assimilated and that are gradually co-ordinated' (p. 37). Athey names schemas according to their characteristics, for example a vertical schema is so called because it relates to up and down movements. As a team we began to use long-hand observations of children's activities: gradually a picture of schemas began to build and we could use this information to plan the next activity or to extend the first one. As part of my own research I began some observations which included observing schemas. One of the positive results of schema spotting is that the adult begins to realize that the child's activity is not as random as it may appear at first. Activities are seen to link as patterns whereas previously they appeared apparently unrelated: this could be a solution for the adult who works with the under-threes and complains 'They don't do anything.' It is the adult's role to recognize exactly what children do, and give priority to planning in order to meet the child's needs. Matching what the adults plans with what the child is doing can promote a child's motivation and development. The anecdote about Peter below illustrates how this can happen if adults are observant and sensitive to children's needs.

Peter was playing on the floor with a large box of cars. Every few minutes he would collect handfuls of cars and take them to another corner of the room. He would then leave them on the floor. When he had emptied the car box he began to collect the cars, a few at a time, and return them to the box. As soon as the car box was filled again he tried to push the box out of the room but he experienced some difficulty because of the carpet and the weight of the box. The nursery officer who was in the room at the time went to collect the dolls' pram, which she offered to Peter with the suggestion that he might like to push his cars around in the pram. Peter moved all his cars from the box into the pram and continued the play by pushing the pram full of cars around the different areas. Every now and then he would take out a few cars and leave them on the floor.

The nursery officer recognized that Peter was using a transporting schema and followed up the planning by providing shopping baskets and some shopping trolleys. These were arranged in the room alongside some real tins of food; Peter was encouraged to transport the tins in the shopping game. With the adults' involvement he played imaginatively, buying the goods and transporting them to the home corner and back again. This activity lasted for 40 minutes, not a bad length of time for a small child about whom some adults in the nursery would say 'they don't do much', or 'they have such limited concentration'.

It is interesting that ideas about schemas and free-flow play have influenced planning and recording. Previously the geography of the buildings and the placing of the furniture had been governing planning. Sometimes planning had consisted of what to put on the carpet, what to put on the table, and what had not been out for a long time. After lots of staff development time we had an approach to the curriculum which was led by the children. The staff developed observation skills which gave a deeper insight into what the children could do rather than what they couldn't do and this in turn has influenced all aspects of our practice.

Conclusion

Change is not easy. It is important to note that there have been various stages to the support and training that staff have received. First, there was an honest attempt to find out about people's experience and feelings. Second, there was support for people attending relevant courses and an expectation that information would be fed back to other staff. Third, and most important, there was a commitment from management to a whole-team approach and a recognition that in order for the whole team to change everyone needed to feel included and valued. All change can be painful, and this chapter has shared some of our success. But of course it's not all perfect – yet! However, we feel confident that with continuing support for each other and from outside agencies we can offer appropriate learning experiences, excitement and fun for our youngest children. We need to create a very honest atmosphere for discussion where staff can feel safe to voice their concerns and then provide a way forward through which change can become a whole-team response.

References

Andersson, B. E. (1990) Intellectual and socio-emotional competence in Swedish school children related to early child care, paper delivered at the European Conference on Developmental Psychology, University of Stirling.

Athey, C. (1990) *Extending Thought in Young Children*. London: Paul Chapman.

Bruce, T. (1991) *Time to Play in Early Education*. London: Hodder and Stoughton.

City of Salford Social Services and Education Departments (1993) *Definition of Educare*. Salford.

Early Years Curriculum Group (1989) *Early Childhood Education: The Early Years Curriculum and the National Curriculum*. Stoke on Trent: Trentham Books.

Goldschmied, E. and Jackson, S. (1994) *People Under Three, Young Children in Day Care*. London: Routledge.

Pugh, G. (1992) *Contemporary Issues in the Early Years. Working Collaboratively for Children*. London: Paul Chapman Publishing in association with the National Children's Bureau.

4 | 'Buildings as well as systems can appear as negative to males in early years settings' – exploring the role and status of the male educarer working with the under-threes

Terry Gould

Following a successful career in industry I gave up a sales directorship to become a mature student training to be a primary school teacher; something I'd been interested in doing for a number of years. People I worked with and most of my other friends at the time insisted I was making a huge mistake, not least financially, but it was something I very much wanted to do. My experiences from being a father of three children made me feel I had something worthwhile to offer to children as a teacher. I was very aware at that time that most primary teachers were female. The decision I made to become a teacher was not based on financial criteria but on ideas of personal fulfilment and job satisfaction. Becoming a teacher, for me, was almost like responding to a vocational call, one that I have not regretted answering.

The training for which I enrolled involved four years of full-time study for a BEd Honours degree. I later opted for the latter two years to involve specialization in the early years. On applying to train I opted initially to teach older children, but having taken the opportunity to work with very young children, decided that the early years were a critically important time in a child's life and was where I felt I wanted to teach. Never did I imagine that one day I would be working with children as young as 2.

At the time of writing I am employed by the teaching service of an inner-city local authority, at one of their community nursery centres. I am the only male teacher in this service but there is also a male nursery officer working at one of the other community nursery centres. These community nursery centres are jointly funded by the Education and Social Services Departments of the authority, and cater for children in need between the ages of 2 and 5 (as identified by the Children Act 1989).

My wife, who initially trained as a nursery nurse, now holds a management post with the Special Support Service of a neighbouring local authority.

The experiences she has been able to share with me, along with my own experiences, have enormously helped my ability to relate to, and empathize with, my nursery centre colleagues; including recognizing the often under-valued nature of their experience and work.

Personal experiences, both in my professional work and in my own family life, have led me to believe that children benefit from having opportunities to develop positive relationships with both male and female educarers. I believe that as a society the UK needs to move as quickly as possible away from its comparatively gender-segregated employment market. This includes, most significantly for me, that of educare and other child-related services.

My experiences of working with 2- to 5-year-olds, and developing relationships with their parents/carers, have been predominantly positive. I firmly advocate that all male teachers should give serious consideration to spending some time working with and learning about this age group; and most importantly that they be given the opportunity and encouragement to do so!

Where are the men?

'The shortage of men in childcare settings is a major obstacle because it conveys the message that only women know how to look after and teach young children, and that only women can be gentle and caring' (Goldschmied and Jackson 1994: 147).

Despite the existence of increased levels of equal opportunity in the workplace it is still unusual to find a male educarer working with 2- to 5-year-olds, and even more unusual to find one working with children under the age of 3. Males remain poorly represented in both educare of under-fives and related occupations. According to collated official statistics of male and female staff working in services for children (childcare and related occupations) in the UK in 1991, less than 2 per cent were male (Jensen 1996: 31).

The question often raised is why should this be the case? What are the reasons that males in the mid-1990s remain so underrepresented at this critically important stage of children's learning and development?

Evidence shows that young children benefit from both male and female role models and influences to support, encourage and nurture their individual personalities and abilities. The male aspect of this influence is recognized as significant by many, including Hancock, who points out (1996: 48) that helping to offer children 'alternative role models [and] encourage greater male participation in the home and gender equality' is important.

The reasons why men appear reluctant to opt for a career working with young children appear complex, and none are comprehensibly able to explain the reality that over 98 per cent of staff in United Kingdom educare services are female. Clearly, difficulties in initial recruitment and training are significant aspects of the problem and may, among other things, be partially due to perceptions of gender appropriateness and gender discrimination against males.

Gender discrimination

Apparently much of British society in the late 1990s still holds deep-rooted, stereotypical views on the role of men working with young children. Indeed as Broadhead reminds us, men can face 'special problems' in gaining employment in nurseries. This idea is supported by evidence including that of 'a man who had been refused jobs in two nurseries [and] was awarded compensation on the grounds of sex discrimination' (Broadhead 1993: 11).

Some years ago, expressing a desire to work with nursery-aged children to an experienced primary school head teacher brought a rather negative response. It was explained to me that a substantial number of governors, male and female, would view it unfavourably owing to their very fixed personal ideas.

Until then I'd seen the biggest obstacle to men working in the nursery as being the lack of qualified men feeling they wanted to, and were able to do the job. At that point the idea of discrimination hadn't figured in my thinking; but here it began to rear its head as I began to realize that, just as there are those who are subtly discriminated against in the job market because of the colour of their skin, their age, or their culture, this can also apply to males working with young children. I admit to being somewhat surprised at that time because many of the advertisements for nursery teachers were boldly decorated with statements such as: 'this authority is an equal opportunity employer', or 'we are committed to working towards equal opportunity'.

Yet despite the rhetoric, and the bold print in the advertisements, I was finding out that perhaps some of the people empowered to employ me as an educarer might make every effort not to do so because of their stereotypical personal views!

Despite how we might like things to be, discrimination does exist against men in areas traditionally seen as 'women's work', such as educare in nursery settings. The 1996 annual report of the Equal Opportunities Agency reveals that today the majority of gender discrimination cases are now being brought by men. These cases seem to arise as a result of the negative influences of past experiences in communities, families and workplaces on those with 'power to appoint'. The way many of those with power respond negatively to males in certain roles sends out powerful false messages about gender appropriateness. So views like those of Michelle Elliot, 'I would look with great suspicion on a man who specifically wants to work with nursery age children' (*Daily Telegraph*, 4 October 1993), though clearly grounded in a positive desire to protect children from being abused by males, can actually become negative influences on young children's opportunities to relate to males and their ideas on gender appropriateness. Such views can have a very direct effect on the recruitment of males to work with young children.

Responses to a male educarer

How some children actually respond to a male educarer can help to broaden understanding of the importance of working towards a more gender-

balanced educare workforce. The following case studies are used for this purpose and can serve as a basis for further discussion of related issues.

A number of very young children when first coming to nursery settings
behave in a way which demonstrates that they are wary, or even afraid, of
male educare staff. Such behaviour contrasts with the way these same children generally respond to female staff. My experiences of the cases of Barry
and Sarah in an inner-city community nursery centre are presented to demonstrate this point, but also importantly to show how, after a period of time,
these children's behaviour usually alters quite dramatically in terms of how
they relate to a particular male educarer. Such cases serve to support the
views of Hughes (1991), Hancock (1996), Jensen (1996) and many others
about the importance of positive male role models in nursery settings as well
as in young children's lives in general.

Barry

Barry (aged 2 years, 4 months) began attending the nursery centre for five
afternoon sessions each week. For the first few weeks on arriving he cried a lot,
clinging onto his mum saying he didn't want her to go. After about six weeks he
had begun to settle much better, so that on arriving he usually quickly got
involved with one of the activities on offer, and mum was able to leave him
playing happily. Barry, however, would not come and play where I (the male
educarer) was situated. On seeing me, Barry would move as close as he could to
either his mum or one of the female members of staff. As the relationship
between staff and Barry's parents began to develop he became less wary of me,
and although he didn't choose to come and play where I was, he didn't run to
the far end of the room either.

Gradually, Barry got more used to me and would come to an activity where I
was involved, but remained hesitant about coming too close. At the end of one
session, Marie (Barry's key worker) and I were talking with Barry's mum about
how he'd settled at the nursery. She told us how that previous day she'd been
asking Barry who he loved at the nursery. He'd named all the female staff whom
he came into contact with but not me. Mum had then said to him, 'But what
about Terry, don't you love him?' The answer had been a definite 'no'. However,
mum went on to say that this didn't really surprise her as Barry found it very difficult to relate to any men and said, 'He's even off with his dad at times!' She
explained she felt it was due to Barry having had very little contact with males so
far in his life.

Some weeks later, Barry has become quite different in his behaviour towards
me. He now often asks where I am and wants me to play with him. Whatever I
am doing Barry wants to do it too. He has even now decided that I get a
goodbye hug and a kiss when he is going home. He comes to find me when he's
leaving, no matter where I am in the nursery. Mum says that at home Barry now
talks a great deal about things he has done with me at nursery and that he says
he loves me now. Mum confesses to being quite amazed at the transformation.

Barry's mum speaks very positively about me, as a male educarer, working with
the children at the nursery. She feels that it has done a great deal for Barry's ability
to relate to males and feels Barry has really benefited from his experiences. Barry,

for his part, has experienced some very positive things about males, including that it is gender-appropriate for men to work in the care and education of young children: he's still only 2$\frac{1}{2}$ years old.

Sarah

Sarah is 2 years, 2 months old. Like Barry she too began at the nursery attending afternoon sessions. She appeared shy and lacking in confidence. She cried very frequently on arrival and her mum, nanna and staff found it very hard to settle her. Marie (Sarah's key worker) has written the following observations concerning Sarah:

> Sarah used to cry and was very hesitant to come into our family room at the nursery. If Terry, our male member of staff, was present we had the greatest of difficulty in persuading her to come and join in any of the activities. While Terry remained in the room Sarah stayed very close to, and was very clingy, with me and a female member of staff near to her. After I spoke about this with Sarah's mum and nanna they explained how Sarah would go hysterical if they ever stopped to speak to a male in the street or on the road. Within a few weeks, Sarah had begun to accept Terry's presence more and could be persuaded to come into the room when he was there. However, she still would not go anywhere near the area where Terry was and appeared very apprehensive of him. She preferred to stay wherever possible at the other end of the room. Gradually, as time went by, Sarah became less clingy to female staff when Terry was present and even began to accept Terry speaking to her from a distance. Sometimes she even responded with a faint smile. Some months later, Sarah now comes into the room when Terry is present without making any of the fuss she used to make. She still seems very aware of his presence but accepts him chatting to her. Mum and nana are in their own words 'over the moon' with the way Sarah is getting more confident in the way she relates to males.

These two cases highlight the fact that both girls and boys under 3 can benefit from having opportunities to experience relating to males in the nursery. Both Barry and Sarah could be identified as learning from an early age that males can be gentle and caring too, and that it is gender-appropriate for males to work with young children.

However, in interpreting what we observe we must, as professionals, guard against making speculative judgements concerning the quality of experiences and role models offered by the males with whom any child has previously been in contact. For example, in many cases it may simply be that their experience of males is extremely limited.

What is highly significant here is that where parents see males working effectively and professionally with young children, even when they themselves might have had initial reservations, they are quick to realize the value that males can bring to the nursery setting.

Gender appropriateness

The European Union, in its recent Green Paper on Social Policy, recognizes that 'The gender based division of family and employment responsibilities not only constrains women's lives but also deprives men of the emotional rewards resulting from the care and development of children' (quoted in Jensen 1996: 5). It has put forward the need for a commitment positively to encourage men to participate more in the care and upbringing of children. This clearly includes males working in the care and education of young children. Such a commitment needs to begin from birth, providing both male and female role models of involvement. There is evidence, from my own experiences, that some children come into nursery provision with emergent ideas about what it means to be a boy or a girl, and that this has often been influenced by parental perspectives and the visual media.

For some this may include ideas similar to those that boys play with guns or cars while girls bake or play with dolls. One of the most important duties of the educarer, male or female, is to ensure that children's learning experiences (everything they do, see and hear) are not restricted by stereotypical ideas such as these. With this in mind the educarer of the late 1990s, and beyond, should be positively encouraged to provide wide experiences/ learning opportunities for all his/her children. Changing gender roles, within society, appears to be highly relevant. Indeed, research into the career choices of secondary school children seems to indicate strongly that they make decisions about careers based on a variety of criteria, many of which have been built up through their experiences during the previous years of their life. Perhaps not surprisingly one of these criteria is the notion whether or not the career is seen as appropriate to their gender. It would seem that our children's lives and other learning experiences influence how they later see themselves as part of their community and wider society. Jensen (1996: 25) highlights a significant aspect of this when finding that 'one of the obstacles to more participation by men in childcare services is the myth that caring for children is not men's work'.

Caring for children appears to be the focus of many such myths, including the myth of the 'New Man'. It was suggested by a newspaper report (*Los Angeles Times*, February 1995) in the USA that American men were changing and sharing more and more childcare duties with their partners, thus creating 'New Man'. A recent study found this to be wildly untrue and just a 'figment of the imagination'. The findings from this study showed that American women spent on average 10.7 hours each weekday caring for preschool children, while fathers take charge without the mother's help for less than an hour a day on average (Stearman and Van der Gaag 1995: 46).

Children need to learn from as early an age as possible that caring for children is as much men's work as it is women's, and they should be encouraged to understand why. Gender should not be used to create artificial barriers in terms of roles in society, not least in the education and care of young children. Having males working in educare and related services for young children can be a significant part of young children learning about gender issues.

Hughes (1991: 146) sums up some of the feelings of those who recognize the value of males, as well as females, working with young children, in her claim that 'it is . . . sad that many children never have the experience of being taught by a male teacher in the early years of their schooling'. She recognizes too that 'this is particularly poignant for children whose experience of men at home is limited or whose feelings towards men are hostile'. Most importantly, we need to understand, as Hughes (1991: 146) points out, that both boys and girls can suffer through missing out on such experiences.

However, even at a time when the importance of having male educarers is becoming more widely recognized, men appear to continue to be disadvantaged by the system and some of those who work within it.

Disadvantaged by the system

Often difficulties encountered by males are not limited to direct personal discrimination. Disadvantage can also be meted out by the system itself: a system that doesn't seem to encourage males to work with young children and in some cases actively discourages them from doing so. Males are often not helped by the design and layout of the buildings and grounds used for nursery settings. Many of these buildings and grounds have not been planned like traditional mixed workplace settings such as offices or factories. They are often designed or, in practice, utilized as female-(adult) only units with, for example, only female toilets or facilities which then have to be adapted to cater for any male employees.

This can, in some situations, cause all sorts of problems including those of privacy and access, which in turn can negatively impinge upon relationships in the workplace between males and females. Male educare colleagues (I haven't had very many, I might add!) have passed on comments to me which they've overheard in establishments in which they've been employed, such as: 'Till he came we didn't have to queue for the loo. Why should he have one loo all to himself when we have to share one between six of us!'

Also, when many of the buildings and grounds were designed this was done in a way which does not appear to have consciously taken adequate account of male workers' potential interests, including adventure areas, growing areas, woodwork areas, etc., all of which can help educarers, both male and female, to offer children wider learning opportunities. In identifying male areas of potential interest it is important to be clear that these areas are in practice not just areas males can be interested in. Many females find them of particular interest too, hence they are, in reality, areas which educarers of both genders can focus on jointly in partnership.

A male applying to work in the majority of nursery settings has to consider that the system can often be anti-male. Even where it does not appear to be like this, he is likely to be the only male working in the building. It can be very off-putting to the male. However, it needs to be recognized that most staff appear to regard the employment of males as positive both for themselves and for the children, even if there are some initial difficulties to sort out.

I can bear witness to this on a personal level. In the majority of settings where I've worked it has not been a major problem for me as a male to join a hitherto all-female team. Indeed, the three most influential people on my career with under-fives, through their support and encouragement, are all females. However, I recognize that there always exists the potential for the existence of major difficulties: those wishing to exercise their discriminatory views can choose from a whole range of other areas to find a reason why the male presence is unsuitable while masking their real reason, that of gender discrimination. Such situations may not always come from within the setting itself. For example, it may be adverse influence or assessment from supporting LEA services, such as advisors or inspectors, who consciously or unconsciously exercise their prejudices against males. Those who address a male educarer's competence or ability are most likely to be female, as very few early years advisers or nursery head teachers are male. The fact that I have felt discriminated against only once for being a male in a nursery setting does encourage me to believe that the occurrence of such situations is relatively rare. However, my experience of personally encountering gender discrimination has also made me highly aware of how difficult a situation males can sometimes find themselves in.

The male educarer can, in some cases, appear isolated and the odd one out because of the existing system. This can be noticeable even from as early as interview stage. Differences can be exploited by some in negative ways, particularly by those who feel very anti-male at that period of time and, for whatever reasons, are unable to prevent this from clouding their judgement. The likelihood is that the majority, if not all, of those who interview the male educarer will be female. Such a situation is borne out by my own experiences and can potentially leave the way open for some level of discrimination to take place. In interviews for nursery posts in which I have participated, only one ever had a male member on the interview panel, and he was outnumbered by the other seven female panel members!

With much appearing to be potentially against males, why do men, such as myself and others, still make the choice to work with very young children? The National Children's Homes Action for Children Report, *What's He Doing at the Family Centre?* (Ruxton 1992: 35) quotes Andrew, an educare worker, as being attracted to work with the younger children because he felt that 'the process of socialization and education is so important earlier on'.

Having taught across the primary age from nursery to upper juniors I feel, similarly to Andrew, that the nursery stage is the foundation for the rest of the child's learning and development, hence of the highest importance.

Men continue to be disadvantaged by a system which doesn't seem to encourage them to work with young children and therefore appears not to support young children having the opportunity to experience being taught by a male in their early years. Such a situation appears symptomatic of the way some would have relations exist between males and young children.

Male relationships with young children

The fact that there are those who treat all men with suspicion can be put down, in the main, to fears or experiences of sexual abuse. Some, though not rejecting the idea of having male educarers, feel that males should have some controls put on certain aspects of their work. These include a female tutor at the Institute of Education who feels that 'men do have to be very careful about when and how they touch a child . . . There are things a woman can do which might be misconstrued in a man' (Hancock 1996: 48).

A male development officer of the National Children's Bureau, who argues that relationships between males and young children may have to be different from those between females and young children, indicates feeling that 'as a male member of staff you may have to be prepared to accept that some restrictions on what you can do with children may be necessary' (Hancock 1996: 48).

While agreeing that there is a need to protect children from sexual, or any other forms of abuse, I disagree most strongly with the balance of such standpoints, not least on the grounds of equality of opportunity including parents', children's and male educarers' rights. My view is that such restrictions on practice should not be allowed to exist because they have extremely negative effects. In the main they serve little purpose except to reinforce existing prejudices; sometimes they distort them still further. They also seriously undermine the quality of the role of the male educarer because they adversely affect both public confidence in the male educarer and the male educarer's own confidence and ability to act naturally and effectively within their role and context. As Hancock (1996: 48) argues, 'insisting that all toileting is done by female workers . . . conveys all sorts of negative hidden messages to children about gender roles'.

Adams (1994: 97) supports this perspective on hidden messages in pointing out that 'Children's attitudes and expectations are influenced by their experiences at home, in their communities, at nursery, playgroup and school.'

Hancock focuses on the legal aspects of such restrictions, pointing out that legislation is beginning to support the abandonment of what she terms 'shortsighted policies', when she refers to a recent case in which an industrial tribunal forced a Norwich crèche to 'scrap its policy preventing men from changing nappies or accompanying children to the toilet after the tribunal upheld claims of sex discrimination' (Hancock 1996: 48).

The potential sexual abuse argument against employing men in childcare services appears to be particularly strong in the UK. However, as Jensen observes, 'it does not appear at all in the Danish debate. This does not mean that cases of sexual abuse in childcare services are not to be found' (1996: 23), but they are not used as an argument against employing males in childcare services.

Significantly, and probably as a result of this, substantially higher numbers of males are employed in childcare-related services in Denmark than in the UK. It seems that in the UK we need to support and value the role of males in educare and related services much more.

Challenging stereotypes

Dowling (1989) identifies the teacher as a role model for children, while Siraj-Blatchford (1992: 121) emphasizes the important function performed by adult role models in addressing issues of discrimination against culture and race: 'An anti-discriminatory policy must involve compensating for the images which constantly surround children in the world outside the nursery.'

Such arguments appear equally true for addressing issues of gender. There are many negative images of males experienced by children in their daily lives outside the nursery setting. In the absence of any positive role models young children may have little or no choice but to absorb these negative images which can, over a period of time, build up into very negative and stereotypical ideas about males in society.

Male educarers can provide positive images and in this way be a vital part of equal opportunity provision, as the case of Matthew demonstrates. This case is offered to highlight just how important it can be for some children to be able to experience positive images of both male and females employed in educare and other child-related services.

Matthew

Matthew attended the inner-city community nursery centre for four full days a week. In his home situation he had been the victim of physical and emotional abuse by his mother's live-in partner whom Matthew calls 'dad', as well as neglect and emotional abuse by his mother. Mike is the male social worker involved with Matthew's case. None of Matthew's drawings at nursery showed any details relating to his mother or his 'dad', but were all related to his relationships with female and male educare staff at the community nursery centre and with Mike his male social worker. Many of his drawings and paintings significantly included me (his male educarer) and Mike (his male social worker) playing with Matthew at football or exploring the nursery grounds or travelling in the car to and from nursery, etc.

Matthew used to talk to staff, including Mike and me, about things which had occurred in his home situation, including physical and emotional abuse. On one occasion he said to me, after telling me how his dad had been aggressive towards him and his mother and hurt them 'but you won't hurt me will you, Terry, 'cos you're kind?'

In Matthew's case he appeared desperate to develop relationships with both female and male staff who weren't going to hurt him and who were predictable in their behaviour. With regard to males, Matthew appears to have learned that they are not all the same in the way they relate to him.

Matthew, having had negative experiences of males, was learning that here were two males who were very different in the way they responded to him in comparison to his 'dad'. Hopefully these positive experiences have challenged his negative experiences of males and helped Matthew to gain a more balanced view of how males can behave, including the fact that they can be kind and gentle. He has certainly not been left simply to absorb the negative images he has experienced.

The importance of being actively and consciously aware, and involved, in offering children positive cultural experiences, including those which are gender related, is publicly recognized by official bodies including the DES (1990). The Rumbold Report recommends that 'every establishment should have . . . a policy on equal opportunities . . . which promotes an under-standing of cultural and physical diversity and challenges stereotypes' (DES 1990: 35).

Educare establishments with males on the staff may wish to consider incorporating staffing issues into their equal opportunity policy. This was the case at one nursery where I was employed. A section of the policy read: 'We aim to offer all our children equal access to all of the activities available regardless of gender, culture, race or disability . . . The nursery has a male teacher on the staff team which enables us to offer positive role models of both genders to all our children.' Such a statement can help to give clear messages, to visitors and the community, that the nursery, its staff and parents/carers, values having a male on the staff and intends to challenge stereotypical gender images.

However, in attempting to make positive statements we, as professionals, need to be wary of inadvertently reinforcing stereotypical images. In this case, without intention, the wording in the above may be interpreted by some as valuing male roles at the expense of female roles, by stressing the point of having a male on the staff. On reflection I feel that it might perhaps have been better if it had read: 'The nursery has both male and female staff and aims to offer positive role models of both genders to all our children.'

Both female and male educarers do appear to recognize and value male col-leagues. Some go as far as to view them as indispensable in meeting the needs of young male children, a view expressed by June Smedley: 'No woman teacher however able can identify from her own experience with the problems of being a boy and growing up into a young man' (*Daily Mail*, 31 July 1996: 12). Others such as Nick Fell simply feel strongly that 'children need male role models. It does create a balance in the school' (*Daily Mail*, 31 July 1996: 12).

Jensen (1996: 21) concludes from his research that 'a single gender staff group has greater difficulty in treating children equally and educating them in equality – because children do not do what we say they should do but what they see we do'. Such an argument supports the idea that staff teams working in the educare of young children need to be composed of more appropriately balanced numbers of both males and females. The issue is not about whether men and women are better, as potentially both are equal in this respect, but that they are, or can be, different in some ways.

In order to achieve a more gender-balanced workforce with young chil-dren, government needs to challenge stereotypes. They can do this by taking high profile measures to encourage and enable men to take a more signi-ficant role in educare provision. This can take the form of helping to reduce the cases of negative or restrictive policies and encouraging greater male entry into the profession; this would be a major initiative in supporting the value of relationships between males and young children.

In the meantime, much can be, and is being, done at a local and individual level by challenging 'closed' thinking and negative practice. It appears that the levels of restrictions on male practice depend to a great extent on the establishment (its local authority, management and staff), and the male and female educarers themselves. I can only speak from my own experience. At the community nursery centre where I currently work I consider that things are as they should be for male educarers. I do not experience any noticeable prejudices against me as a male undertaking my duties in the same way as female staff. There are no restrictions on practice. I am able to sit children on my knee and to comfort them and also to change them. Parents speak only positively of having me, as a male educarer, working with their children.

Relationships with parents

At a recent staff appraisal (May 1995) of my performance relating to aspects of communication, parents' views were sought. The following list comprises just some of the comments parents made regarding me as a male educarer. All the comments, apart from being 'like a second dad', could most certainly just as easily have been made about a female educarer:

- He is easy to talk to.
- He is very approachable.
- He listens well to us and to our children.
- He's like a second dad to my child.
- It feels like he really knows your child.
- He makes my child feel really welcome at the nursery.
- He has explained a lot of things about education.
- I feel I can speak to him at any time.
- My child really loves him.
- He is so good with the children, they all like him.
- He uses first name terms; that's important.
- I wish he could move to my child's next school as his teacher.
- He's easy-going and easy to talk to.
- He involves us.

All of the comments made were very positive. As all were made in confidence, of course, I am unaware which parents made them and cannot research them further. What they clearly show is that parents of children at this inner-city community nursery centre feel extremely positive about having this male on the staff, both for themselves and for their children. They feel valued by this male and extremely happy for their child to be in his care. The comments are really more about the person – me – and not so much, if at all, about my gender.

In this nursery centre setting no parental concerns appear to exist about the safety of their children with me – a male educarer. Yet there is evidence of concern created within society about potential relationships between men and young children involving the likelihood of sexual abuse.

The level of such a concern is, in my view, having a highly detrimental effect on the provision for young children because males are being increasingly put off choosing a career with young children. They are being made to feel that such a career choice is no longer gender-appropriate. My concerns have been echoed by others, including most recently the Chief Executive of the Teacher Training Agency. She is alarmed at the current shortage of males in primary education, which seems to be getting worse, based on statistics that the number of men entering this area of the profession has dramatically declined over recent years. Her current view is that, based on current trends in the primary section, 'we shall have no men left in the profession by 2010' (Jensen 1996: 12).

As we have seen, parents of children in nursery settings can have very positive perceptions about a male educarer working with their child. However, this may depend very much on the individual male. I would question whether it is not just the same regarding parents' positive acceptance of female educarers? Perceptions and viewpoints do appear highly relevant: for example, some single female parents seem particularly pleased and approve of me as a male interacting with their child. I have also found that in some cases a male presence can be influential in helping to develop more positive relationships with fathers as well as with mothers. For example, some fathers appear to feel more relaxed dealing with or talking to a male when first coming into the nursery setting. Because of this it may be that these fathers are more willing to become involved in talk with staff when bringing or collecting their child.

At our nursery centre last year we had one father who didn't respond positively to the efforts of female staff who tried desperately hard to develop a relationship through dialogue with him. When I, as a male, approached him to try to develop dialogue he appeared more relaxed and responded positively. Over a period of several weeks I did manage to establish a relationship with him through which we were able to help both his family and his child much more. As staff, we all noticed that as this father grew in confidence in coming in to speak with me, he also spoke more to female staff and importantly his son developed more confidence and appeared happier attending the nursery.

This father needed to bring and collect his son as his partner was in and out of hospital and unable to do so. Jensen (1996: 27) in his research found that some fathers preferred their child to attend a nursery where there were some male workers. This may be because of cultural reasons or due to a lack of confidence or just that some men feel awkward in talking or dealing with female staff. Not all fathers or male carers, however, are able to bring and collect their child from nursery settings. As professionals, we must remain mindful of the importance, in our work with children and their families, of involving fathers/male carers as much as possible. The research of Ghedini *et al.* (1995: 29–30) and others underlines this point.

Reflections

Since my appointment to the community nursery centre almost two years ago I have had time to reflect on my own situation. I feel that, initially, settling in was made easier by the fact that the centre had previously had a male teacher for a short period and also I'd had previous experience of working in settings where I was the only male. The staff team was a very experienced one who, as a whole, recognized the value for the children, parents and themselves of having a male educarer on the team. The management team was particularly aware, committed and supportive of me. I was made to feel welcome and to feel valued.

The head teacher and interviewing panel members, though fiercely committed to equal opportunity, made my appointment on merit but recognized the value of a male member of staff as helping to reflect the community more fully in terms of gender. As a local by birth, a parent of three children – two girls and a boy, and lately grandparent of a 3-year-old grandson – I have been able to bring cultural and life experiences to the fore which have greatly helped me to empathize with the children, parents/carers, staff and the community. What I have experienced appears to contradict some of the experiences of other males in educare settings, such as Trevor Chandler (1990: 31–5), but I find no problems with such variations of experience. I have functioned within a different role to Trevor and others in that the majority of my work has been with the children on the 'shop floor' as part of the team. It has not been difficult for me, as a male, to come to work at my current community nursery centre. This has been, in my view, mainly for the following reasons:

- I had a highly positive attitude of wanting to be there, coupled with a set of life and work experiences which greatly contributed to my conceptual understanding, perceptions and thinking concerning the role of the teacher and the team at the centre.
- Because of the level of experience and development of the staff at the centre they did not find it difficult to relate to me as a male team member. This support of colleagues has been the single most important aspect of being able to develop within my role.
- I was able to value and respond positively to other staff members' skills and training, particularly as my partner trained initially as a nursery nurse.
- Mothers did not see me as a threat because I was a man even though some had been victims of violence from a male partner. On the contrary, they saw me as a person to whom their children could relate and respond to positively. Any anger women have towards men has not been directed at me. It appears I am accepted as being the professional educarer I am.
- The high level of support and encouragement from parents/carers has been highly significant in making me feel welcome and valued.
- There has been some teasing of me as a teacher but not in a way which threatens me merely as a male. Staff have got to know my strengths and my weaknesses and generally feel happy to seek my advice as I seek theirs. We recognize as a team that no one person has all the answers.

- My presence, though altering the dynamics of the centre in some respects, I consider that it has done so positively and in a whole-team way.

Increasing the numbers of males in educare and related services

We need more males in educare services to address issues of both equality and quality of those services for children and their families. Having appropriate numbers of males and females in educare services plays a critical role in supporting and ensuring equal opportunities within that provision for all our children. Even as the idea takes hold, that more men are needed in these services (as appears to be happening), it needs to be recognized that we must be patient as it is likely to be a lengthy process. The level and speed of success in achieving the goal of higher numbers of males will, I feel, very much depend upon the actions taken to encourage them to take up the profession. While the status of young children in our society remains low, their care and education will continue to be a low priority.

An important question is who is likely to be most influential and successful in altering this situation? Which organization, authority or institution? Or is it a much more fundamental question of values? This is always a difficult question to answer as each of those involved needs individually, as well as jointly, to take up the issues and integrate them into their own policies and practice. I have already considered the role of the LEA, but here is also a list of some other bodies with the power to influence males to take a greater interest in working with young children:

- local authorities
- trade unions
- training institutions
- careers officers
- the government and political parties
- childcare centres and educare settings
- parents' organizations
- voluntary organizations.

The level of research and knowledge about males in educare services seems extremely limited. What is needed, therefore, is large scale funding for research to be undertaken to ascertain what the advantages and disadvantages are of employing more males in this professional field, along with exploring barriers which exist to male recruitment. From this it is important to investigate the most appropriate and efficient policies which, when implemented, will enable recruitment of appropriate levels of males into this area of work.

My view is that training institutions are probably one of the most powerful agencies to influence and promote greater levels of male recruits into educare services. I say this because unless there are sufficient numbers of qualified males available to work in these services it is pointless and ineffective for local authorities, other organizations and educare settings, to create policies themselves and have high ideals about employing a more gender-balanced workforce. Again, this is related to the status of work with young children and the career prospects of all workers in this field.

Career officers and teachers in schools and in local authority offices are also extremely important as they have the advantage of being in a position to influence young adults positively to consider a choice of further education in order to qualify to enter such work. They can inform students, and other young people they are in contact with, that educare work is for males just as much as it is for females.

The small percentage of males in educare and child-related services is part of a national problem reflecting and involving a gender-segregated labour market. Those jobs which are stereotypically dominated by males have much higher status, and importantly higher pay, than those dominated by females. Educare work is dominated by females and as such, like that of welfare and care work, has lower status and pay. We need to influence those with the power to make efforts to change how things are so that the status and pay of any job is not determined by the gender of those engaged in the work but more by the nature and importance of the work itself. For this to happen, a shift in people's thinking needs to take place so that men and women become considered just as important as each other in life and work generally.

The United Kingdom might do well to emulate campaigns such as that launched in Viborg, Denmark, in 1994 called 'Children also Need Men'; in Kalmar, Sweden, entitled 'Come into Childcare Services You Men!' and in 1995 by the Employment Office in Aarhus, Denmark, entitled 'The Recruitment of Men for Pedagogic Training'. The aim of the latter is to have 33 per cent of those entering training to be male by the year 2005.

The 1994 Danish campaign (Children also Need Men) was run in cooperation between the Ministry of Employment, the Employment Office, training colleges and two unions for pedagogues. The campaign was promoted in all the training colleges in Denmark and involved the distribution of a huge poster and colourful brochure along with major press and media coverage.

A course was set up for men-only to train as pedagogues, and special training material was prepared. Success was achieved through this in attracting more males in work with young children.

What has been a common feature in all of these three campaigns is that they have been well funded, on a large scale and nationally promoted. Most noticeably, however, the most important source of impetus appears to be national government. They are the only organization with access to sufficient funding for campaigns and training on such a large scale that they can be effective in driving home the message that 'children need males too!'

'Children need males too!'

While this chapter has concerned itself with the importance of males in the educare of young children it is important to remember that this is within a context that the role of females in educare is highly important too. Young children need to be able to interact with, and respond to, both males and females.

In this short chapter it is impossible fully to address all the issues related to males working with young children. What we need is more literature and research which explores this sometimes sensitive area of male employment. It is most important now that having read this chapter you think and talk much more about the issues involved, and seek to make your views not just known but acted upon!

Here are some questions you might want to think about having read this chapter:

- What in your view are the reasons why males remain so under-represented in educare and child related services?
- Is there a need for some kind of positive discrimination to encourage more males to train and work with young children as educarers, social workers, etc.?
- How important do you feel positive male role models, as well as positive female role models, are for young children?
- What changes could be most effective in creating a more balanced work-force in educare and social work and how might these be best effected?
- Do you feel males often respond to children differently from females? If this is the case then why might this be so? (Quoting examples from your own experiences might perhaps be most useful here.)
- How important do you feel it is to reflect the aim of providing positive role models of both males and females in an establishment's equal opportun-ities policy? Is this always possible without male members of staff?
- How many males does your own local authority employ in its early years provision? If you don't know, why don't you find out?
- How might the individual seek to challenge the negative images of, and discrimination in practice against, males working with young children in educare and child-related services?

References

Adams, J. (1994) 'She'll have a go at anything': towards an equal opportunities policy, in L. Abbott and R. Roger (eds) *Quality Education in the Early Years*. Buck-ingham: Open University Press.
Broadhead, P. (1993) Men in Childcare, *Child Education*, March: 11.
Chandler, T. (1990) *Men Caring for Children*. London: National Children's Bureau.
Department of Education and Science [DES] (1990) *Starting with Quality, the Report of the Committee of Inquiry into the Quality of Educational Experience Offered to 3 to 4-year-olds*. London: HMSO.
Dowling, M. (1989) *Education 3–5*. London: Paul Chapman Publishing.
Ghedini, P., Chandler, T., Whalley, M. and Moss, P. (1995) *Fathers, Nurseries and Childcare*. Brussels: European Commission.
Goldschmied, E. and Jackson, S. (1994) *People Under Three*. London: Routledge.
Hancock, P. (1996) Men in Childcare, *Child Education*, March: 48.
Hughes, P. (1991) *Gender Issues in Primary Classrooms*. Leamington Spa: Scholastic.

Jensen, J. (1996) *Men as Workers in Childcare*. Brussels: European Commission.
Ruxton, S. (1992) *What's He Doing at the Family Centre?* London: National Children's Homes.
Siraj-Blatchford, I. (1992) Why understanding cultural differences is not enough, in G. Pugh (ed.) *Contemporary Issues in the Early Years*. London: Paul Chapman Publishing in association with National Children's Bureau.
Stearman, K. and Van der Gaag, N. (1995) *Gender Issues*. Hove: Wayland.

5 | 'We need to know' – identifying and supporting very young children with special educational needs

Sylvia Phillips

This chapter sets out to show that even though there is legislation which should ensure that children who have special educational needs (SEN) should be identified at a very early age, their educational needs met and their parents supported, there are great discrepancies in actual practice.

How are children's special educational needs identified when they are under 3 years old? What are the responsibilities of educarers? How do parents react to learning that their children have special educational needs? Why is it that the experiences of both parents and children with SEN can be so different?

There is general acceptance that early detection of special educational needs is important in order to improve a child's quality of life, by making early intervention possible. This chapter argues also that early diagnosis or clarification of a child's special needs, provided it is conveyed appropriately and accompanied by support, is essential not only to a child's development but also to parents' feelings and capacity to support the child. Clearly, the ability to identify SEN, understand the nature of a child's difficulties and suggest appropriate methods of intervention is also of great significance to all those who work with young children.

Special educational needs and children under 3

In most local authorities there is a well-established network of services for the under-fives, where health authorities (including NHS trusts and family health services), social services departments, voluntary agencies and LEAs work closely together to make provision for young children with SEN. Local authorities have a duty, under the Children Act 1989 (implemented in 1991) to 'Safeguard and promote the welfare of children in need and to promote the upbringing of such children by their families, so far as this is consistent with their welfare duty to the child by providing an appropriate range and level of services' (Department of Health 1991: 5).

Under the Children Act 1989, a child is 'in need' if:

- s/he is unlikely to achieve or maintain, or to have the opportunity of achieving or maintaining, a reasonable standard of health or development, without the provision for her/him of services by a local authority under this part;
- his/her health or development is likely to be significantly impaired, or further impaired without the provision of such services;
- s/he is disabled.

Although there is some overlap, there has been concern that this Act does not refer to the term 'special educational needs' which had been introduced in the Education Act 1981 and confirmed in subsequent Education Acts (1988, 1993 and 1996).

The Code of Practice (DfE 1994) contains a section on the under-fives and includes a particular reference to children under 2. Under the 1993 Education Act an LEA may assess the educational needs of a child under 2 subject to parental consent, and *must* assess if requested by a parent. As a result, if necessary, a statement may be produced specifying the nature of special educational provision to be made. The Code of Practice suggests that statements for children under 2 'will be rare' but makes it clear that the LEA should make appropriate educational provision such as home-based teaching (for example the Portage system), a developmental play programme (perhaps at a nursery or assessment centre) or home-based support from a peripatetic service (for children with learning or visual impairment, for example).

There is an emphasis on close liaison with the health service and the need for careful monitoring. Where a child between the ages of 2 and 5 is not attending a nursery class, school or centre, then it is envisaged that parents, health or social services will remain the major sources of referral for assessment of special educational needs.

Where the child is attending a nursery school or class, however, there is an expectation that the procedures for identifying and meeting SEN outlined in the Code of Practice will be followed. This involves noting concern, notifying parents and working closely with them. There may be referral for multidisciplinary assessment involving an educational psychologist and, in particular, a child development team involving child health services to establish whether or not there is a physical explanation for the difficulty (such as hearing or visual impairment), or to obtain help and advice on the management of difficult behaviour.

Emphasis is put on parents' rights to be informed about, and involved in, all decisions when a child is under 5. Health services and trusts are central in identifying children under 5 with SEN, and they are asked to supply parents with the names of voluntary organizations who may offer a variety of forms of assistance. Similarly, under the Children Act 1989, local social services departments must provide written information on the full range of services in their area for children 'in need' and ensure it reaches those who might need it.

Identifying the SEN of under-threes

Hall (1996) usefully distinguishes between *low prevalence, high severity* conditions which include conditions for which a pathological basis has been demonstrated or can be presumed (such as cerebral palsy, aphasia, severe learning difficulties, severe language impairment, autistic spectrum disorder) and *high prevalence, low severity* conditions in which there is a combination of genetic, constitutional and environmental factors, sometimes including neurophysiological or neuropsychological dysfunctioning (for example dyslexia, moderate/general learning difficulties). Clearly, while the former are more easily identified at an early stage, the difficulties should be seen as a continuum not a dichotomy. Four criteria may be used in deciding that a 'condition' exists. There must be a 'distinctive'

- response to interventions;
- aetiology (causation);
- pattern of presenting symptoms;
- prognosis.

It is important to note that 'high prevalence' needs are more easily identified after a child has reached the age of 5+ and concern is expressed as a result of difficulty or even failure in learning. However, many difficulties experienced in later learning may arise from physical, sensory or other impairments which could be identified earlier (for example, a high proportion of children experiencing dyslexia manifest speech and language difficulties below the age of 5). While some caution must be exercised over 'predicting' potential difficulties, there can be no doubt of the need to identify a child's SEN as soon as possible so that they can be enabled to make the most of their abilities. With the aid of speech therapy, physiotherapy, teaching and medical intervention where necessary, their independence, cognitive, physical, motor, social and emotional development can all be promoted. At the same time, the burden of stress on parents can be reduced, together with feelings of isolation. Financial support may be available, and the need for this should not be ignored.

In many cases, identification of SEN will be a matter of complex professional judgement which may have begun before the child was born; several local authorities have a comprehensive assessment system. Soon after birth there is a medically based assessment in hospital. This will be particularly thorough if any adverse signs have been noted at prenatal examinations. Babies showing particular conditions, Down's Syndrome for example, will be referred to a child development centre or be visited by a senior medical officer and specialist health visitor. They will examine the baby and outline an intervention programme, often involving other professionals, such as physiotherapists. Thus the beginning of this early assessment process is *medical* – doctor, paediatrician, specialist health visitor.

At 3–6 months parents take their babies to the child development centre for further assessment where they are likely to be seen, interviewed and the child assessed by various members of a multi-professional team. Possible members of such a team are: paediatricians, doctors, specialist health visitors, orthoptists, occupational therapists, speech therapists, educational psychologists, audiologists, dieticians, dentists, social workers, teachers and Portage workers. (Not all local authorities have such a centre, but they should provide a similar *service*.)

Emphasis is placed on the need for professionals to work with parents as partners and the contributions which parents can make to an informed and full assessment of their children are widely acknowledged. Despite the expectations under both the Children Act 1989 and Education Acts, parents are not always aware of their rights and often have incomplete understanding of the nature of their involvement. Gross (1996) reports on some parents in one LEA who, when asked if they wanted to contribute to their child's assessment, wondered how much the contribution might be as they were not sure if they could afford it!

Traditionally, and even with the establishment of child development centres, assessment has taken place in settings which are unfamiliar to child and parents, and this in itself has highlighted the power differential between professionals and parents in determining outcomes. The Code of Practice proposes: 'Young children should be assessed in a place where the child and family feel comfortable' (DfE 1994: 99).

In the same way, if parents have 'access to other parents and to family centres and other local services, play and opportunity groups and toy libraries, then they might have direct impact on the effective implementation of any assessment process or educational programme' (p. 99).

Simeonsson *et al.* (1995), in a comprehensive discussion of family involvement in assessment, emphasize that if parents and professionals are to act as partners there must be *mutual* awareness of respective skills and attitudes. It is important when we work with parents of young children, and are seeking their advice about a child for whom we have concern (or about whom they have expressed concern to us), that we appreciate that they enter into any interview situation with both apprehension and expectation. These will include expectations:

- as to the manner in which the assessment will be carried out;
- about the nature of information they will be asked to provide;
- of a clear diagnosis (identification of difficulty);
- that there will be proposals for intervention.

If their expectations are not met, then the involvement will be perceived as unsatisfactory and incomplete. Moreover, this experience is likely to affect their views of the professionals/services involved and any future encounters. It is worth remembering, when working in a nursery with very young children, that a negative experience with a professional involved earlier with their child may be generalized to all professionals, thereby adversely affecting your interactions with the parents.

Simmeonson *et al.* showed that there was a strong mismatch between the professionals and parents' perceptions of the assessment process: 62 per cent of professionals said they always asked personal questions of parents whereas only 6 per cent of parents anticipated such questions. In terms of involvement in the process:

- 44 per cent of professionals expected parents to 'wait in the lobby' while the child was assessed;
- 27 per cent wanted to see parents actively working with the child;
- 13 per cent invited parents to 'validate' assessment results;
- 13 per cent invited sharing attitudes and feelings.

Clearly, even where multidisciplinary teams do 'involve' parents there are different constructs of involvement and partnership, which require reconsideration.

Nevertheless, more than 80 per cent of parents found the experience helpful overall. However, a significant 33 per cent disagreed with the results.

In some local authorities, all children are assessed by a multi-professional team at 3–6 months, 9–12 months and again on school entry. Children who are identified as having SEN will have their development assessed and monitored by this team until the age of 5, when they become the responsibility of the LEA and its associated health services. They may well still be seen by a multidisciplinary team but not necessarily involving the same people. Developmental plans are reviewed every three to six months. The plans may involve:

- other tests/interviews with particular professionals;
- advice as to what other professionals may offer;
- a 'teaching/learning' programme.

Not all authorities observe the above practices, as illustrated in the studies below. It is often considered that the provision and coordination of services for young children is at its best in the pre-school years. Unfortunately, there is still evidence that 'breaking the news' to parents is not always handled sympathetically. Thus there are reports of mothers/carers being told without the presence of a partner or family member or friend for support; of parents' own fears being belittled; of information known to the doctors and nurses being withheld, only to be 'let out' inadvertently, by junior staff on some other occasion.

Parents' perspectives

Since the 1970s much has been written about the needs of parents/carers of children with special needs, particularly those children with a physical, sensory or learning disability. There have been several attempts to produce taxonomies of parental reactions to learning about their child's difficulties, and it is important not to generalize about parental reactions and feelings.

The Audit Commission (1994) noted that parents are frequently the first to detect that their child is not developing normally. In their survey, 40 per cent of the sample parents were the first to identify a problem but over 50 per cent of them were not believed or taken seriously by the professional to whom they turned for advice. General practitioners were cited most frequently as failing to take the parents' concerns seriously.

Sometimes, of course, conditions such as Down's Syndrome are identified at birth, although it may be impossible to predict future development for some time. Parents tend to feel dissatisfied when a professional's answers appear inconclusive or indecisive: they are anxious to know what the future may bring and may, as a result, feel that the professionals they meet

- are professionally inadequate – they don't know enough (and therefore the parents seek 'another opinion');
- are trying to protect the parents from learning some 'bad news';
- don't understand parental concerns;
- are patronizing them and 'gatekeeping' knowledge.

What parents really want is a basis for planning their lives and that of the child. It may well be, of course, that they also have some hope or need to believe, that the child will one day 'improve'.

Often this leads them to follow *any* suggestion about 'methods' which appear specifically designed for children with similar difficulties. It is important for anyone who works with very young children with SEN to be aware of the range of reactions their parents may experience, in order to work cooperatively with those parents. The plea of 'we need to know' does not mean that the information given will necessarily be welcomed, although there are numbers of parents who react with apparent calm acceptance and are able immediately to plan to meet needs successfully and obtain maximum support for their child from within and outside the family. However, the following reactions to learning about a child's disability were noted by Mackeith (1978):

- feelings of protectiveness (of 'the helpless') which could become overprotection;
- 'revulsion' at the abnormal (a strongly emotive term, but possibly experienced by some people);
- anxieties about parents' own competence in caring for the child and about the possibility of having future children with a disability;
- feelings of bereavement – some people go through 'grief' reactions which have been compared to bereavement, for the loss of the 'normal' child they might have had. This often gives rise to anger but then is usually replaced by adjustment to the situation;
- shock – the surprise of the news – which can lead to denial of the disability or of the professional's diagnosis, anger (general or directed towards professionals) and resentment;
- guilt – a feeling of personal 'blame' for producing a child with difficulties and fear that the child will blame them as parents. This reaction is probably far less common than was once believed;
- embarrassment – fears of social reaction.

It should be noted that this categorization may be misused and educarers should be wary of trying to identify reactions in this way. The final category here, for example, may not be 'embarrassment' but fears that society and different social groups will not 'accept' their child. In other words this taxonomy does not reflect a 'social model' of disability.

Implications for educarers

The 'news' that a child has a special need may produce any (or a mixture) of the above emotions, to varying degrees. Many parents may need support in working through these emotions, and workers with very young children must be aware that even where parents have known of the special need since their child's birth, they may still be experiencing difficulties in adjustment. Any transition point – entry to nursery and later, entry to school – marks a significant stage in their child's development and their inclusion within, or exclusion from, social settings. For many parents, the ages of 18 months to 3 years is the period where their children's needs are first identified, and therefore parental feelings may be at their most heightened. Sadly there are still examples, as will be shown later, where parents are not informed of their children's difficulties in a way which shows any consideration for their feelings – in the words used to them, the time they are given or the situation in which the information is conveyed.

In some cases, teachers and nursery nurses may be the first to voice concern to parents about a child's difficulties, and indeed they are requested to do so in the Code of Practice. It is important to plan carefully how to do this, giving thought to the timing and setting of the occasion and the language used and the support offered. This should show you have thought of possible action that can be taken and where appropriate advice and support is available. Educarers should also be prepared, not for one of the earlier reactions, but for some *relief* to be expressed by a parent who might have had concerns and been afraid to voice them, or who, as in the case of one of the mothers described later, had not been listened to by another professional.

When there are other children in the family the effects on them also need to be considered, as the case studies later in this chapter show. Parents will be concerned about the amount of attention and time which are inevitably spent on meeting the needs of a child with SEN and which might adversely affect the intellectual, emotional and social development of other children. Where there are older siblings, then there will probably be a certain amount of jealousy and expectations of 'looking after younger brothers and sisters'. How is the family to decide what is normal and what is placing undue burdens on all members of the family? I know of several families where older children feel that their teenage years were fraught because they were expected to spend a lot of time helping parents to care for a younger brother or sister with severe learning difficulties. They echo the teenage mother of a child with SEN who said, 'There'll never be a time when I'm young and free!' They have to test out their friendships by seeing whether or not their friends can 'accept' their brother or sister; they may also feel guilty if they express frustration or resentment even to themselves.

The birth of a baby with special needs (or the existence of an older brother or sister with SEN) may begin affecting parental interactions with the 'normal' 2- to 3-year-old child in a nursery: and educarers should not become so preoccupied with their responsibility for recognizing and meeting the needs of a child with SEN and their parents, that they ignore the fact that they may be teaching the siblings of children with SEN.

Identifying young children with SEN in the nursery

Not all children under 3 entering nursery provision will have had their SEN identified by health authorities and child development teams. Responsibility for early identification and assessment therefore lies with nursery staff.

Assessing very young children and predicting their future development is made extremely difficult by the very varied nature of normal human development. All that can be said for certain is that while there should be a general increase in complexity and integration of behaviour and sophistication of problem solving abilities, the normal development of any one child will show much individual variation, at times appearing to stand still, at others to show very rapid advance. Emotions will come and go. Children with SEN may show either general developmental delay or 'disordered' development usually resulting in a 'spiky' or uneven profile. Thus some may have poor spatial or motor abilities yet have an extensive vocabulary and advanced use of language. Some may seem uncommunicative yet demonstrate comprehension far beyond their use of expressive language. Some may build towers and bridges with blocks, but appear unable to recognize a rhyme; some may sit and look at picture books, happily turning pages or 'share' a story with an adult; others squirm and run away before the first page is turned. It is important not to take too simple a view of 'general developmental delay'.

At no time does development take greater strides than in the first three or four years of life. We therefore need to expect greater diversity in levels of development of children aged 2 to 3 without affixing a label and assuming a set of 'expectations of development' will automatically follow. Hall (1996) refers to the following rates for particular problems in pre-school children:

- waking and crying at night – 15 per cent;
- overacting – 13 per cent;
- difficulty settling at night – 12 per cent;
- refusing food – 12 per cent;
- polymorphous pre-school problems – high activity, tantrums, disobedience, aggressive outbursts, tearfulness, clinging – 10 per cent of 3-year-olds.

In many cases these disappear and most can be managed successfully, but Hall points out that nearly half the psychiatric disorders in 14- to 15-year-olds represent conditions which have existed for many years. What is important, therefore, is to note 'concern' about children's difficulties, devise intervention strategies and monitor progress. The Code of Practice provides useful guidelines.

The key to assessment of children under 3 lies in close observation, which includes listening to and interacting with children in all their activities, including play. Particular attention should be paid to their development of language and communication skills, physical and motor development, self-help skills and increasing ability to interact with other children and adults. Where progress gives rise for concern then the child's teacher or key worker should prepare a written report setting out the child's strengths and weaknesses and noting evidence for the concern. The use of parent assessment material and developmental checklists should be considered.

Parents should be fully informed and the child's name should be placed on the nursery's SEN register.

Many nurseries already have their own systems in place and have often been supported by health visitors and special schools or support services in devising checklists and guidelines. Where the difficulty persists over five or six weeks (or is very severe) then the nursery may either devise an individual programme and place the child at stage 2 or 3 of the Code of Practice or refer for external support or further assessment. Because the child is so young, this will nearly always involve contact with health services and a hearing and sight examination.

It is possible to obtain statutory assessment which may lead to a statement for children under 3. Where a child over 2 is attending a maintained nursery or school then the LEA expects that Code of Practice procedures are followed. Many very young children, however, attend provision made by social services or voluntary or independent sectors. They are urged to share concerns and involve appropriate services and the LEA as early as possible.

Children with very complex needs may be given a statement (in some LEAs this may be necessary to access a particular service). A statement must include:

- all available information about the child, with a clear specification of the child's SEN;
- a record of the views of the parents and any relevant professionals;
- a clear account of the services being offered, including the contribution of the education service, the educational objectives to be secured and the contribution of any statutory and voluntary agencies;
- a description of the arrangements for monitoring and review.

The LEA should ensure regular review of any specific educational targets. There should be close collaboration with non-educational service providers to ensure good record keeping and to 'avoid duplication of investigations when the child is over 2 years'.

Statements for children under 5 are subject to review at least every six months to ensure that provision is appropriate to meet the child's needs, in addition to carrying out annual review in accordance with the regulations.

Special educational provision for children under 3

This might include full- or part-time attendance at a nursery school or class playgroup or opportunity playgroup. For a description of one such 'opportunity group' see Brenda Kyle's chapter in *Working with the Under-threes: Responding to Children's Needs*. There may be additional support from a learning support teacher who may give one-to-one help, or from a peripatetic hearing or visual impairment service. In some cases there may be a home-based learning programme – the Portage system is used in several LEAs – or a locally devised teaching service, perhaps based on 'play' and involving parents in teaching their child. In cases of behaviour difficulties, support may be available from an educational or clinical psychologist or a peripatetic support service. In some cases, there may be access to non-educational services: speech therapy is by far the service most often identified for young children with SEN.

So far, the chapter has considered what provision there should be to identify and meet children's SEN, emphasizing the importance of procedures for assessment in order to obtain access to health and educational services. The chapter has highlighted the need to work in partnership with parents and to identify children's SEN early. Two case studies give contrasting examples of practice.

Mark Smith

Mark is the second child in a family of three children. His elder brother Daniel was just over 3 years old when he was born. His mother was a nursery nurse who had stopped working when Daniel was born. His father works in a bank in the large industrial town where they live.

Mark developed normally until he was about 15 months old, by which time he was walking, had normal language development and showed a lively curiosity. His mother cannot remember exactly when she became aware that Mark had started walking around with his head down, and started bumping into chairs and the doorway, and falling over things. 'I remember one day suddenly thinking that's the fourth time today I've told him to look where he's going.' Her husband tried to allay her fears by saying 'It's just a habit', but agreed that Mark should be seen by the doctor.

Their GP immediately referred Mark to the local hospital for further tests. Mrs Smith recalls that she was fortunate in having her own parents living nearby who could look after Daniel while she began what seemed like 'a nightmare of not knowing – not knowing whether he was brain-damaged, blind, or both; not knowing whether he would "get better" or whether the condition could be cured by an operation'.

The family was fortunate in that the hospital was also the location of the regional child development centre, which made a full assessment, suggesting that the eye condition was only temporary, and arranged a return check-up visit for five weeks' time.

On return to the hospital, the specialist prescribed an ointment to be administered four times daily. Mark's mother had great difficulty applying this, because Mark cried and tried to fight against it. His father administered it in the morning and evening before and after work. But there was no improvement. Mark's mother noticed that Mark began to sit in one place and hardly move. He showed no interest in his toys, even when handed them.

At this stage, Daniel, nearly 5 years old, started primary school, and Mrs Smith took him to school, pushing Mark in a pushchair. On the way she talked about things she could see, trying to draw Mark's attention to them. She began, however, to feel guilty that Daniel was being neglected during this very important period of his life because she could only think of Mark. Mark was now about 18 months old.

After using the ointment for six weeks, with no improvement, Mark was referred to the nearby city's Royal Eye Hospital, where infantile glaucoma was diagnosed.

Mrs Smith describes her feeling as 'one of relief'. 'Although it may sound strange, I thought at last I've got someone who knows what he's doing. I'd heard of glaucoma, although only among old people. I was told that he would have to have an operation to reduce pressure.'

Mrs Smith then went through a stage of apprehension and anxiety about how lonely Mark would feel in hospital. There was open visiting for parents and a lot of support from hospital staff.

Mrs Smith's parents cared for Daniel, in his own home, to try to reduce the stress on him and his parents. Mrs Smith recalls trying never to cry in front of Daniel and making great efforts to help him learn to read, and playing with him whenever possible: 'I remember screaming at John, my husband, "that's just what Mark will never do".'

At this time she was contacted by a visiting teacher from the peripatetic support service for the visually impaired. This teacher had been alerted by the local child development centre, and visited Mrs Smith before Mark's operation and arranged a visit to follow the operation. Of all the professionals, doctors, consultants, nurses and psychologists encountered by Mrs Smith during these months of uncertainties, she found the visual impairment (VI) support teacher, Mrs Lee, the most helpful and supportive. 'She was very matter of fact and never tried to offer false hopes. What she did, however, was start to make me plan for the future. She told me what was available.'

Mrs Lee carried out an assessment of Mark's development, within the home, using the Sheridan and Oregon checklists. She offered suggestions for improving motor and language skills and began to visit weekly. She also began procedures for assessment which might lead to the provision of a statement of SEN. Mr and Mrs Smith were able to contribute to the assessment and a statement was completed within three months. At the age of 2, Mark was given a place in a mainstream nursery school near Daniel's primary school (which unfortunately had no nursery provision) and provided with a special support assistant (a trained nursery nurse).

The head of the nursery, the teacher and special assistant all met with Mr and Mrs Smith before Mark started, and discussed the parents' concerns for their son.

While at the nursery, the VI support teacher visited weekly to monitor progress and advise staff. Mark settled quite well at the nursery after a tearful first week. The nursery staff discussed a toilet training programme with the mother and this was put into operation within three weeks. By the middle of his second term he was completely trained, wearing normal pants and was proud to be 'a big boy'. By this time he became more independent in dressing. The VI teacher taught him the positioning of the main pieces of furniture so that he could move around the room. Although there were some difficulties when children were enjoying floor-play or equipment was left on the floor, staff and other children became far more conscious of the need to enable Mark to gain confidence in moving around, and he was taught to use particular paths to the main resource areas. He began to talk to other children and be included in their play. Advice

A report on Mark aged 2 showed:

Physical development	Average height and weight for age.
Social skills – self	Feeding skills poor – uses fingers adequately. Tries to feed self but not well coordinated. Help needed at meal times from special support assistant. Not toilet trained – still in nappies. Informed mother/NNEB after the event, i.e. wee-wee/pooh meant that he had done it. Can't dress self fully, but can put trousers, jumper, socks on. Trouble with shoes.
Social skills – others	Seems to enjoy being with other children. Play – has soft toys – all have names and he can identify them all. He also plays with toy cars and lorries.
Learning skills	He knows what a book is and likes to be told stories. 'Tactile' books/pictures were enjoyed.
Language development	Good for age – can use some whole sentences, asks questions, some baby talk words. Intelligible and articulate. Knows a few simple rhymes, for example 'Round and round the garden'.

Figure 5.1 An assessment of Mark's skills aged 2

was given to the nursery nurse on how to be vigilant and how to increase Mark's independence, as there was a tendency for him to rely on adults. Mark loved being told stories, and by the age of 3 could retell stories and invent them. He learned to identify and name objects by feel and touch. He located people by listening to their voices and finding the direction by sound. The VI teacher emphasized the need for him to keep his head up and directed to the front of his body, to try to prevent him from picking up any 'unusual' mannerisms which might impair social interactions.

The aim was to transfer Mark to a school with resourced provision for children with VI as soon as he was 3. There he would not have one-to-one support, but there would be a high adult–child ratio and an environment where special resources could be found to meet his needs. Mark had very little residual vision, although he distinguished light and could see and name some colours. A priority area would be to start on pre-Braille (and then Braille) teaching and mobility skills. Mark had developed normally in terms of language and ability and it was anticipated that when he went to primary school he would be given access to the full National Curriculum.

Although Mark's parents still find it very hard to accept the limitations faced by Mark, they now accept his difficulties and feel that Mark is being helped to achieve his potential.

Mark's parents believe that good educational provision has been made for him in his very early years and that this has led to good emotional and social development as well as fostering his independence. Once more he plays with toys, and his intellectual and language cognitive and linguistic skills are well developed.

Anna and Charlotte

Anna and Charlotte, twins, were born when their sisters Gemma and Hayley were 3 1/2 and 2 years old. The twins were delivered normally after an uneventful pregnancy of 40 weeks. Their mother recalls that they were 'very good babies' for the first 12 months, and that although they made noises, they did not cry much. When they were about 18 months old, their mother was concerned that it was difficult to start toilet training and also that although they were walking, they spoke no recognizable words. Finding this unusual after her experiences with Gemma and Hayley, she reported it to the health visitor who said that late language development was quite normal for twins who often developed their own form of communication. Their mother was uneasy about this as she had not observed *any* signs of communication between them.

Busy with four children, the eldest of whom started at school when the twins were 18 months old, the mother did not worry unduly. When the twins were just under 2, and Gemma and Hayley were at a local nursery, their mother joined a mother-and-toddler group, but because Anna repeatedly tried to leave the room, this was discontinued and the twins gained places at a nearby nursery, attending mornings only. Here they were placed in separate classes because staff believed separation would enforce communication skills. Both were still in nappies. At first they appeared to settle well (staff reported that they didn't cry when their mother left!) but within a week or so problems were reported. Anna destroyed the paintings and work of other children, threw water around and would not sit still for stories or games. Charlotte appeared to be less trouble, but mother thought that this was because she was allowed to wander round the classroom unchecked by the teacher. Their mother recalls 'I hated going to pick them up, because there was always a complaint. I felt they [the staff] thought I was a bad mother because I couldn't control them. They never offered any help, just told me what a relief it was when I arrived.'

At home, other problems emerged. The twins began to smear faeces over their bedroom; they tore wallpaper and broke ornaments and their sisters' toys. Parents removed all ornaments and pictures from within the girls' reach. They still had no speech. Their mother telephoned the health visitor who came and 'reassured' the parents that this was all 'normal behaviour' for twins and they would 'grow out of it'. (This attitude towards parental fears has been noted in literature on professional–parent relationships.) However, after four weeks, the parents felt they needed more help and contacted the health visitor again, who sent the health visitor responsible for SEN. She was immediately concerned about their language development and arranged for them to have speech therapy for half an hour each week in a group with three other children. She also arranged for them to have a hearing test. The local authority in which she works does not have a child development centre, but there is a team of designated professionals working across local clinics and hospitals to provide child health services.

In the meantime the mother had been asked to remove the children after five weeks in the nursery; they were now attending a 'Scallywags' group. She noticed that the twins did not appear to recognize the differences between objects: dolly, teddy bear, pretend foods were all treated the same and any could be given as a response to a request for any one of them. The experiences of the previous nursery were repeated – the twins interfered with the activities of other children, threw objects around and bit other children. Eventually the children were separated and Charlotte was sent to a different nursery. In a few months, the children had attended three or four different pre-school groups.

After failing an initial hearing test, they were retested and their hearing found to be normal. A consultation with a paediatrician was arranged. During this session, Anna remained silent, but Charlotte kept saying, 'stuck, stuck', which was her word for food. During the consultation, an attempt was made to assess each child independently. When Charlotte, who had been outside with her father, came into the room, crying, her mother picked her up and cuddled her. 'What did you pick her up for?' queried the consultant, 'You're reinforcing her bad behaviour.' The mother considered this a most unsympathetic response, and lost confidence in the consultant and any of her later deliberations. The specialist health visitor and speech therapist were all consulted, but no 'cause' was found for the twins' delayed development.

At the age of 2½, although they attended the Scallywags nursery, no one had specifically mentioned 'special needs' to the parents. The twins were still in nappies and continued to misbehave. Their mother said, 'Picking up Charlotte was like before – I dreaded going. I felt they thought it was my fault – that I wasn't a good mother.' Anna developed the habit of beating her head on the floor. No one at any of the nursery groups ever alerted the mother to any difficulties in ability, understanding or learning, or made any reference to intellectual, perceptual or motor development. All comments were concerned with 'misbehaviour'. The health visitor devised a 'discipline programme' for use in the home, but it was deemed a failure.

If the twins' difficulties had been identified as 'special educational needs' then even aged 2 appropriate provision could have been sought. No one informed Anna and Charlotte's parents of their rights: they were, in fact, grateful for what they saw as some attempt to find out 'what was the matter'.

When the twins were 3, a teacher from a local special school visited at the request of the health visitor. The LEA agreed, without the need for a statement, to provide part-time attendance (mornings only) at the special school. A taxi, with attendant, collected and returned the twins. At about this time, the mother's sister (who was taking an NNEB course) brought her a book which contained a description of autism and autistic behaviour. After reading it the mother said, 'It's just the twins. I knew then, really. We didn't mention it to the doctor, she'd said it was just language delay. It was the end of everything – they were never going to be normal, there was no future for them. My husband only read two or three pages. He couldn't bring himself to read it all.'

A month later, the consultant arranged for an assessment at the school. The mother's memory of this consisted of the girls coming into the room one at a time: Anna touched her mother's legs and then wandered docilely round the walls. When Charlotte came in, she sat on a 'horse-thing – she loves animals'. There was some discussion of the difficulties and then, as the parents got up to go, the doctor said, 'I think they show characteristics of autism – no communication, and behaviour difficulties.' With that, they left. The letter they received said 'signs of infantile autism'. 'We just came home thinking – our life's over. They're never going to get better. You try and be strong, 'cos it's coming up to Christmas, but you know it will just mean wrecked toys.'

The family now has support from social services: someone to 'watch' the children from Monday to Friday from 2.00 to 4.00 p.m., and every other Sunday someone comes from a voluntary service. On Wednesday, a carer from the Crossroads scheme stays with the twins from 6.00 to 8.00 p.m. so that the parents can take the other children out.

These parents only started accepting that their children had difficulties between the ages of 2 and 3. Confirmation of the problems and support has come only after the age of 3, and even then it is not adequate. The effect on the older girls is as yet unknown; major problems occur because the twins destroy their belongings and take a tremendous amount of attention. Moreover Charlotte has killed the family guinea pig – 'loving it, squeezing it and dropping [or throwing] it'. Anna has squeezed the hamster so tightly that it died. Neither girl is toilet trained. Anna is described as 'docile, laughing a lot, twirling until she is dizzy and imitating what you say'. Charlotte is very 'bossy and stubborn'. Since the diagnosis, the parents have been in touch with other parents through the National Autistic Society and have found this contact very supportive. However, their mother does feel bitter about the lack of information and support when the children were under 3. She says:

> The health visitor should have listened to me and known there was something wrong when the children were smearing and had no speech . . . The main problem with doctors is they should listen to parents a little bit more . . . Playgroup and nursery teachers should pick up problems earlier and inform parents. They shouldn't treat you as if you're not a good parent.
>
> We needed to know earlier. No one told us. The mother has to do all the running – I had to contact the health visitor and say 'you'll have to come' . . . We knew something was wrong but we didn't know what . . . There's a special school in a nearby town, but [there is] a two-year waiting list – now we might not get a place.
>
> It helps to know what's *wrong*. We *need* to know.

These two case studies illustrate how much any system depends on local applications and the quality of the professionals. Both sets of parents experienced similar feelings of distress, loss and confusion. Both families were subjected to stress because of inaccurate diagnosis and incomplete information in the early stages. However, Mark had a condition which, while causing a permanent and severe disability, meets all four of the criteria for a syndrome. It also creates a disability which comes high up on the scale of 'social acceptability'. His LEA had good, focused services for visually impaired pupils and the support service had sufficient time to provide an excellent level of support.

The twins, in contrast, had a condition which was, in its early stages, at the far end of a continuum of infant behaviours. Far less is known about autistic spectrum disorders than visual impairment. The point at which behaviour should be considered as sufficiently 'different' to warrant being considered as needing special support and intervention is a matter for multi-professional judgement. However, even when the concerns of the parents were taken seriously and a consultant paediatrician became involved, there was a clear failure to coordinate the multi-professional work. No one appeared to find the time or inclination to listen to the parents seriously and see what was happening from a family perspective. No one coordinated all the contributions to make a complete picture. What happened was a series of individual actions none of which could, in isolation, be an effective response to the special needs of Anna and Charlotte. Certainly, no one addressed the feelings of the parents that 'their life was over'. Many of the obligations placed upon local authorities and area health authorities went unfulfilled. Voluntary organizations were found by informal means, reports were delayed, parents were less than fully involved in assessment procedures and they were left in the dark about what the professionals were thinking.

The stories of Mark, Anna and Charlotte, their parents, and other family members remain unfinished, but from these early beginnings we can see just how significant early identification is for children with SEN. There are important implications for the role of all those involved in educare for the under-threes and the way they impact on the future lives of children with SEN *and* their families.

An interesting issue arising from the second case study concerns attitudes towards SEN. While children with language difficulties, a sensory impairment or physical disability may often evoke a sympathetic response from teachers and nursery nurses, those presenting challenging behaviours do not. Autistic spectrum disorders vary considerably, but some are manifested as behaviour difficulties. All too often the response of professionals is to seek the removal of such children, or, in the case of very young children, 'blame' parents: they do not make the same supportive response that they would for a quiet, socially conforming child whose learning may be impaired. All those working with children need to examine their own attitudes towards the nature of behaviours presented by children with SEN.

In the same way, a further problem is related to our beliefs about 'maturation and development'. While an earlier cautionary note has been expressed about individual differences in development, the study of Anna and Charlotte provides a warning against believing a child 'is going through a phase and will grow out of it'.

References

Audit Commission (1994) *Seen but not Heard*. London: HMSO.

Department for Education [DfE] (1994) *Code of Practice on Identification and Assessment of SEN*. London: HMSO.

Department of Health (1991) *The Care of Children: Principles and Practice in Regulations and Guidance*. London: HMSO.

Gross, J. (1996) The weight of the evidence: parental advocacy and resource allocation to children with statements of special educational need, *Support for Learning*, 11(1): 3–8.

Hall, D. M. B. (1996) *Health for All Children*, third edition. Oxford: Oxford University Press.

Mackeith, R. (1978) The feelings and behaviour of parents with mentally handicapped children, *Developmental Medicine and Child Neurology*, 15: 24–7.

Simeonsson, R. J., Edmondson, R., Carnahan, S. and Bucy, J. E. (1995) Family involvement in multidisciplinary team evaluation: professional and parent perspectives, *Child: Care, Health and Development*, 21(3): 119–215.

6

'I'm like a friend, someone to chat to . . . but a professional friend' – how educators develop positive relationships with parents and children

Chris Marsh

Introduction

As an educator of children aged between 3 and 11 who now teaches adults at a university, and as a mother of three teenagers, it has always seemed to me that the relationship between educator and taught significantly influences what is learned, particularly in the early years. My previous research highlighted ways in which positive relationships were developed in a nursery school (Marsh 1994). Research in Finland has also shown that when children were asked about the important features of their experiences when they were younger and were attending early childhood centres, the quality of relationships was a major aspect (Huttenen 1992). A child in an early childhood centre can, during the course of one day, be with six or more different adults, none of whom have any specific responsibilities for her. Taken together, these issues pose an interesting research question: how do educators develop and maintain positive relationships with parents and children? (Smith and Vernon 1994). This question is explored with particular reference to the key worker system whereby one worker has overall responsibility for particular children and their families. Research in a children's centre operating this key worker scheme included observations of parents and children arriving and departing and of children involved in activities with staff during sessions, as well as interviews with parents and staff using a structured interview schedule.

A parental perspective

I knew about the centre because I live in the neighbourhood and I pass it regularly. I'd heard it was a good place so you need to put your child's name down early, so as soon as Hannah was born I went and filled in a form. When it was nearly time for her to start I got a phone call inviting

me to take her to have a look round. I met the coordinator who
explained which sessions Hannah could come to and gave me a booklet
about the centre. She introduced me to our key worker who showed us
round and arranged other times for us to visit. These were so she could
find out a bit about our family, Hannah's routines and likes and dislikes
and our ideas on how we wanted to bring her up.

When Hannah started at the centre her key worker met us when we
arrived and she'd have a chat. Hannah would start to play with one of us
or on her own. Then I'd give her a cuddle and go and make myself a
coffee in another room. Later someone would come and ask me to go
and pick Hannah up while she was still playing happily – before she got
upset and asked for me. These times away from her grew longer until our
key worker suggested I left her for the full session.

Hannah's been here for over six months now and she loves it. She
runs in and goes straight to her key worker who picks her up and gives
her a big cuddle. If Hannah's woken up and been fretful – teething or
something in the night – I'll tell our key worker so she knows Hannah
might be tired or out of sorts later. If she is fretful at all when I leave
they'll phone me later at work to let me know she's settled down.

Then when I or my partner collect Hannah later they'll tell me anything special she's done or said or if she's been out of sorts. If we chat for
too long Hannah'll come to be picked up and cuddled by me or our key
worker or she'll go off to play again. She loves it here, and I really trust
them.

This toddler and her parents are very happy with their centre. What are the
factors that have helped to make the process of inducting Hannah and her
parents to the centre such a positive experience? What can we learn from this
that might be useful in facilitating this process for other parents and their
babies and toddlers in other establishments?

The centre where this study was undertaken is a children's centre close to
the heart of a large city. It operates an extended day, although most children
attend for a core day arriving between 9.00 and 9.30 a.m. and leaving
between 3.00 and 3.30 p.m. There are approximately 14 workers including
those involved in senior management plus support staff who are involved in
cooking, cleaning and maintenance. The centre is open all year except for a
week at Christmas. As well as the provision for under-fives without their parents being present, which is my concern here, the centre operates an after-
school club, a holiday play scheme for children aged 5 to 11, parent and
toddler sessions and a similar session for childminders and their toddlers.
The provision for under-fives which I have been examining consists of three
units, one for babies aged 6 months and children up to 2 years old, and two
for children from 2 years old up to school age. The under-twos unit uses one
room and has a bathroom attached; the others, over-twos units, consist of
two rooms with a bathroom situated in-between them. As the centre is open
almost all year and operates on an extended day basis, staff work shifts and
holidays have to be staggered.

The centre's system of admitting children is similar to that of many settings catering for the under-fives. A key worker system operates whereby one adult is the primary contact person for an individual child and their parents. This key worker will be with the child for a large part of each day, and will be responsible for collecting information about the child and their family, updating records on the child's development, and passing relevant information about the child on to colleagues. The key worker will also meet parents on a three-monthly basis to discuss the child's progress over this period. This way of working accords closely with that described by Siraj-Blatchford in her discussion of issues of quality in combined nursery provision. She uses the term 'primary educators' – in the centre under discussion here these are usually the key workers:

> Centres can strengthen and support children's development and learning by establishing a day-to-day, one-to-one link for parents and children. This can be with a primary educator who is responsible for monitoring the quality of care and education a child receives. Primary educators should have a key responsibility to liaise with the parent/carer, to collate records of the child's development and to act as a significant reference point for information on the child and her family.
>
> (Siraj-Blatchford 1995: 12)

The system which operates at this children's centre follows these recommendations closely. The key worker is allocated to the child and their family before the child begins to attend the centre. The key worker will be one who will be in the room the child will have as their base room. Each room has two key workers. The under-twos room has two key workers with a ratio of one adult to three or four children, the maximum being seven children to the two adults. The other rooms each have two key workers with a maximum of ten children making a ratio of one adult to five children. However, in these over-twos units there is some freedom of movement for some of the day, so the four adults will encounter up to 20 children.

When the parent(s) come to look round the centre with their child it will be the key worker who gives them a guided tour, who records the information on their child and their family and who oversees the process of inducting the child and their parents into the centre. Knowing who their key worker is from the beginning is reassuring for the parent and gives them one special person to relate to (Cowley 1991). This is particularly important in the over-twos rooms where several workers may be present at the beginning and ending of a session. Knowing which adult is your key worker gives the parent the security of knowing which person to approach, confident that any messages or important information will be passed on to other workers. The key worker system also provides a focus for discussion at a time of significant developmental change in the child's life. Meal times and eating habits, sleeping times during the day and toilet training are clear examples here.

On one visit it was interesting to see a group of older toddlers each eating and drinking in the manner suitable for their current stage of development. Children were using a beaker, a feeder cup or a bottle depending upon their individual needs, and implements included a plastic fork and spoon and a fork and fingers. The use of terry towelling bibs was encouraged, but not enforced, and these bibs were elasticated so children could easily remove them themselves. The atmosphere was relaxed and informal with conversation taking place naturally – much like a family meal at home.

The balance between children having some autonomy over aspects of their lives while encouraging them to become socially adjusted in ways regarded as acceptable by the wider society can be a delicate one to achieve. Staff and parents work in harmony to adapt to individual children's changing needs and routines.

For example, one independent 2-year-old (Hannah) was no longer keen to settle down at the centre for an afternoon sleep. Her parents discussed this with her key worker; together they adapted her routine, at the centre and at home, to accommodate her wishes. On one session observed, the children who had a sleep were being settled in their usual places – most had a 'bed' on the floor, one had her own pram. Hannah said, 'I don't have a sleep do I?' 'No, you don't have a sleep', came the reinforcing reply of her key worker and Hannah, happily reassured, went off to play quietly. In this instance the change in routine was suggested by the parent. In other cases it might come from the key worker.

One child was being toilet trained by her parents at home. They had explained how they were going about this to the key worker, who had agreed to follow the same procedure in the centre. Another girl, seeing her friend using a potty and not wearing nappies, had asked if she could do the same. The key worker had mentioned this to her parents, and her father had brought in several pairs of knickers as 'spares' for her to try instead of nappies.

In the under-twos room, where there are two key workers and few other staff are involved (except for the two workers who cover for lunch breaks), both parents and staff tend to think of both workers as key workers for the children in their care on a daily basis. Here the shiftwork system also means that if a child stays from 8.00 a.m. until 5.00 p.m., the same worker will not be there to greet the child on arrival and to see them leave. Neither parent nor staff saw this dual key worker role as a difficulty: indeed, both saw it as having potential advantages. Some parents said that they thought their child needed to get used to several adults in addition to themselves, although they did not like their child to be involved with too many adults during the course of a day.

One worker felt that a potential disadvantage of the key worker system was that a child whose main experience of the centre was with her key worker might feel overprotected. As she pointed out, 'Just because I'm her key worker doesn't mean she likes me more than my co-worker – she may prefer her even though she gets on well with me.' This worker felt that the key worker system should allow for some flexibility, which it did at this centre, whereby both the child and the parent could form friendships with other adults on the basis of need or preference while still operating the key worker system successfully. There were several examples of this happening at the centre, although workers acknowledged that this might lead to resentment on the part of a key worker.

The central play area is another area in the centre which is staffed by two workers who do not have a key worker role. The staff offer valuable opportunities for groups of children to have different experiences with other adults and other children at specified times. However, at times, with staff breaks, holidays and absences due to illness, it must seem to some children as though their special adult has been away for a long time.

The number of adults involved with individual children during the day was seen by staff as something which needed careful monitoring, as children can be with six or more different adults in a day.

A recent study of three independent nurseries raised this issue of the large number of carers involved as a particular concern in relation to babies under the age of 6 months (Barnes 1996). The child's age is crucial here. As Elfer and Selleck (1996: 10–11) point out,

> Children can cope well with having several adults looking after them, provided that it is the same adults over time and those individuals with whom they have an attachment relationship, for example, staff in the nursery are available in times when they are distressed, for instance, when arriving in the morning, or facing challenging circumstances.

Against this background, it was observed that relationships between workers and parents in the centre were positive, friendly and respectful. Such relationships are extremely important because parents can feel guilty about leaving their very young children. One member of staff commented on parents coming to collect their child and staying for a cup of coffee: 'I'm like a friend, someone to chat to . . . but a professional friend.' This professional aspect, and being able to distance oneself if necessary, for instance where child protection issues arise, is crucial.

On another occasion, a mother brought her child in and stayed to show some photographs to her key worker and the researcher. The key worker sensitively included a 2-year-old in this looking-and-talking session, helping her to be gentle with the photographs, while chatting to the mother and keeping a vigilant eye on her 7-month-old son as he crawled around and played happily on the floor. When the photographs had been looked at, the mother stayed for a further chat – her son was playing contentedly but she was eager to stay for her own sake.

Sometimes it is the need of the parent rather than the child which has to be considered. A worker mentioned this in discussing the gradual admission process when the child first starts to attend the centre, and gradually stays for longer periods without their parent in the room with them. As she put it,

> Sometimes it's the parent who finds the process hard, not the child. The child settles perfectly happily but you have to let the process go on longer because the parent isn't ready to 'let go'. There's a skill to knowing the 'right' moment when the child and the parent are ready for the child to attend without the parent present in another room on the premises.

In the centre children are segregated by age into under-twos and over-twos rooms. Thus a child starting at the age of 6 months will begin their life at the centre in the under-twos room and, at around the age of 2, will gradually transfer to a room for over-twos. This division into age groups is due to the enormous physical, emotional, intellectual and social differences children undergo between the ages of 6 months and 5 years.

This centre introduced an under-twos room when the number of babies and toddlers started to increase following the provision of workplace nursery places for mothers working for the local authority. It was considered that very young children needed a higher proportion of adults to children and a more protective environment than that appropriate for adventurous 4-year-olds. The smaller area, the lower numbers of children and the quieter atmosphere are evident on visiting this room.

Whatever the setting and the physical layout or the similarity or mix of age groups, very young children need a higher proportion of adults to children – adults who are supportive of their needs. For example, in another setting, a day nursery, Oliver, a 12-month-old boy, had chosen to crawl out of the babies' area into a room with predominantly older children. He 'grizzled' quietly yet persistently. A worker gently picked him up and talked to him reassuringly while she carried him comfortably – straddled across her hips. His 'grizzling' stopped instantly. The worker, whom he knew very well, chatted to him and others as she moved around tidying toys away.

Elfer (1996) points out the young child's need to explore and to be curious but to be able to return to a secure base, be it a parent, childminder or nursery worker, when they become anxious or face a new situation. The important points are that this adult is available when needed, and that the child feels secure and attached to them – if the relationship appears detached the child will not be reassured. One example of a child with a positive attachment to her key worker in the centre was demonstrated on a visit where Claire, 12 months old, was happily playing on the floor at a distance from her key worker. If this person went too far away, Claire would crawl closer to her. After a while a game developed whereby Claire would waggle her index finger as the signal for her key worker to pass her a small toy. Having done this the adult would waggle her finger in turn, smiling all the time. After a few minutes Claire struggled to stand up, pulling at the leg of the key worker who helped her gently. Later Claire lifted her arms to indicate that she wanted to be picked up, and received an immediate response. The interaction was non-verbal on the child's part; the adult chattered easily, sometimes providing a running commentary for Claire. Clearly the young child's communications were being responded to and her needs met sensitively.

The quality of such interactions reinforces a point Barnes (1996: 27) makes about the importance of the adult as a responsive caregiver: 'I believe that this is singularly the most important feature if babies are to be cared for appropriately within a group care setting.' Honig (1989) stresses the importance of workers allowing babies to get close to them; what she refers to as 'bodily dominion'. She suggests early security is developed through cuddling, hugging and touching, and recounts her experience of seeing a worker lying on her back on a carpeted floor jogging a baby on her legs. Honig recommends that if we regard such interactions as conducive to developing intimate relationships with children, we need to introduce key worker systems which will facilitate the development of such relationships. Rouse and Griffin (1992) also recommend the key worker being closely involved with their key children at some time during the nursery day.

At the centre, a key worker explains about her role with a new baby who had recently started. Samuel is 7 months old. He does not like the difference between home food and that on offer at the centre – this is being dealt with. His key worker has been temporarily released from some of her duties during the period of his gradual admission so that she can form an attachment with him. Hodges (1989) notes the importance of this flexibility for laying the foundations of the future relationship with the new parent and the new baby. Normally Samuel is a happy baby, but he has demonstrated his displeasure at two aspects of the centre's provision: the food, which he has refused to accept, and being placed in a specially enclosed area to keep non-mobile babies separate and safe from the activities of toddlers. This area is bounded by a plastic-covered, foam, semi-circular shape placed against a wall. There is a mirror placed for babies to look at themselves and cushions on the floor with toys safe for babies to explore with their mouths. When placed in this area Samuel grumbled quietly but continuously. His key worker now places him in the middle of the floor, at least for some of the time. This is an area where he needs constant supervision as older toddlers are walking past him; in essence he is in the centre of a thoroughfare. In the centre of this bustle and activity he is happy. This consideration of Samuel's needs and the adult's ability to see life from the child's perspective is important in helping him to feel happy and to be receptive to learning. Babies need affection and sensitive attention to help them develop their feelings, emotions and intellect (Miller 1992).

Now his key worker has adapted to his routines for feeding, playing and sleeping, she will gradually resume her other duties. Importantly in this adaptation process the baby leads in establishing a routine that suits his needs. Being sensitive to children's needs, even if they cannot be met instantly, is important in establishing and maintaining the child's emotional well-being. As Elfer (1996: 33) says, 'although we may not always be able to respond to children's emotional needs as quickly or as much as we would like, we can know about these needs, rather than denying them. Within the constraints of our work setting we can at least think about how we can respond in the most creative and sensitive way.'

At the centre under study children are segregated into age groups for most of the day, but there is some flexibility within this. The children in the over-twos rooms, for instance, regularly spend some time in the central play area with two other workers. These staff liaise with the children's key workers in planning the activities children undertake in this area so as to enrich and complement the curriculum on offer in the other rooms. Often a structured play environment will be set up with the children's active involvement. Activities within this might be designed to target special skills a child needs to develop. Equally the number of children present might relate to the level of the child's social skills or to the age of the children.

These two workers often work in the under-twos room to cover for the key workers during their lunch break. Consequently these central play workers are known to the children in this room. When a child from the under-twos room is due to make the transition to an over-twos room the child is often taken into the central play area with one or two children from the room into which they will be moving. Here they can meet and get to know some of their new peers in a smaller group, together with familiar adults. This makes the transition process more gradual and easier to cope with. The central play area can thus be one means whereby continuity of adults can be provided within a smaller group setting than the usual routine in the over-twos rooms.

There are several other ways in which the transition from the under-twos room to the units for older children is made as natural as possible. There are many similarities with the gradual admission process. The parent is consulted about the child's transition from one room to another and a suitable time is agreed. For example, a child would not be transferred if it arose at a traumatic time in their life, for example, around the time a new baby is due. Currently one girl is ready to make the move in terms of her developmental stage and chronological age, but she is not moving for another couple of months because her mother is going into hospital; her parents and staff agree it will be more appropriate for her to make the transition when her home life is more stable again. Consequently, she will be almost 3 years old when the transition is successfully accomplished.

When the child changes room they also change their key worker as, under the system the centre operates, the key worker is always in the room where the child is based. The child moves to their new setting on a gradual basis with their initial key worker accompanying them and staying with them. After a time in the new room the child will return with their key worker to the under-twos room. As with the initial gradual admission process the periods in the new room will get longer, and the original key worker will cease to stay as the child becomes settled. The child may also choose to go outside and play with children from the new unit at lunch times. Equally, children from the over-twos rooms often call in to see the younger children.

Before the transition process begins the parents will be consulted and will meet their new key worker. A child staying from 6 months to school age will thus have two key workers (there may be more depending upon staff turnover). Interviews with staff and parents did not show this to be a problem. The reasons for this appeared to be because parents were confident that key workers consulted each other and discussed the child's current achievements and needs in detail with them, and that they were confident that the child's written records were frequently updated. The flexibility whereby parents felt happy to chat to a worker (whether or not they were their key worker) about general issues or concerns was important here too.

Because the child has already undergone the transition from home or childminder to the centre, and they may have attended one of the centre's toddler groups or visited with an older sibling, the transition from the under-twos room to an over-twos room generally takes place without too much difficulty. If a family already has a child attending the centre and a younger sibling starts attending they may or may not have the same key worker. This depends upon which key workers have a vacancy, parents' wishes and the ages of the children concerned. For example, while the parent may appreciate the continuity and familiarity of having the same key worker for both children, if they are both in the under-twos room the older child may not react positively to sharing his key worker with his new brother or sister as well as sharing his parents! If the children are both in the same over-twos rooms they may benefit from being in the same room with the same key worker, or (depending upon their relationships) they may be better in the same unit but with different key workers so they would see each other for parts of the day but not all the time. Much depends upon the siblings' relationships and their parents' views.

How can we tell if children are happy in this centre? Body language, actions and comments were all cited by parents and by staff. Observations of children were undertaken on arrival, during the day and on leaving. Opinions were unanimous. Parents said: 'She runs in', 'She wants to come at weekends!' 'He doesn't want to leave.' The quality of staff and their stability in staying at the establishment are both important here. This was also shown to be very important in interviews with parents in a nursery school, where the stability of staff was greatly valued (Marsh 1994). Similarly, they found continuity of staff, together with frequent adult–child interaction, were highlighted by parents as important elements in provision for babies and toddlers.

Children too were important in helping to establish other children's happiness. I observed a 2 1/2-year-old girl, Sarah, run in and grab another girl in a friendly hug – no words were uttered – but Sarah's delight in finding her friend already there was evident. The importance of children's peers in helping children feel at ease in a setting away from home has only recently been recognized as a significant factor. Yet, as Elfer and Selleck (1996) highlight, children are often not able to rely on their friends attending a centre at the same times as they do.

This was demonstrated to me when Kelly, a 2 1/2-year-old girl, entered the under-twos room one morning. 'Is Louise here today?' she asked her key worker. 'No, it's Thursday – she doesn't come on Thursdays', came the reply. 'She was here yesterday', Kelly followed up the exchange. 'Yes', came the reply. 'You were both here yesterday, but Louise doesn't come on Thursdays. She'll be here with you tomorrow.' Kelly had clearly made established friendships in her nursery room. These may be fleeting or more long-term with young children: either way it is difficult for workers to help children to consolidate friendships other than by explaining a child's absence, as in this case, because of the intermittent nature of children's attendance at many centres.

Practical difficulties affecting relationships

The provision of places to as many children as possible, in ways which fit in with parents' wishes and work-related needs inevitably affects the composition of the group of children in any one room – this will vary from day to day and session to session. It is difficult to cater for the child's needs in terms of sustaining friendships with a self-chosen peer, especially as friendships may change frequently. The only way to ensure relative continuity in the composition of children in rooms in centres would be to offer all places on a five-day week, full-time basis, but to do this would severely reduce the number of places available, thereby restricting access to nursery places. Access, as Penn (1995) points out, is a major issue for both working parents and employers; this affects centres and the provision they are able to offer.

While continuity of people, children and adults is desirable in nursery settings, it cannot be guaranteed. Moving house may affect both groups, while children may move on to another stage of education; workers may change job or decide to make a career change. Parents who were interviewed stated the importance of staff staying for several years and appreciated knowing key workers over a long period of time. However, stability of staffing is hard to achieve in settings where the majority of staff have nursery nursing qualifications which are not viewed highly by the general public, where salaries are relatively low and the possibilities for upward movement in a recognized career structure are somewhat limited. Higher status and pay for staff engaged in work with very young children is necessary in strengthening staff development and creating the reflective culture envisaged by Elfer (1996) where educators can support each other and develop.

Conclusion

Research into day care suggests six major factors which enhance the quality of the experience of the child. These are:

- adult-child relationships based on affection and sensitive responsiveness, whereby the communication from the child receives an appropriate response;
- continuity and stability of caregivers and of adult relationships, including the use of a key worker system and low staff turnover;
- peer relationships;
- developmentally appropriate learning experiences;
- health and safety;
- enjoyment.

(adapted from Melhuish 1991; Sheriff 1995)

Of these criteria the first three are of overriding importance because neither 'appropriate learning experiences' nor enjoyment will occur unless the first three criteria are at least partially fulfilled; and 'health and safety' should be covered by legislation and the enforcement of minimum standards through the process of inspection. As Sheriff (1995: 5) emphasizes, 'the adult and the child and their interaction and relationship are of central importance to the quality of learning before school'. The preceding study of one children's centre and its key worker system would seem to support this conclusion. Further research would be valuable in considering how we can maximize such fruitful relationships now we realize and accept that they do not have to be between parent and child only, they can also be between a responsive worker and the child. Such relationships with primary carers contribute to the successful development and emotional well-being of children.

It is now acknowledged that care and education cannot take place separately but must take place together for the child to be nurtured successfully (Ball 1994). The key worker is one mechanism which can help to create positive bonds between workers and parents, which in turn will help the child to feel comfortable and at ease in the setting. Whatever system is used, however, it is imperative that open, honest communication takes place between parents and workers so that both are informed of any changes that are going to happen, thus helping the child to cope. In busy nursery settings with a large number of staff, children and parents around, clear understandings and procedures for passing on information are an essential element in providing a high quality service (Siraj-Blatchford 1995). Establishing at the outset a single worker as the major link between the home and the nursery context for both the child and the parent is a significant way of helping to establish a fruitful two-way communication system, to the benefit of all involved.

References

Ball, C. (1994) *Start Right: The Importance of Early Learning.* London: Royal Society for the Encouragement of the Arts, Manufacture and Commerce.

Barnes, S. (1996) *Provision for Babies in Daycare Settings.* Manchester: The Manchester Metropolitan University.

Cowley, L. (1991) *Young Children in Group Day Care: Guidelines for Good Practice.* London: Early Childhood Unit, NCB.

Elfer, P. (1996) Building intimacy in relationships with young children in nurseries, *Early Years*, 16(2): 30–4, Spring.

Elfer, P. and Selleck, D. (1996) Look who's talking, *Nursery World*, 15 February: 10–11.

Hay, S. (1995) Developing services for children under eight: responding to parents, *Children UK*, Autumn: 12–13.

Hodges, M. (1989) The first workplace nursery, in V. Williams (ed.) *Babies in Daycare: An Examination of the Issues.* London: Aldgate Press.

Honig, A. (1989) Quality infant/toddler caregiving – are there magic recipes? in D. Rouse (ed.) *Babies and Toddlers: Carers and Educators Quality for the Under Threes.* London: NCB.

Huttenen, E. (1992) Children's experiences in early childhood programmes, *International Journal of Early Childhood*, 24(2): 3–11.

Marsh, C. (1994) People matter: the role of adults in providing a quality learning environment for the early years, in L. Abbott and R. Rodger (eds) *Quality Education in the Early Years.* Buckingham: Open University Press.

Melhuish, E. (1991) Research issues in day care, in P. Moss and E. Melhuish (eds) *Current Issues in Day Care for Young Children: Research and Policy Implications.* London: HMSO.

Miller, L. (1992) *Understanding Your Baby.* London: Rossendale Press.

Penn. H. (1995) The relationship of private daycare and nursery education in the UK, *European Early Childhood Education Research Journal*, 3(2): 29–41.

Rouse, D. and Griffin, S. (1992) Quality for the under threes, in G. Pugh (ed.) *Contemporary Issues in the Early Years – Working Collaboratively for Children*. London: Paul Chapman in association with the NCB.

Sheriff, C. (1995–6) What is quality? *Childcare Now*, 4: 3–5.

Siraj-Blatchford, I. (1995) Expanding combined nursery provision: bridging the gap between care and education, in P. Gammage and J. Meighan (eds) *Early Childhood Education: The Way Forward*. Derby: Education Now Books.

Smith, C. and Vernon, I. (1994) *Day Nurseries at a Crossroads: Meeting the Challenge of Child Care in the Nineties*. London: NCB.

| 'There are lots of activities for him to do and plenty of help and care from the educarers' – supporting under-threes and their parents in a parent-toddler group

Jenny Lively and Karen McMahon

> It is the blend of different and realistic perspectives of both staff and parents which builds the best environment in which children can grow and develop.
>
> (Laishley 1983: 208)

Introduction

This chapter traces the development of a toddler group at Hollywood Park Combined Nursery in Stockport. It is written by two of us who are the 'educarers' who work with the under-threes; we trace our own development alongside that of the toddler group. The chapter is written as a personal account of our experiences and those of the parents, children and researchers who have worked with us.

Karen

I completed my training as a nursery nurse in 1971. Since then I have worked in day nurseries, nursery classes and infant schools. In 1991 I furthered my training by studying for a Diploma in Post Qualifying Studies. This course involved continually evaluating one's practice, identifying areas of need in the workplace and effecting change. My chosen elective study during this course was equal opportunities with a particular focus on gender issues.

After gaining this qualification, I applied for the post of deputy head of care in Hollywood Park Combined Nursery. Here I have had the opportunity to attend a wide and varied range of social service courses.

My community role involves liaising with health visitors, social workers and family resource workers. I also make arrangements for health visitor drop-in sessions, welfare rights drop-in sessions and our Friends of Hollywood group, and prepare our community room and soft play area for fun time sessions for children with special needs. Along with Jenny I organize the running of the toddler group and preparation for nursery sessions.

Jenny

My career with under-fives started in 1968 as a nursery assistant in a day nursery. On completion of a two-year NNEB course in 1973, I became a nursery officer and later deputy officer. In 1980 the day nursery amalgamated with the nearby nursery school to become the first combined nursery centre in the authority. I became a senior nursery officer within this new establishment.

My personal and professional development has been continually enhanced by the opportunities available in the centre. Gaining the DPQS has made me aware of changes in policy and practice in early years provision, and its effects on the role of those working in that environment.

I often draw upon my own life experiences which have given me a deeper understanding of the difficulties and problems that many parents experience when bringing up a young family. Through this I feel that I am able to demonstrate a non-judgemental approach.

I have been involved in a number of initiatives which have been both stimulating and of great benefit to staff and users of the centre and which will be discussed more fully in this chapter. These include:

- setting up our thriving toddler group;
- the opening of a toy library;
- fund-raising activities which rely on carers' participation and support;
- involving carers in the centre which gives us the opportunity to share knowledge and skills;
- arranging drop-in sessions for carers which have been well supported;
- producing a newsletter in which staff, carers and children contribute equally and enthusiastically.

These new ideas could not have been implemented without the commitment of our head teacher and staff team, and also the solid relationships that have developed with carers and users of the centre.

The centre

The centre is unique within the authority. It was established in 1980 as a result of the amalgamation of an existing nursery school and a day nursery run by the Social Services Division. The centre is housed in a former primary school building and provides 100 full-time equivalent places. There is a notional split of 60 'education' places for the normal school day and year, 10 places for children of students at the local further education college and 30 'care' places (mainly long-term care). The age range for which the centre is designed is 3 to 5 but because children are admitted to primary schools in the September or January of the school year in which their fifth birthday falls, the major client group are 3- and 4-year-olds. However, the need for some form of provision for the under-threes and their parents became increasingly apparent.

The centre itself is open 49 weeks of the year and provides day care facilities out of term time for up to 30 children per day, and offers day care between 8.00 a.m. and 3.00 p.m. on Monday, extended to 6.00 p.m. from Tuesday to Friday, according to individual children's needs. Staff work shifts to cover the longer day.

All staff are employed by the Education Division which funds the centre. The establishment comprises a head teacher, deputy head teacher, deputy head of care, one teacher, one senior educarer and ten educarers, together with a part-time non-teaching assistant, a caretaker, cook, domestic assistant, kitchen assistant and secretary.

The deputy head of care and educarers work shifts to cover the extended day and extended year facility. Teaching staff are entitled to the normal number of weeks' leave as other nursery school teachers, but these may not be in normal school holiday patterns.

An admissions panel which includes representatives from education and social services meets to discuss applications for places. The centre is a borough-wide resource and attracts families from a wide catchment area. Many of the children attending the nursery have younger siblings who often accompany them into the nursery as they arrive and come along with their parents to collect them at the end of the session. This constant contact with the under-threes was one of the reasons which led to the identification of a need for some kind of provision for this age group.

Staff development is central to the efficient running of the nursery centre. There is a firm commitment to collaboration, support and team work. Members of the team continue to update their initial training via award bearing courses, in-house development and attendance at local authority courses.

In-service training also includes study at diploma and masters level and involvement in research projects. There are many visitors to the nursery including students in training from colleges of further and higher education, other professionals from a range of services and support agencies, researchers from the university with which we have close links, and recently from Granada Television when the work of the centre was highlighted in a focus on the early years.

Carers have always been welcome and often share in their children's experiences in the nursery. It soon became obvious that there were other needs to be met within the centre, i.e. those of the under-threes, carers and the wider community.

The toddler group

The way we developed the toddler group was founded on our commitment to the 0–3 age group and our awareness of the issues influencing their educare. Other factors included the size of the building, the provision of stimulating experiences for the children, the constant involvement of

Figure 7.1 Advertising the toddler group

families with babies and children under 3 and the clearly identified need within the community for an educare facility for very young children.

We advertised the facility (Figure 7.1), inviting parents, nannies and child-minding groups to book in for sessions. The flyers were displayed in clinics, health centres, parents' noticeboards, newsletters, etc., but we found that booking out sessions to individual groups was too limiting, and decided to incorporate all groups coming together to the same session.

The number of people attending rapidly increased. We found we were serving a variety of people, i.e. single parents, childminders, parents with older children attending the nursery, and we needed to look again at the facilities we were offering. We considered limiting attendance to one session per week, but this was not popular because they wanted to attend more, and so we ended up with the majority of carers and children attending all three sessions. We both felt that with the number of families now using the toddler group we were unable to provide the level of service and standards we were used to and it soon became obvious that in order to continue with the high quality service we needed more space.

Developing the group

After much discussion and careful thought we decided to make use of a much larger room in the centre in order to accommodate more children and carers. We aimed to provide a place where children and their carers could learn how to work and play cooperatively with others, within a group other than the family. Staff and carers discussed together what we wanted to achieve and what carers hoped that they themselves and their children would gain from attending these sessions. Carers said that they wanted a place where they could feel comfortable and their children could play together in a safe environment. They welcomed the opportunity to build up relationships with other carers. One particular request was for a round table which they could sit around and chat. Another parent suggested buying new mugs just for the use of the carers. We looked at different aspects of the room together. Karen was aware of issues relating to the much needed floor space, particularly availability and the safety of the wide age range of the children for whom we were catering. She also suggested attractive shelving to house our different resources. Jenny suggested a children's book case in the home corner so that children could sit quietly on their own with a book if they wished. Another book case could be for carers to share books with their child, perhaps to read to them.

We both discussed the layout of the room, where different areas such as the wet areas for paint, water, sand, etc. would go and where the quiet areas would be situated. We talked to carers and other staff and came up with a plan for the room (Figure 7.2).

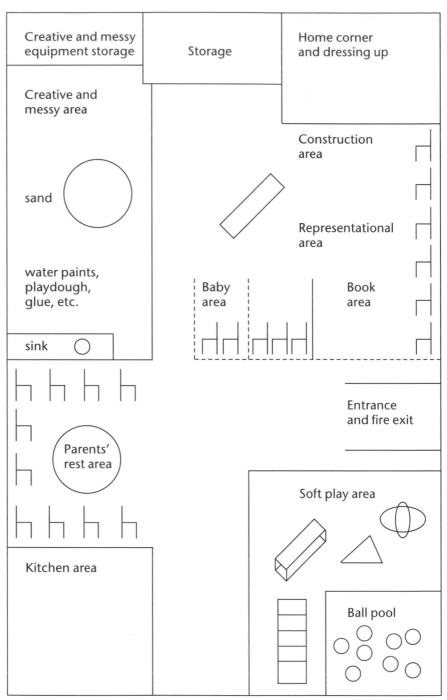

Figure 7.2 The layout of the room

Sharing information

We both discussed different methods of display in the room and decided to use some of the boards for information and some to display children's work. We backed the boards with attractive textured fabric. Much care and thought was given to the types of messages we wanted to portray. We wanted carers to be aware of how children learn through play and first-hand experiences. A large board was set aside for this purpose on which we displayed some of the quotes about play which we encourage parents and other carers to read and discuss with us. These include:

Play is a powerful motivator, encouraging children to be creative and to develop their ideas, understanding and language. Through play, children explore, apply and test out what they know and can do.

Children learn through play, developing social, physical, emotional and imaginative skills as well as finding out about the world around them.

Parents are able to share with their children the joys of learning through play, asking questions, providing encouragement and praise.

In line with our commitment to, and policy on, equal opportunities we also included posters and pictures of children playing from different countries and cultures. Throughout all the displays positive images are portrayed, reflecting the diversity of cultures, roles and abilities in our society.

Another board offers information about the local authority's admission policy to nursery schools, nursery classes and to our centre, which at the moment is the only combined centre in the authority.

Information booklets and admission forms are available for parents and guardians to complete at the nursery or to take home and fill in at their leisure.

We also point out and explain to carers our 'planning board' which is available for them to read at any time and to add any comments they wish to make. We feel that explaining to carers how and why we plan helps them to understand and support our aims.

There is a large wall at child level specifically for children to display their own work, but we do find that even at this young age children prefer to take their work home to show to other members of the family and no pressure is put upon children to leave their work at nursery.

Parents and other carers also have their own board where information regarding events happening in the community is available. Other facilities offered at the nursery are also advertised here. People also display their own items of interest such as toddler group 'nights out', coffee hours (Figure 7.3) and items for sale.

Carers quickly took the opportunity to share their views about the group and to offer suggestions. Pamphlets and information on health issues, welfare rights and parenting skills are also displayed on this board (Figure 7.4).

We are looking to arrange for an outreach worker from Welfare Rights to come into the centre so that carers will be able to call in and get information at first hand.

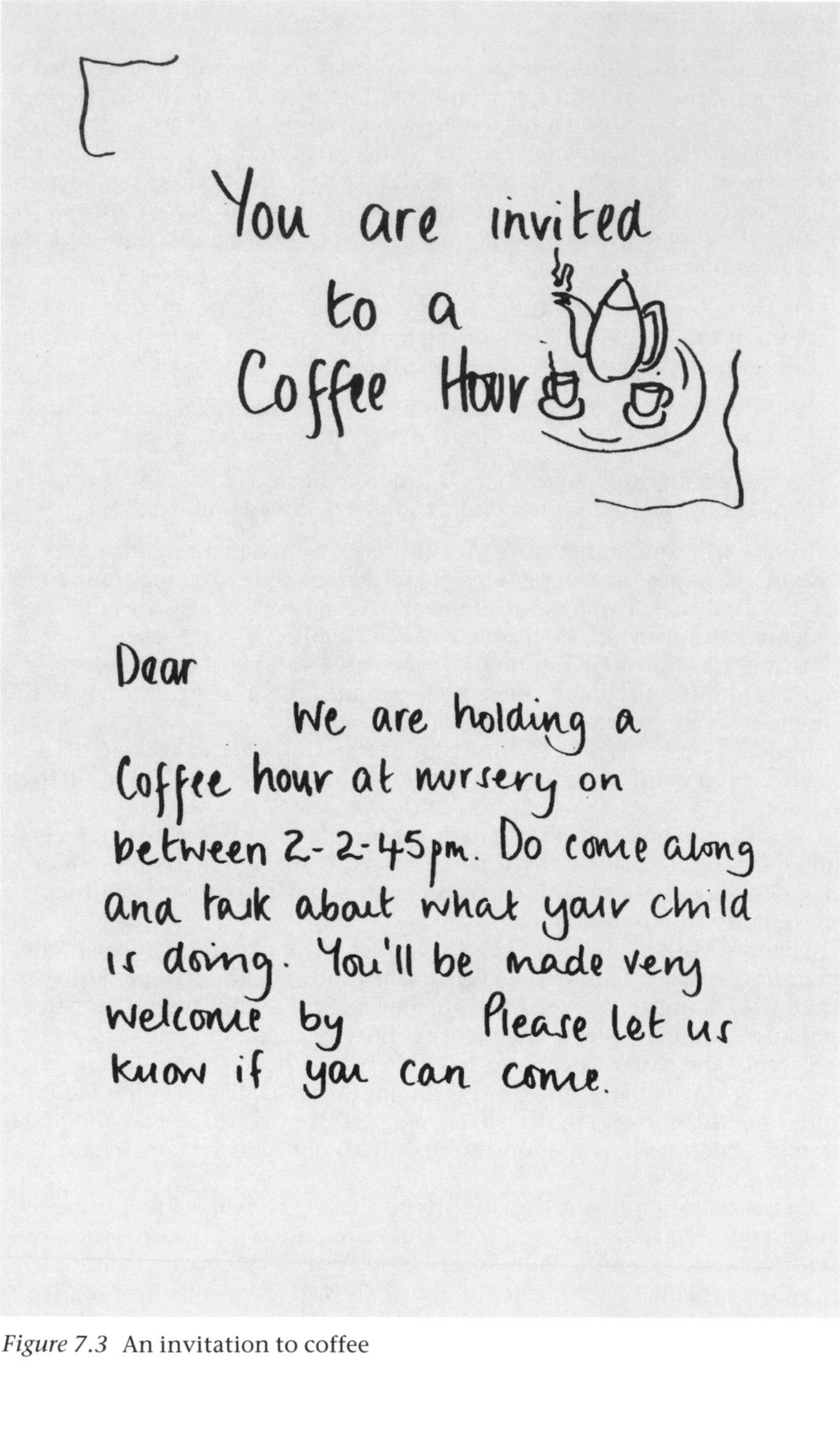

You are invited
to a
Coffee Hour

Dear

We are holding a
Coffee hour at nursery on
between 2-2-45pm. Do come along
and talk about what your child
is doing. You'll be made very
welcome by   Please let us
know if you can come.

Figure 7.3 An invitation to coffee

STOCKPORT M.B.C. ✓ EDUCATION DIVISION

EDUCATION PSYCHOLOGY SERVICE

Coping with the
Under-fives

A short course for parents/carers to
be held at Hollywood Park
Combined Nursery Centre.

Wednesday 28th	February	1996	9.45am - 11.00am
Wednesday 6th	March	1996	9.45am - 11.00am
Wednesday 13th	March	1996	9.45am - 11.00am
Wednesday 20th	March	1996	9.45am - 11.00am
Wednesday 27th	March	1996	9.45am - 11.00am

Course Leaders
Lynda Dodd - Educational Psychologist
Sheila Aris - Teacher (Behaviour Support Service)

Please see Jenny or Adriana for more details.

Figure 7.4 An example of an invitation to a course for parents and carers

Meeting everyone's needs

We both feel that first impressions count and that the welcome given to both adult and child is all important. Nobody slips into the room unnoticed. It can be physically difficult when working with a child or a group of children to get up and greet the carer, but as soon as possible one of us will introduce ourselves and find out as much information about the child as they want to tell us.

Some of the parents and other carers come to meet their own needs, to find a place where they can belong, become part of a group and contribute in their own way. This can sometimes prove difficult as people come from all over the town and are not from a close-knit community where all are neighbours.

Sometimes the group gels well and there can be a really good atmosphere. Carers can chat about experiences with their children and are able to help each other through shared experiences. On occasions when this does not happen so easily we have devised strategies where we introduce subjects into the conversation which we feel will be of interest to carers. We are also able to offer advice or assistance when needed. We have found playing varied music to suit different tastes helps to create a welcoming atmosphere. This seems to help carers to relax and be more receptive to friendly advances from other people.

We are delighted that so many men are coming along to the group, but we have found that men do not always seem to talk as easily to each other as women, and we have had to find ways of making men feel welcome and at ease in the group. For example, we have added to our magazine selection as this used to contain mainly women-orientated magazines. It now contains a wider selection of reading material such as newspapers, train magazines, car magazines, etc. As staff we have found that our topics of conversation have increased, and we have had our horizons broadened and enriched by working alongside fathers as well as mothers, and other family members. Some of the topics of conversation have included walking the Pennine Way (with one grandfather), orbits of the moon and other planetary systems, pilot training, and how demoralizing it is for the main breadwinner to be in long-term unemployment with little hope of any change. Lee's comments (Figure 7.5) bear witness to the value of the group for the men who come along. As a team we are now considering whether there is a need for a men-only toddler session and whether it would be attended.

Following our attendance at the National Association of Nursery Centres' conference on the 'Quality in Diversity' project, linked to the Early Childhood Education Forum, we discussed the importance, for the group and for the nursery centre as a whole, of the five foundations for early learning which the project identifies as:

- belonging and connecting;
- being and becoming;
- doing and being active;
- contributing and participating;
- thinking, understanding and knowing.

PARENT AND TODDLER

What is your experience of these groups?

Do you have positive memories of how the activities were planned to develop your child's social skills?

Were the people in charge of the centre involved totally in the planning of the activities to ensure that each child had a structured and stimulating experience whilst at the centre?

Were you made to feel welcome by everybody?

If you cannot answer *YES* to each of these questions, you must not be attending the Parent/Toddler group at Hollywood Nursery.

I am a father who works night shifts, and since my wife returned to work I have taken over the responsibility of ensuring that our son is given the benefit of the excellent facilities on offer at the Nursery.

I was not too keen on the idea at first, but after just one visit, and after witnessing the joy that the centre brings to my son, I cannot deny him the experience offered by the Toddler Group even after a 12 hour shift.

Not only has James benefited from the Toddler Group, but I find I actually enjoy going and meeting the other Parents and Carers at the Nursery!

If you are looking for a new and stimulating environment to challenge your child, a place for you to go and meet other people who want to be involved in the activities on offer rather than those who prefer a coffee whilst the children entertain each other without the necessary adult input, then come along to the Parent and Toddler Group at Hollywood Nursery.

> Tuesday - 9.15am to 11.15am
> Wednesday - 9.15am to 11.15am
> Thursday - 1.30pm to 3.00pm

Hope to see you there!

Lee Howard

Figure 7.5 A parent's views

We have found all of these foundations to be equally applicable to all who attend the parent-toddler group, be they children, carers, new staff, students or existing staff.

Carers' development

Our aim is to meet the needs of carers and children in equal part. A non-judgemental approach is used when working with carers. We accept that they come for their own reasons and give and take what they need from the group. Some attend purely for the benefit of their child, some for themselves to chat to other people in similar situations, and some are referred by their health visitor or social worker. If a parent, for example, is going through a difficult time and perhaps making negative comments or displaying negative behaviours towards their child, staff show support for the parent and child and look for, and draw attention to, positives in their child's behaviour in the hope that, in time, the parent will be able to see and display positive behaviour for themselves.

It is heartening to see a parent who might not have known anyone in the group when first starting and who initially sat quietly by her/himself, eventually becoming sufficiently confident to chat with new arrivals, putting them at their ease and explaining the aims of the group. The development of such skills enriches the group as a whole. It is encouraging to see parents as they begin to move with confidence around the room and play with their own and other children. We are now looking at ways of encouraging parents to observe and possibly write up their observations on their child to share with us.

Parents within the group have a thriving social calendar and arrange trips out for those who are interested. At other times the opportunity just to chat is sufficient. One parent studying for a degree takes the opportunity to use the parents' room to study and sometimes has to be encouraged to become involved with the children.

We recently set up a course for parents, led by the child psychologist and the head teacher. This proved very popular, helpful and informative; parents were able to share their feelings, worries, anxieties and ideas with each other. They offered each other advice and exchanged ideas, with the psychologist offering her expertise and suggestions. The course was conducted once a week for eight weeks. The last one was on 'play' and was led by the head teacher. The parents who attended the course were presented with a certificate which was valued by those who received it. This course was so popular that not only have we another group of parents waiting for the next one but the group who have already been involved are requesting more input. We also have a health visitor who holds drop-in sessions on a regular basis – this is open to any parent or carer seeking help or advice about their child. The health visitor also puts on specific courses such as feeding, behaviour problems, toilet training, etc., where anyone interested may attend.

What are we providing?

As the group developed we considered ways in which we could improve on what we were offering and re-examined our aims. We decided that, for us, the group is a place for carers and children to:

- play together;
- share together;
- have fun together.

We believe, along with *Starting with Quality* (DES 1990: 7) that:

At this early stage, children gain a great deal from interaction with others, both adults and children. As the child moves from the close relationship of family life into new situations, the close involvement of parents can supply both important continuity for the child and information for the educator about the child's interest, experiences and needs. Establishing a partnership with the home at this stage provides a firm foundation on which subsequent educators can build.

For children to build up a lasting relationship with staff/educarers at the nursery is of utmost importance in their overall development.

In looking more closely at our own practice and at what our parent/toddler group provides, we decided that it offers:

For the child

- lots of varied activities and experiences suitable for each individual child, planned daily according to the needs of the group;
- opportunities for the child to explore and investigate the world around them – lots of tactile, hands-on activities and experiences;
- the opportunity for children to socialize to play, share and take turns with other children, to learn social skills – i.e. taking off and putting on socks and shoes, becoming responsible for their own toilet needs, washing hands, etc. This includes learning to communicate both verbally and non-verbally, to share and care about each other and to interact with other children;
- for children to become familiar with simple routines – i.e. sitting down for a snack, singing together as a group, listening to a story;
- for children to familiarize themselves with the nursery building, to meet other members of staff and other children, to become acquainted with the facilities within the nursery, i.e. toilets, soft play area, resources.

For the carer

We try to encourage carers to build up relationships with each other, in particular those who feel alone and isolated. We will introduce them and draw them into the group, and encourage them to talk and make themselves a cup of coffee. We discuss with carers the child's background, the opportunities their child has at home, what they expect from us, and what they would like us to provide, and most importantly, *we encourage carers to play with their child.*

For the educarer

We aim to provide a positive role model while working with children, parents and other carers. Working alongside parents in particular, we are conscious that some may themselves not have had these experiences as a child and may find it difficult to play with their child. We need to be consistent: while parents have responsibility for their own child, we allow time out for parents to talk and have a coffee. We consider how adults are positioned in the room and where chairs are placed. When newcomers arrive at the beginning of term it may be best to place the adults together to enable them to get to know each other. As the term progresses, we place the chairs with the activities to encourage carers to work with their child. We need to be friendly and welcoming to carers and children to show that we value each individual child; we want to make them feel special. We must develop a child's self-esteem and confidence with praise and encouragement, and be aware of equal opportunities, regardless of gender, race or culture. It is possible to detect any problem in a child's speech and development at an early age: we are aware of the responsibility and work closely with other professionals and support agencies.

Working as members of staff in the toddler group, we find ourselves in a dual role, working both as an educarer and meeting the needs of the carers. This can sometimes be a difficult task as both sides can be equally demanding. We need to be continually aware of each individual child's needs and ensure that those needs are met, but we also need to be aware of a carer who feels lonely, needs advice and support, or who just wants someone to talk to. Carers sometimes need to let off steam and exchange experiences, ideas or problems with other carers. We, as educarers, are aware of this and need to provide the opportunity for this to happen, while at the same time making sure the children are safe, secure and involved with their carers in stimulating play.

Some parents or carers find it more difficult to interact with others, especially those for whom English may be a second language, males coming into a predominantly female environment and those who, for a variety of reasons, may feel lonely, isolated or vulnerable. We are particularly aware of this and make sure that any difficulties in communication are not overlooked. We achieve this by close observation of parents and children, and by creating a friendly, caring atmosphere where all are made to feel welcome.

Planning and provision

The member of staff working in the toddler group plans the activities for each session. Careful thought is put into these sessions, and the needs of children are considered first. The types of activities on offer must be suitable for children aged 3 and under: the room must be safe, clean and comfortable, with special defined areas for babies and toddlers. We have found the first lesson learned is to be flexible and adapt to and work with the age and stage of the children who attend, since we cannot be certain of the age range or numbers for any one session.

Originally the planning sheet used to plan the week's activities for the toddler group was the same as the one used in the nursery but we quickly discovered that this did not always meet the needs of the toddler groups. We may plan to do one particular activity (such as potato printing) but find that eight babies have arrived and this would then not be suitable. Flexibility and adaptability are key words for us!

For the younger children, especially babies, we provide a comfortable and stimulating environment with cushions and bean bags, activity gyms, bells, rattles, mobiles, musical toys, fabric shapes, textured objects for the children to touch, feel and explore.

We provide an area for messy play – for example sand, water, etc. – where careful thought is given to providing suitable tactile resources appropriate for the age of the children using them.

An area for creative play offers opportunities for painting, glueing and playdough. Large sheets of paper and thick paintbrushes are used at the easel for the children to gain confidence and to experiment with paint, splodging, blobbing, watching it drip, etc.

A structured home corner is provided where children can role play, dress up, use the telephone, puppet, dolls, etc. This is an area where children can use their imagination and act out situations familiar to them – for example making tea, washing up, dressing dolls, using telephones, etc.

We have an area for large and small construction to develop manipulative skills and hand–eye coordination. We make sure that the children are able to use the construction materials that have been provided – whether it has a sliding, pressing, slotting or hooking facility – again being conscious of each child's developmental stage and ability level.

We provide an area for representational play where children can use resources such as dinosaurs, farm animals, zoo animals, garage and cars, airport and aeroplanes, house furniture and people, train and track, plus many others, and these can be used by the children in an imaginative way, building on the child's existing knowledge and extending language.

Physical play, soft play, jigsaws, simple lotto, shape sorters, and many other tactile activities are available for carers and children to use. We also have a separate soft play room to which the under-threes have access.

We have a book area with a selection of books, from simple board books and picture books, to books that carers can read with their child. There is a comfortable place to sit, with a carpet, cushions and bean bags.

We aim to promote equal opportunities at all times in the group and are conscious that it should reflect the multicultural nature of our society, particularly in the activities and equipment we provide. We are anxious to welcome people of various abilities, class, status, race, gender and cultural or religious backgrounds. There are ways in which we can promote equal opportunities and encourage multicultural awareness through the resources we use and the activities we provide. Equal opportunities is given high priority. The discussion of our policy within the nursery centre has helped us in the toddler group to consider the kinds of resources we provide. For example:

- *Books* – we provide a choice of quality books demonstrating positive role models, i.e. a man washing up or ironing, mum mending the car, children who are disabled, music and rhymes from around the world. There are books displaying positive images and books about ethnic cookery as part of our parent programme.
- *Home corner* – the dressing-up clothes provided include saris, kimonos, kilts, etc. The cooking utensils include a wok, chopsticks, balti dish, tandoori, etc. We taste food from different cultures, for example Italian, Indian, Chinese, Caribbean, etc., as well as providing a broad range of pretend food from different cultures; examples include matzo, croissant, chapatti, poppadom, star fruit, passion fruit, mango, etc.
- *Dolls* – there are multicultural dolls, boy/girl dolls, dolls with different disabilities, differences in size, shape, colour and dress.
- *Games* – we provide, for example, those which can be adapted to meet individual needs so that no one need feel excluded from the activity, whether carer, child or educarer.
- *Other people* – we invite visitors from a variety of different cultures and professions, such as male nurse, policewoman, etc., to share in the group. The celebration of different festivals, for example Christmas, Diwali, Eid, Chinese New Year, Easter and Ramadan, helps to promote understanding and cooperation, leading to exciting and interesting developments and activities.

We aim to meet the children's emotional needs by providing a safe, secure environment for the child to experience and explore through play. Social needs are met by providing the opportunity for children to interact with others and to develop self-help skills.

We provide activities for music and movement, musical instruments, action rhymes, finger rhymes, dancing, physical activity and exploration of space and rhythm.

Health and safety

We are always aware that part of our role in the toddler group is to ensure the health and safety of our children and their families. An attendance register is taken at the beginning of each session and is kept available throughout in case of an emergency. This register includes children, adults and staff, and also includes relevant information about children on the register. Care is taken to ensure that the children are safe and cannot leave the building unsupervised. They are not allowed in the kitchen area and care is always taken with hot drinks.

It is also important that toilet facilities are satisfactory for adults and children, with provision for hand washing and baby changing, for example a changing mat near to the toilets and a separate bin for nappies. We have a safe place for prams and pushchairs; we make sure that no fire exit is blocked. There is a set procedure in case of fire, with fire drill information placed in a prominent position.

An accident book is kept and any injury, however slight, is recorded. A first aid kit is available with a full contents list attached. We ensure that all equipment is clean and safely laid out and that all equipment is cleaned and checked regularly.

Most children sometimes suffer minor injuries and bumps and bruises due to energetic play. However, a child may suffer injuries that have been deliberately inflicted by adults. It is important that every member of staff is aware of this possibility, and follows the nursery procedures if they think a child may be at risk. This would include contacting social services if we were not comfortable with any explanation given. A much fuller discussion of the complex issues surrounding child protection, together with information and support, is offered by John Powell in the following chapter. We consider our role within the toddler group to be an extremely important and sensitive one in this respect, and both in-house and in-service support play an important role within both the toddler group and the nursery.

Roles, partnerships and professional development

We have had continuous discussion about our role within the toddler group. We both agreed that we felt a little self-conscious when originally working in the group with parents and other carers, as this was something we had not been involved in so closely before. However, with time and experience we have grown into our roles and have become used to being observed by carers and directly questioned about what we are doing and why. We now find our roles both enjoyable and rewarding. As educarers, we have found our own professional development has accelerated while working in the group. This has motivated us to find out more about the development of under-threes, and we have begun to read and research for our own satisfaction. We are also involved with the Manchester Metropolitan University in a research project on educare for the under-threes; discussion with, and observation by, researchers has helped us to reflect on our practice. We have had to observe children and carers, think about what we have observed and question the way we work – whether certain activities have been appropriate, whether we have been as fair as we can in the way we have allocated our time to particular people and situations. We have listened to carers and gathered knowledge from their experiences and we have been able to pass this on to others. In particular, we have become more aware of parents' and other carers' individual needs and the different reasons why they come to our toddler group. Most of them come both because they recognize the value of the activities on offer for their child and because it gives them an opportunity for talking to other people.

Parents' comments about the toddler group have been positive in identifying what they and their children gain from attending the sessions; they have made us both feel that our work is rewarding and worthwhile. Comments such as the following are particularly encouraging:

> I like the parent/toddler group because the educarers work alongside the parents and help in the activities that are provided. My son Keir loves it.

> Since my daughter joined the toddler group she has calmed down a great deal, and also plays better with other children.

> Elizabeth is learning to share and mix with other children in the group and seems to be more confident and sociable. She really enjoys coming here.

> Thomas has learned how to mix with other children, and to share his toys. There are a lot of activities Thomas can do here that he could not enjoy at home.

> It is great for me to spend time with Bill and other children his age in a relaxed, small group. There are lots of activities for him to do, and plenty of help and care from the educarers.

> I feel that since bringing Jamie and Steve to this toddler group Jamie's communication and both their learning is improving greatly. They are both able to experiment and be creative and play at the same time.

> My son is happily occupied, and he enjoys meeting other children of a similar age group. I also find the toddler group is convenient as it is within the nursery where my other son attends. I also feel that his co-ordination skills will improve because he has so many toys to play with.

By working with other professionals we have gained a deeper insight and understanding of some of the worries and problems experienced by parents within the family: we both feel we are better equipped to help deal with them. When we were first given the responsibility of running the toddler group after working within a nursery setting our first reaction was 'What are we going to do with these children and what can they do?' After playing with each child and observing their individuality we began to notice small signs of progress taking place – we have both now become hooked on the under-threes.

New developments

We are always keen to develop new ways of working and to introduce the children, parents and carers to the facilities available for the over-threes. One such development is the toy library which, as the publicity leaflet (Figure 7.6) shows, now provides opportunities for all children and their families to benefit from a range of carefully selected toys and equipment, to which they may not normally have access.

HOME/SCHOOL LINKS

As part of our policy of developing home/school links the Toy Library has been established

The Toy Library caters for children aged from 6 months - 5 years

Each toy in the Toy Library has been selected for their high quality, attractiveness and safety

The toys in the Toy Library have a high educational value and are therefore especially useful for helping to develop learning skills

THE TOY LIBRARY OFFERS:

The opportunity for you and your child to play with a variety of toys

Educational toys develop your child's abilities

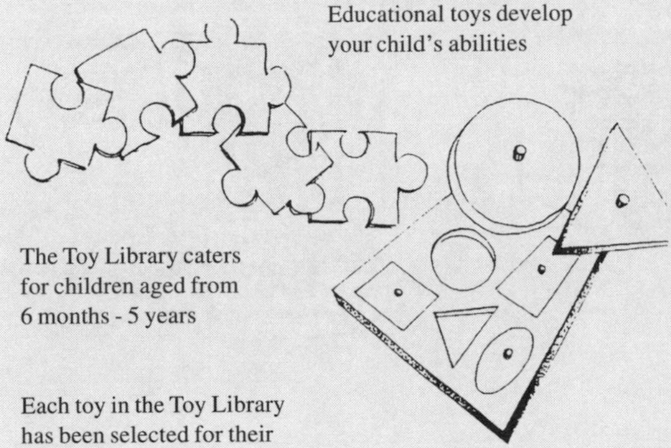

Toys and activities that reflect the many races and cultures in our society. Our toys also challenge racist/gender stereotyping

DON'T FORGET:

Playing with toys enables you and your child to have an enjoyable time together

Whilst playing with your child you could perhaps talk about

different - shapes

different - sizes

look at - colours

and **count** together

Please inform Hazel if any of the toys get broken or any parts are lost

If you have any ideas or comments about the Toy Library please pass them on to Hazel who will be pleased to hear them

Figure 7.6 The toy library

Carers are encouraged to take responsibility for running both the toy and the book library and for selecting those books and materials which appeal to them and their children (Figure 7.7). Of course staff are always on hand to help and advise, and the development of literacy skills has an important place on our list of aims.

We also consider it important that everyone involved in the life of the nursery centre is kept informed about activities, events and user groups. The Timetable shown in Figure 7.8 is just one example of the way information is shared. A noticeboard is another way in which all stakeholders are able to share information, express their concerns, share their feelings and celebrate their successes.

Figure 7.7 Welcome to our library

	Monday	Tuesday	Wednesday	Thursday	Friday
9.30 **11.30**	Crèche and adult classes for parents	Parent-toddler group Welfare rights once per month	Parent-toddler group	Preparation for nursery group	Crèche and adult classes
1.30 **3.00**	Open for informal use by parents	Friends of Hollywood and parent use Health visitor drop-in once per month	Preparation for nursery group Health visitor drop-in once per month	Parent-toddler group	Open for informal use by parents
3.30 **5.30**	Staff meeting	Maintenance Display Preparation Setting up	Input session by various groups	Funtime for children	Cleaning up Preparation for next week

Figure 7.8 Timetable of events

Preparing for nursery group

While working in the toddler group we both noticed how confident some of the older children who had attended toddler groups for quite some time had become. Carers had also been saying how they would have liked some time for themselves. After discussion between ourselves, the head teacher and other members of staff, we felt there was an additional need both for carers and children that we might meet. We considered whether a separate group where carers could leave their children for up to two hours would be worthwhile. In the toddler group carers are required to stay for the whole session; this would be a step towards an easier and smoother transition into nursery.

Parents and carers responded well to this idea; so the new group became the Preparing for Nursery Group and is a popular part of the facilities on offer at the nursery centre. The group provides places for up to eight children aged 2 years 9 months and over, who have regularly attended the toddler group. There are three places allocated to children who have social services input into their families. Children are welcomed and settled into the group: as their confidence in themselves and with the staff grows they will gradually be introduced to and shown nursery life. This is done by events such as walking through the nursery with familiar staff, talking about what they see, being introduced to nursery toilets and hand dryers and occasionally using outside play areas and equipment. The children will also begin to recognize and say hello to all the nursery staff. In this way we feel a link has been made between children and staff that will ease the transition into nursery life.

Because this is possibly the first time some children will have been cared for by anyone else outside the immediate family we realize it is a big step for the child to take: sensitivity is shown to both children and carers. The group provides consistency and security with familiar routine and staff. There is an active approach to learning with emphasis on the use of the senses and by giving praise and encouragement. Because of the high staff:child ratio (1:4) there is a lot of time to talk both as a group and individually; children are encouraged to extend and enrich their language development, and to foster positive self-esteem and personal self-help skills. Because staff know the children who will be attending the sessions of the Preparing for Nursery Group we are able to provide activities appropriate for their age and stage of development.

Some popular activities have included observing and feeling ice in the water tray, blowing bubbles, using the musical instruments, using scissors – although at this age children usually need a lot of help. Preparing and eating a picnic together is another outdoor opportunity for carers and/or other staff to be involved.

Carers have appreciated this time and used it in different ways, some to catch up on housework or devote time to a younger member of the family, some to socialize or use the nearby fitness centre, others to study for further qualifications, using the group and the staff as a resource and support.

When these children are offered a place in the nursery, written records are then passed on to the members of staff with whom the child will be placed. And of course both carers and children have the security of returning to the parent-toddler group as and when they need it. In providing what we consider to be two 'pre-pre-school groups' in the Toddler Group and the Preparing for Nursery Group, we are meeting the needs of carers, children and educarers. Collaboration, continuity of experience, ease of transition, development of confidence, self-esteem and increased knowledge and understanding are key elements in providing a firm foundation for young children and their families and carers. As one parent remarked: 'Whatever goes on here is great . . . it's having a positive effect on the children – I mean, if the kids come out confident, that's all you can ask for.'

References

Department of Education and Science [DES] (1990) *Starting with Quality, the Report of the Committee of Inquiry into the Quality of Educational Experience Offered to 3 and 4-year-olds*. London: HMSO.
Laishley, J. (1983) *Working with Young Children*. London: Paul Chapman Publishing.

8 | 'Who is listening?' – protecting young children from abuse

John Powell

Introduction

It is important for the reader to know where I, as the writer, am coming from and what experiences and concerns are foremost in my mind.

My involvement in working in early years education began when I was a social work practitioner working with families with young children. As a result of this I came into contact with many situations relating to child protection. In addition, I was in regular contact with other practitioners who were representative of all the relevant different vocational areas. As a social work practitioner I was in constant touch with primary carers in families and in different day care settings.

Later I moved into teaching in a college of further education and was responsible for the social studies input to people on the nursery nursing courses. For the past two years I have been at the Manchester Metropolitan University developing multi-professional courses and projects. One of my chief concerns is to hear the voice of the primary care practitioner, one to be heeded in all multi-professional contexts as a voice of status!

This chapter will consider issues relating to the communication required to offer protection to very young children from harm and/or abuse. The title of this chapter particularly identifies listening as a key skill in protecting young children from abuse. When I refer to listening it has for me a sense of 'heeding the other', a central concern in making sense of a situation. However, I do not mean solely heeding the child, but also paying heed to one's self and self-perception. This includes our personal ways of constructing notions of what is harmful or abusive. There are also other 'voices' which are important to listen to when sharing concerns: these are the voices of others such as colleagues and practitioners from varying multidisciplinary settings who may be able to offer some insight which could lead to a clearer understanding. In addition, the voices of procedures and guidelines as well as advised working practices must be heeded if we are to respond adequately to the situation of concern for the young child.

I will refer to a case study as a useful vehicle to develop some of the ideas and concerns raised about the process of listening. This case study is recognizable as a likely scenario of a child abuse situation and is based upon my practice as a social worker with families including young children.

Emma

It was a pleasant morning in September with the sun shining, giving an impression that this was to be a problem-free day. The phone rang and the social worker reluctantly picked it up. After giving his name he waited to hear what the problem was and whether it would merit investigation. The manager of a local day nursery had phoned to ask for advice about a 2-year-old girl in her care. The nursery manager said: 'The nursery nurse, Sally, has a very good relationship with this mother and her youngest child, Emma. Emma has not been with us for long'. She then checked her records and added, 'in fact she has only been here for two months. Usually Emma is a very active and involved child, she just loves being with us. I would say she is an interested and curious child who gets into everything. However, this morning the nursery nurse, Sally, noticed that the mother just sort of left Emma with us and then rushed off. Sally said that Emma's mother's behaviour was quite different from usual because she seemed so offhand – though she does work and we thought she might have been late. Emma seemed very quiet, not like her usual self and also she seemed very clingy to Sally.'

The social worker listened carefully; without being asked, he knew not to interrupt. He felt that this beginning amounted to Sally being aware of a sense of difference in the way that both the mother and daughter related to each other. In addition, he felt Emma's behaviour according to the nursery nurse had appeared different from what was expected as being usual for her.

These moments reflect the introduction of often important information which may give useful clues confirming possible ill-treatment and are relevant to any referral. What is being said by the nursery manager is a way of signifying that concern for another is being constructed. The early information also may express the special relationship between the primary care practitioner and the child. This relationship, though perhaps fraught with interpretation and assumption, is linked to personal agendas of care and concern for another, often defenceless, human being and is being expressed through the special professional context of the referring practitioner. What must be heeded is that this relationship with the primary care practitioner is extremely important in the eyes of the child, the parent or legal carer in ensuring the day-to-day quality of life and its routines. The relationship between the child and her regular nursery nurse or other caregiving practitioner is one of high status in that child's and carer's eyes.

The nursery manager went on to say that Emma took her tee-shirt off to put something on from the dressing-up box and Sally noticed a series of small, regular bruises running along her spine from just below her shoulder to just above her lower back. The social worker asked the nursery manager to describe the marks. They were difficult to describe, being small, about two to three centimetres long and stretching in a long line down Emma's back. The nursery nurse had not made a fuss about Emma showing them because she was concerned that Emma did not feel upset or embarrassed.

What had happened to Emma must have been at the forefront of the social worker's mind. In addition, the social worker may have wondered whether the noticeable difference in Emma and her mother observed by Sally and reported as part of the referral by the manager implied some tension existing between them. Alternatively, perhaps the nursery nurse after seeing the marks on Emma's back formulated a construction of events that supported a view that Emma had been ill-treated. Perhaps the special relationship between Emma and Sally, while denoting positive and supportive features of caring, also contained other judgemental attitudes that Emma was not being cared for adequately?

The social worker believed that it was an essential requirement that he made a visit to the day nursery and discuss the matter further.

Some thoughts for consideration

What might Emma (a child just under 3 years old) be able to tell? As Pugh and Rouse Selleck (1996: 123) point out, 'Although most infants do not learn to talk until their second year, their voices are there for us to hear from birth.'

A child's voice need not be solely verbalized in language; it also exists in all the various means that young children have to communicate a sense of their needs through verbal and non-verbal ways to the listener. Pugh and Rouse Selleck (1996: 127) also comment that 'listening to young children through observing their play and talking about their drawings has a particular significance for those working with children who have been abused and neglected or traumatised; and that . . . play is a powerful means of developing a relationship with a child and providing opportunities to observe the child's concerns and preoccupations.' In addition to the verbal presentation of the world through language there are other channels through which young children may represent symbolically their feelings and concerns. Play is another way to access a child's concerns and to respond appropriately – or at least in what seems an appropriate manner. The voice of a child may be silent or non-verbalized but still be recognized; it may represent a more rounded expression which can include play and non-verbal communication as well as verbal expressions of feelings.

Accessing a child's voice in a child protection scenario

It is important to consider the relative status of the different concerned professional practitioners and the family members to the child, and how very young children may be encouraged to speak out. Many parents/family members will feel intimidated by the presence of a social worker and by the questions being asked. Most young children will find it impossible to answer direct questions unless the context is one in which they feel comfortable and the questions are designed to encourage interaction. Young children may voice their concerns or feelings in a role play situation by interacting with play objects which appear non-threatening and familiar. It is important when practitioners communicate with young children that they do not ask leading questions, and that the words familiar to the child are used in the interaction. In my experience it is unusual for a young child to reveal what has happened in a spontaneous account: for example it may take some time before something is shared or what is shared seems meaningful to the practitioner. Any recording that takes place should be verbatim and in the child's own words. There are clearly many difficulties for children to speak out or for practitioners to heed what is being said. The feelings of the practitioner need some acknowledgement since they may act as a barrier to communication in some situations while positively supporting communication in other contexts. Learning to communicate with young children is a long-term process for practitioners and should be part of their ongoing skills development.

Practitioners need to be clearly representative of an 'official' voice while at the same time being able to communicate at a personal level. The contradiction often remains in the minds of family members, that because a social worker (for instance) appears approachable and interested in them as people, they are somehow not as official as social workers who do not appear to be so. Of course social workers are not just agents of social services organizations, they are also people who make judgements based upon their values and beliefs.

It is the early years practitioner responsible for the direct care of the child who may be able to establish a rapport with the child based on their longer-term relationship and to whom the child may give voice to their concerns.

None of these points should be overlooked, because they contain some useful indicators for consideration; they highlight the potential difficulties implicit when considering child abuse. I will raise these concerns as questions for consideration:

1 Why is Emma's change of mood relevant?
2 What does Emma's mood signify?
3 What agenda relating to child protection does Sally hold?
4 Why should Sally relate her concerns to her manager?
5 Why should the manager pass the concerns to the social worker?
6 Why should the social worker take notice of the concerns raised?
7 What is the agenda of the social worker in relation to child protection, the family in question and the nursery staff?
8 Why should the social worker take this matter any further, and what are the consequences in relation to Emma?

The first three questions raised are significant in the sense that if mood or behaviour are an expression of the voice of a young child, what is there in these moments that allows Sally to believe that Emma might be suffering from ill-treatment? There are a number of indicators which might well evoke concern of a general nature and therefore would come to the attention of most practitioners wishing to see a young child flourish and develop. The chief of these concerns is the rather unusual bruises which deserve further questions. However, the earlier concerns which Sally felt, which were concerned with the relationship exhibited between Emma and her mother, may be about Sally's expectations of child/mother behaviour. These expectations of behaviour may relate to Sally's own familial and cultural experiences of how mothers and children should relate. The access that each of us has to expectations of relationships may be strongly influenced by our own experiences of being a child or parent. These impressions can be extremely subjective and moralistic, and really need to be questioned to ensure that judgements are not solely being passed on the basis of one's own personal prejudice. On the other hand, however, it is important to be able to recognize the part that personal values and belief systems have to play in decision making, and the responsibility each of us has to respond to a child's needs.

The point which the third question alludes to, namely that of agenda, is a complex one to interpret but essentially is about personal and usually undisclosed positions which may influence any action. Sally's agenda might be made up of her own subjective values, her relationship with Emma and Emma's mother/father, and her relationship with any other siblings of Emma who she may have had contact with in the past. Sally's relationship with her manager and the way that she may be perceived in the organizational structure might also be influential, as well as her awareness of child protection procedures. These points could be expressed in the following way: that Sally does not like Emma's mother because she does not care for Emma in a way which Sally approves of. In addition, Sally may know that social workers have been involved in the family in the past because of suspected ill-treatment. Sally might be concerned to impress her manager that she is aware and sensitive to the needs of the children in the nursery, especially if her manager has just provided in-service training about child protection and how to recognize it. This is just one set of possibilities relating to understanding the first three questions and, in particular, the influence of personal and practitioner agendas. *Personal interpretations are strongly and actively present at every moment of decision making within child protection cases. Practitioners need to reflect on any prejudices they may be developing.*

Other questions raised issues about why Sally should inform her manager and her manager should raise this with the social worker. There are clear guidelines which practitioners involved in direct work with children are expected to follow.

Referral and recognition

In the case study Emma is being referred by Sally to the manager and then to the Social Services Department because that is the required course of action in line with childcare procedures according to the Home Office Guidance (Home Office 1991: 27 – 5.11.1): 'any person who has knowledge of, or a suspicion that a child is suffering significant harm, or is at risk of significant harm should refer their concern to one or more of the agencies with statutory duties and/or powers to investigate and intervene – the Social Services Department, the Police or the NSPCC.'

The discussion prior to the point of referral has raised the question about how knowledge or suspicion may be constructed by different practitioners at different points along the expected procedure route.

Discussing a preliminary concern (as Sally has, in this instance with her manager) resulted in her manager expressing concern that this set of circumstances – including the bruising – may constitute knowledge or suspicion of significant harm or risk of significant harm. Once the manager has contacted the social worker there is an obligation that he or she should investigate.

Investigation and initial assessment

'There is a duty to investigate whenever the Social Service Department has reason to suspect a child is suffering or is likely to suffer significant harm' (Home Office 1991: 28 – 5.14.1). The 'reason to suspect' is the critical point here, but clearly when an injury which is seemingly suspicious is noticed and a referral has been made, then a social worker has a duty to investigate. There are a number of questions being raised from this latest invocation from the *Working Together* guidelines. These include: what is 'significant harm' as presumably opposed to 'insignificant harm'? What is an investigation and how does a social worker gain adequate reason to suspect?

There are legal interpretations of what 'significant harm' might be which includes the way a child's health or development may be impaired. Section 31 of the Children Act 1989 states 'where the question of whether harm suffered by a child is significant turns on the child's health and development, his health or development shall be compared with that which could reasonably be expected of a similar child'. There are clearly numerous moments when personal and professional interpretations will come into play to influence the actions of the social worker. The moment that the social worker receives the referral might be deemed to be the start of an investigation. The social worker in the role of investigator has the concern of trying to find out more about what may have happened to the child and what various concerned parties may have to say about the child's welfare.

In the case study the social worker visited the day nursery and discussed the concerns expressed by the manager and by Sally about the bruises on Emma's back. The social worker also asked whether the mother or father had been informed that a referral had been made. The parents had not yet been informed of the inclusion of a social work element although it was legitimate for the nursery manager to discuss her concerns before involving parents. However, it is then, of course, important to include the parents to ask them what had happened and advise them of the seriousness of the situation.

The social worker asked Sally if she had talked to Emma about the bruise. Sally confirmed that she had said to Emma, 'Oh dear, you've got some marks on your back, how did that happen?' Emma had said nothing though Sally felt that her body language had given cause for concern. Emma had bowed her head and looked away from Sally. The social worker did not feel that it was appropriate to see Emma's back without a parent being present. The day nursery manager invited the social worker to phone Emma's mother from her office. Emma's mother was asked by the social worker to come to the nursery or if it was more convenient to meet the social worker at her home to discuss the bruise. Her reaction over the phone was that she did not know what had caused the bruising but that she thought that Emma bruised easily and that she was constantly being told by people about little marks on Emma. However, Emma's mother agreed that she would leave her place of work and come into the nursery.

When parents and carers who have the day-to-day responsibility for looking after children are told that a social worker is investigating an incident where their child may have been ill-treated, they often react with anger or disbelief. In this situation, however, a ready excuse was being offered, almost as if the mother had been expecting this call. There is, of course, a heavy sense of judgementalism being placed on the initial parental response in this case. It is sometimes difficult for practitioners concerned in the professional care of the child to appreciate how parents may feel when they receive a phone call similar to the one just described. It might be argued from the parents' position that the social worker involvement already implies an oppressive manner, having required the mother to leave her job and to come to the nursery to answer questions. There is perhaps also a sense of the mounting status of these injuries as more practitioners become involved. From the social worker's perspective (which relates to other practitioners in the early years), however, there is a duty to remember the general principles of the Children Act 1989, particularly that 'the child's welfare shall be the court's paramount consideration' (Children Act 1989 section 1.1).

While the child has made no complaint or given any indication of wanting any intervention, by a social worker or anybody else, the child's welfare is deemed to be understood by those surrounding her. What is emerging perhaps is that there is a strong disparity between the different actors in a child protection context, with the legal duties and responsibilities conferring significant power on the investigating practitioner to look into the situation and to ensure that the child is given proper consideration. In this instance the bruising to Emma's back is the most vocal part of her voice. Emma is not necessarily asking for the attention which is being given her, but her bruises do ask for such attention and involvement.

In the case study, Emma's mother agreed that she would accompany the social worker to the local hospital where Emma could be seen by a paediatrician. The resulting examination made the paediatrician feel that the marks had probably been inflicted but it was difficult to understand how it had happened.

Categories of abuse

The following categories of abuse are included in the *Working Together* manual (Home Office 1991: 48) as a guide to 'those using the register' and are as follows:

Neglect: the persistent or severe neglect of a child, or the failure to protect a child from exposure to any kind of danger, including cold or starvation, or extreme failure to carry out important aspects of care, resulting in the significant impairment of the child's health or development, including non-organic failure to thrive.

Physical injury: actual or likely physical injury to a child, or failure to prevent physical injury (or suffering) to a child including deliberate poisoning, suffocation and Munchausen's Syndrome by proxy.

Sexual abuse: actual or likely sexual exploitation of a child or adolescent. The child may be dependent and/or developmentally immature.

Emotional abuse: actual or likely severe adverse effect on the emotional behavioural development of a child caused by persistent or severe emotional ill-treatment or rejection. All abuse involves some emotional ill-treatment. This category should be used where it is the main or sole form of abuse.

The definition relating to physical injury seems to apply to Emma in the case study but the concern of the social worker investigating must also consider that section 31(2) of the Children Act 1989 is satisfied that 'the child concerned is suffering significant harm or is likely to suffer significant harm' (Clarke Hall and Morrison 1990: 77).

The term 'significant' refers to a situation that is 'noteworthy, considerable or important and conveys that harm should be "sufficient to justify public intervention"' (Clarke Hall and Morrison 1990: 79). Further, Clarke Hall and Morrison explain that 'harm means ill-treatment or impairment to health or development and ill-treatment includes sexual abuse' (p. 79).

The concern at this point within the investigation is for the social worker to decide whether the child is at risk of further ill-treatment if she returns home. This is an important moment in an investigation because the child's safety must be considered on the one hand while the child's emotional needs must also be at the forefront of the social worker's concerns. Often where there is no specific diagnosis from a medical practitioner of an injury having been inflicted it may be difficult for a social worker to convince a magistrate that an emergency protection order which would place the child in an alternative setting to her home is necessary. Social workers will also have in mind that removal from home and from regular caregivers may be emotionally damaging and confusing for the child. In effect the social worker is required to predict whether the child is likely to suffer harm or not and respond appropriately.

Reflection on the case study

What does the case study tell us about the child protection procedures and the intervention of different professional practitioners in the early years with their differing roles and responsibilities?

At each moment in the case study scenario assumptions and key decisions have been made about Emma and her family. The way that Emma initially presented to the nursery nurse as 'different to her usual self' was perhaps the moment that a construction was developing that Emma was possibly the victim of child abuse. Once the bruising was discovered and the nursery manager as the designated staff member decided to refer the incident to the Social Services Department and a social worker was allocated, the investigation gathered momentum. The social worker began to investigate by asking questions and developing insights into what may have occurred which resulted in Emma's bruising. Emma's mother did not shed much light on the cause of the bruising and Emma was not able to say what had happened either. The pursuit of explanations resulted in the social worker taking Emma to be medically examined at the hospital.

It is interesting that as the focus of examination moves from place to place (such as from the day nursery to the hospital), the different practitioners are involved in developing an argument (which may be informative about what had happened) as what likely action might be best taken to protect Emma. Certainly there is a sense that a bureaucracy has been activated which is concerned to gather information which may lead to a better understanding of what has happened to Emma. It may perhaps assist any decision making in considering actual or suspected risks of further ill-treatment. There is also a question of power to act on behalf of a child, raising concerns about what is happening to Emma, her family and primary care practitioners. Emma has for instance not spoken but is assumed to have communicated that she may have been the victim of child abuse through the behaviour she has exhibited and, most significantly, through the manifested injury.

The mother's voice is heard in the context of the ability she has to explain what may have happened, as well as the opportunity she has to give permission for the medical examination. These are noticeable as potential features of cooperation with the investigation. If the mother changes her story, a different set of constructions will be activated by the practitioners involved.

There are a number of issues arising from the consequences of disempowering the child's voice so that children become objectified and constructed as victims of abuse but too young to speak out.

Each practitioner has a duty which is embodied in childcare legislation and is present in child protection guidelines to report their concerns of suspected and actual ill-treatment; social workers, police and NSPCC practitioners also have a duty to investigate and seek assistance from parents as well as childcare practitioners. Each of these practitioners should, however, attempt to reflect on their own personal agendas which may unwittingly be constructed through bias and prejudice based on their beliefs, values and experiences.

There is a feeling among many day care practitioners that they have a part to play in working for children's welfare which is acknowledged by other practitioners in the early years field up until the point that a referral is made. In written reflections on past incidents of possible child abuse in their experience, some primary care practitioners have reported to me that they felt a loss of control as more and more outside practitioners became involved in the developing investigation. Nursery nurses, for example, who are primary care practitioners in such cases, find that their contribution radically diminishes as the focus for concern develops from the immediate caregiving contexts, including the day care setting. Experienced nursery nurses with strong relationships with the child are likely to be totally excluded from investigations which involve managers, even if these have little or even no direct knowledge of the child. Yet it is important to remember that in the majority of cases the child will return to the day care context after the investigation is completed and the involvement of practitioners external to the child's immediate care needs have ceased. The ability of primary care practitioners to listen to the child's voice should not, therefore, be abruptly truncated or ignored during the time of the investigative and decision making process.

Who is listening? This question was the starting point for this chapter and has been its central concern also. In child protection situations the concern of all the different professional practitioners is the welfare of the child. Children have a voice and may speak out, depending on their maturity and ability. However, this is not an easy thing for any child to do, since they may feel unhappy, or unable to do so. If a child does say anything when asked it is important for the primary care practitioner to write down what is said as a verbatim statement. A child's own words are important in gaining an awareness of her personal expression and access to language, as well as giving a sense of an authentic experience.

The case conference process

As the case study investigation progressed, the child was represented more as a focus of multi-professional interest rather than that of a single childcare practitioner. The opportunity for all parties – including the parents – to meet together to share their concerns and decide on a plan of action for the future only takes place at a case conference. It is at the case conference that all of the different representatives of those concerned with the child's welfare will meet together to share their perceptions. There are usually three noticeable stages to a case conference process:

- the investigation and the sharing of interdisciplinary involvement;
- a general discussion covering concerns and issues;
- a set of outcomes which will be supportive of the child in the future.

During the case conference those present will tend to be: parents, direct care practitioner and manager, investigating social worker and line manager, medical representatives, police representatives and the child protection coordinator as chair. (Note that if a nursery nurse rather than qualified teacher is the primary care practitioner, they will very likely not be included as 'the direct care practitioner'.) Other appropriate practitioners may be invited as the need arises. It can be argued that such a team with a seemingly clear focus on the needs of the child will work cooperatively towards that end. However, the parent often feels in a position of defending themselves against the concerns and questions raised by the other practitioners. It is not surprising that the very presence of such a powerful group makes it difficult for a parent to speak with ease and many parents will feel they are merely being set up as scapegoats.

It is not really clear how well the different professional practitioners listen to or heed each other since they have different roles to fulfil, with different value systems to relate to. In many ways the child's voice is best heeded by those who provide regular care both in families and in day care facilities. It is in these contexts that familiar routines can be organized and which the child will probably feel most comfortable with. The voice of the parent and the caregiver in the day care context are the voices which the child hears and interacts with but they are the voices which tend to be overlooked in settings such as the child protection case conference, where more status is given to practitioners such as the social worker and the paediatrician.

The caregiver in day care usually becomes the young child's attachment figure 'to whom secure (or insecure) relationships may be formed that supplement the secure or insecure attachments formed to parents' (Thompson 1995: 32; also see Howes and Hamilton 1992). In other words the day care practitioner may offer a buffer of security away from home or act as a continuation of security from home. As Thompson argues, the caregiver's role may be to develop ongoing monitoring of the child's development outside the child's home and to provide assistance to parents about the child's needs and capabilities while answering questions about child rearing. There is also the possibility that the caregiver practitioner can act as a broker making contact between parents and other community agencies. These possibilities though are contingent on the quality of the childcare setting and the training and orientation of the child's caregivers.

Conclusion

This chapter has attempted to identify some of the concerns surrounding protecting young children from ill-treatment and abuse. It has clarified the necessary procedures which must be instigated to protect a young child adequately while at the same time recognizing the complexity and differences in the way power is perceived between the various actors and professionals. While the ability to hear the voice of a child tends to lessen the more professionals are involved, the day care practitioner's role could be crucial as an intermediary between the child and family members and the family and the professional community. Clearly there are dangers in such a relationship of being caught in the middle between two possibly antagonistic groups, but this is an area where the future status for caregivers in day care could professionally develop: they might find that their voice will be recognized in this role.

Emma's story is one of continuing concern and professional involvement. Eventually the case was submitted to court and a supervision order was granted. Emma is now 7 years of age and I believe still has a social worker visiting the family.

References

Clarke-Hall, Sir William (1990) *Clarke Hall and Morrison Law Relating to Children and Young Persons – Special Bulletin, A Guide to the Children Act 1989*. London: Butterworth.

Home Office (1991) *Working Together – Under the Children Act 1989 – A Guide to Arrangements for Inter-agency Cooperation for the Protection of Children from Abuse*. London: HMSO.

Howes, C. and Hamilton, C. E. (1992) Children's relationships with child care teacher: stability and concordance with parental attachments, *Child Development*, 63: 867–78.

Pugh, G. and Rouse Selleck, D. (1996) Listening to and communicating with young children, in R. Davie, G. Upton and V. Varma (eds) *The Voice of the Child. A Handbook for Professionals*. London: Falmer Press.

Thompson, R. A. (1995) *Preventing Child Maltreatment Through Social Support – A Critical Analysis*. London: Sage Publications.

| 'Our very best show' –
registration and inspection,
implications for work
with under-threes

Rosemary Rodger and Shirley Barnes

Introduction

Nationally a great deal of attention is currently being given to the ways in which quality is measured in the early years of education (Abbott and Rodger 1994; Pascal 1994). In the first part of this chapter Shirley Barnes outlines the registration and inspection requirements for nursery settings subject to the requirements of the Children Act (DoH 1989). She shows that nursery settings subject to this legislation are concentrating on general issues relating to training, equal opportunities, parental involvement, staffing, quality of care in the areas of child development, and the rights and expectations of children, parents and people working with young children. In the second part of the chapter Rosemary Rodger considers the possible implications on a nursery of inspection under the requirements of section 10 of the 1992 Education Act, both from her own perspective as a registered inspector, and from the perspective of the staff of the nursery. These inspections use a different quality framework from those undertaken under the Children Act, although their aims and outcomes are in some ways similar. Both registration and inspection procedures are aimed at enabling providers to meet acceptable standards. However, both writers feel that it is very important that all parties are involved in the process and that registration and inspection is not seen as something that is 'done to you' as opposed to 'done with you'.

Part 1: Registration and inspection under the Children Act 1989

With the implementation of the Children Act in October 1991 came many changes and reorganizations. Part X Schedule 9 of the Children Act has strengthened the regulatory powers of the local authority and states clearly that the care of young children is not simply a private matter between parents and the providers of care but is one in which the local authority has a duty to ensure that adequate care is being provided to young children. The range of services which are now subject to regulation include:

- childminders;
- crèches;
- playgroups;
- nurseries;
- out of school clubs;
- playschemes.

The aim of registration is:

- to protect children;
- to provide reassurance for parents whose children are being cared for by someone outside the family;
- to ensure that services for young children are provided within an agreed framework.

However, the Children Act also presumes that registration will be granted unless there are very good and clear reasons why it should not be.

The main purposes of inspection of registered provision are:

- to enable the local authority to satisfy itself that services are being pro-vided to an acceptable standard and children are appropriately cared for;
- to provide reassurance to parents about the involvement of the local authority;
- to ensure that the facilities provided are consistent with the information held on the register;
- to encourage day care providers and childminders to raise standards.

Once registered, all services and childminders must be inspected by the local authority at least once a year. The local authority has a duty to ensure at least minimum standards of childminding and day care for under-eights by means of this registration and inspection of the care provided. In order to meet their statutory obligations, local authorities have had to recruit suit-ably qualified and experienced personnel.

The stereotypical view of a registration and inspection officer is, I suspect, a middle-class white female, slightly 'matronly' with a brisk and authori-tarian aura, who wears sensible shoes, carries a briefcase and a clipboard and takes copious notes. Although I can think of some officers who may have some of the above characteristics, most of us come from a variety of back-grounds and are all shapes and sizes. Many, perhaps predictably, are female, although there are a number of male officers and I am sure that this propor-tion will increase as, we hope, more men are recruited into the early years field.

I must own up and declare that I do indeed carry a briefcase (essential for all the advisory leaflets and useful addresses I need) and I frequently use a note pad, as it is crucial that I collate accurate information, and therefore I cannot rely on memory alone to retain the vast amount of information that is collated as part of my everyday work.

Having qualified as a nursery nurse in the 1970s, I have since spent all my professional life working in a wide variety of early years services, both within the public and voluntary sector. I have managed individual establishments, such as nurseries and family centres, as well as having management responsibility for the children's day care services within a social services department. In addition, as a parent of four children, all of whom have attended and continue to attend a range of day care facilities, I have the insight of a consumer. As a student on one of the new interdisciplinary degrees (BA (Hons) in Early Childhood Studies), I am able to enhance my existing knowledge of a multidisciplinary view of early childhood services. Having recently completed the Ofsted training for registered nursery education inspectors, I believe that I have a holistic approach to all aspects of early years provision. Like Rosemary, I believe that my work as an inspector provides both myself and early years workers inspected with valuable professional development opportunities.

The guiding principles which underpin all educare governed by the Children Act are as follows:

- children's welfare and development are paramount;
- children should be treated and respected as individuals whose needs (including special educational needs) should be catered for;
- parents' responsibility for their children should be recognized and respected;
- the values deriving from different backgrounds – racial, cultural, religious and linguistic – should be recognized and respected;
- parents are generally the first educators of their children; this should be reflected in the relationships with other carers and providers;
- parents should have easy access to information about services in their area and be able to make informed choices.

(DoH 1991: Chapter 6, section A 6.2)

The Guidance defines factors which influence quality of care as:

- the interactions between adults and children;
- the interactions between children;
- the size of the group and the number of adult carers available;
- continuity, training and experience of carers;
- recognition of children's developmental needs;
- quality of partnership between parents and the carer(s);
- the ability to structure and support children's learning;
- the programme of activities, including elements of imagination, challenge and adventure;
- equality of opportunity policy in employment and service delivery;
- children's involvement in the planning and choosing of activities and projects;
- the organization, display and accessibility of equipment, suitable toys and materials;
- attention to health, safety and type of physical environment.

I am now going to take each of the factors in the Guidance and discuss how I view them and the ways in which I assess their implementation. Like all registration and inspection officers I am influenced by my own cultural beliefs, personal values and professional training. However, I aim to show how the Guidance can be used as an appropriate framework.

The interactions between adults and children

Moss *et al.* (1995) survey and summarize some of the relevant research:

> Quality of interaction between adult and child has been identified as the single most important factor in the intellectual development of young children in group day care . . . Good quality interactions involve caregivers, parental or otherwise, whose behaviour towards their charges is responsive and sensitive. They are likely to respond to children's verbal and non-verbal signals/provide activities which are developmentally appropriate, elaborate and expand children's language and play where appropriate and be sensitive to children's feelings. Children who receive such care are likely to be more advanced in language, cognitive development and social competence than children whose carers are less responsive. Poor language development, less complex levels of play, aimless wandering and lower levels of attachment to the caregiver have been demonstrated to be associated with caregiver behaviours such as harshness and detachment.

During my many observations of interactions in nurseries and other settings I have seen many loving and sensitive approaches to relationship building. My personal preference in group day care settings is for some form of key worker system but it is not the only way to work; I am always looking for a child-centred approach which puts the needs of children first, where staff treat children and parents as human beings with as much right to respect as themselves.

The interactions between children

All experienced early years practitioners will recognize that children are very sociable little people, and given the opportunity will develop friendships and demonstrate care and concern for one another as well as the usual disagreements and battles for control. Even very young children will show recognition and pleasure when interacting with familiar adults and children, even though their spoken 'language' is not easily understandable.

Inspection and registration officers will need to assess how friendships are supported and developed between children, and how responsive the carers are to using such knowledge in the implementation of play opportunities.

As children become more aware of themselves, they begin to understand about the 'family' and wider social community, as well as what is acceptable and unacceptable behaviour. Children undoubtedly learn positive attitudes to others through their own experiences and the 'role' models around them. In some settings children are able to meet and become friends with children from a variety of cultural backgrounds; in others, children with disabilities may play with able-bodied peers. In all settings we look for acceptance of diversity and the provision of a range of opportunities for social interaction.

In a 'good' day care facility – whether it be with a childminder or in a group setting such as a nursery or playgroup – opportunities will be provided for children to play both on their own and alongside other children, whether in parallel, associative, cooperative or organized play (where the purpose is perhaps a task, i.e. constructing something or a dramatic play experience).

The size of the group and the number of adult carers available

The Guidance pertaining to the Children Act sets out staff to child ratios (based on the ages of the children) and recommends that in larger establishments (over 50 places), the children should be organized into self-contained units of no more than 26, with the recommendation that 3- to 4-year-olds should be in groups of around six to eight, with smaller groups for younger children. The Act also specifies how much indoor play space is required per child, again based on the ages of the children. I have found that in many group day care settings children are being grouped according to their ages. For example many nurseries will have 'baby units' accommodating, in some cases, babies from a few weeks old until they are about a year old. The second group may accommodate babies from a year old until they are rising 2. The toddlers are usually the 2- to 3-year-olds, who then move on again to the pre-schoolers (usually 3- to rising 5-year-olds).

Some sessional facilities, playgroups, crèches, etc. where the children are on a part-time basis (less than four hours per session) may be in mixed age groupings.

The Guidance specifies the following staffing ratios for group day care settings:

1:3   children aged 0 to 2
1:4   children aged 2 to 3
1:8   children aged 3 to 5.

In addition, if more than 20 children attend the facility, the officer in charge/manager should be supernumerary (not included in the staff to child ratio).

The ratios for childminders are as follows:

1:3   children aged 0 to 5
1:6   children aged 5 to 7
1:6   children aged under 8 of whom no more than three are under 5.

One of the realities of the implementation of the Children Act appears to be that, particularly in full day care settings, children have very little planned opportunities to socialize with children of different ages. However, carers express concerns that non-mobile babies can be hurt by older, more adventurous toddlers, and that older children's needs can be difficult to meet if in the same group you have demanding toddlers.

Continuity, training and experience of carers

It is clear that responsive, familiar caregivers are crucial to the well-being of all children receiving non-parental care. The Guidance states (section A 6.4):

> As working with young children is demanding and complex, caregivers require a wide range of skills in order to provide good quality services. Training produces benefits for a variety of reasons. A trained person will understand how to respond sensitively to young children's needs. Parents are usually good at such responsiveness without any special training, but because of the difference in their emotional commitment, such responsiveness may not be so automatic for caregivers. To some degree sensitive responsiveness will reflect personality characteristics but appropriate training will help to improve it for most caregivers. Training can make caregivers more aware of stages in children's development and the need to adjust to the child's changing developmental needs.

The Guidance stipulates that for full and sessional day care facilities at least half of the care staff should hold a relevant qualification in: childcare, early years education, social work, health visiting, or children's nursing. In addition, they should also have experience of working with young children.

What is also crucial is that professional training and development is not static. All childcarers, from whatever sector or type of service, need access to ongoing training and development opportunities. In Chapter 3 Jean Coward discusses the benefits of this continuing professional development in working with the under-threes.

Recognition of children's developmental needs

There has been quite a lot of debate recently among early years practitioners and researchers about the developmental milestones that one can expect children to attain if they are developing 'normally'. However, if you accept that children are individuals then it is also reasonable to accept that the way in which they reach such milestones may also be individual. Jean Coward also discusses the ways in which observing what children actually do can help staff decide on appropriate next steps for individuals. In inspecting we look for educarers' awareness and appreciation of how young children learn and the ways in which they use this awareness to support and facilitate development. We also look for the consideration that is given to the religious and cultural background of the child.

Quality of partnership between parents and the carer(s)

In order to ensure that there is consistency in the relationships with children and that carers develop an intimate knowledge of the children and understand the child's family background and culture, it is crucial that regular and open dialogue exists between parents and the child's carers. Parents need to be kept fully informed about all aspects of the child's care and development.

All early years practitioners need to recognize and value the fact that parents are the primary educators of their children.

I have seen many effective examples of partnerships with parents and I would recommend that all group day care settings should have a policy regarding their partnership commitment to working with parents. A number of nurseries will regularly arrange a 'parents evening': here staff and parents can discuss in a relaxed manner all aspects of the children's care without the usual pressures of time, and without having to look after children at the same time. Some groups have set up home/nursery or playgroup books where snippets of observations and information are shared. This system can be especially beneficial if the parents do not collect the child from the setting.

Inspectors look for educarers who are open and willing to listen to and take on board some of the expectations of parents. For example, parents of a baby may want to ensure that the caregiver will be responsive to the child with lots of nurturing and loving care. On the other hand, parents of children in the 3 to 4 age bracket may be more concerned with the range of curriculum activities available and how these experiences will support and extend their child's knowledge. The Rumbold Report (DES 1990: 13) states:

> What is needed is for educators to be able and willing to explain to parents how the experiences offered to children contribute to their learning, and how their children are progressing. They need to be pre-pared to share responsibility with parents. This places considerable demands upon the educators: they need to be ready to spend time on it, and to exercise sensitivity: they also need to have enough confidence to invite parents to share in their children's education. They must ensure that they have the necessary skills to work effectively with parents.

The ability to structure and support children's learning

In order to provide a stimulating environment for children, educarers need to have an awareness and understanding of how young children learn and play. The individual needs of the children should be taken into account when preparing and organizing the play areas. The play environment must be 'child-centred' to enable a range of play experiences/activities to take place. Children need the opportunity to test out their ideas, to have a go, to take risks, to make decisions and to choose for themselves.

On a recent visit to a playgroup, I observed a lovely example of an educarer responding to these needs. A group of children and a playgroup worker were discussing a birthday party. When discussing what food they like to eat at parties, a number of children mentioned jellies. The playgroup worker asked the children if they knew how to make a jelly, and most of them said no. The worker then set up an activity for the children to make a small jelly, each using yoghurt pots. They used both jelly cubes and crystal jellies. The children were encouraged to use all their senses of touch, smell and sight. They described and discovered what happened when the jelly dissolved in the water, discussed what would happen and why the jellies would set when they were put into the fridge. They were finally given the choice as to whether they wanted to eat the jelly at playgroup or take it home.

The richness of this experience and the learning opportunities available to the children was made possible both by the playgroup worker's ability to respond creatively to the children's interest and the flexibility within the daily routine to respond to the children's initiative. One can see how, from this initial conversation with the children (some of whom were only 2 years old), this topic could have been extended and developed even further.

The programme of activities, including elements of imagination, challenge and adventure

If you consider that some children may spend up to eight or nine hours a day in the care of either a childminder or within a group day care setting, it is crucial that the range of play activities and experiences are wide enough to provide ongoing challenges for the children while at the same time providing opportunities for the children to practise and build on new skills and knowledge.

Many providers have taken advantage of the vast array of commercial play equipment available, most of which is beneficial and does provide learning opportunities for the children. However, as an inspector I am also looking for creative use of improvised play materials and natural materials. I am also looking for opportunities for outdoor play which involve children developing gross motor skills through physical adventure. I am also pleased to see children being given opportunities to refine similar skills in soft play areas. Consider the play and learning opportunities involved in, say, a pop-up toy, which is very popular for younger children. Most young children learn very quickly how to make the 'object' pop up and derive great pleasure from practising the skills needed to achieve the desired result. Yet, I ask, how long will this piece of equipment continue to stimulate and extend the child's knowledge? Compare this with the learning opportunities involved in a child exploring some everyday objects such as a range of containers made of different materials plus shells and pine cones, and how these will give interest and stimulation.

Equality of opportunity policy in employment and service delivery

A care provider's most important resource is the personnel involved in caring for the children. As part of the registration process, the local authority has to satisfy itself that all persons involved in looking after the children or in the proximity of the children are 'fit' to do so. The following points are taken from the Guidance (section 7.32) and should be taken into account when assessing fitness:

- previous experience of looking after or working with young children or people with disabilities or the elderly;
- qualification and/or training in a relevant field such as childcare, early years education, health visiting, nursing or other caring activities;
- ability to provide warm and consistent care;

- knowledge of and attitude to multicultural issues and people of different racial origins;
- commitment and knowledge to treat all children as individuals and with equal concern;
- physical health;
- mental stability, integrity and flexibility;
- absence of known involvement in criminal cases involving abuse to children.

Children's involvement in the planning and choosing of activities and projects

Planning a developmentally appropriate curriculum is one of the most important factors in quality care and yet is one which presents the most difficulties to a lot of childcare practitioners, whether they be childminders, playgroup workers or nursery personnel. It is easy to plan a curriculum which meets more of the adults' needs than the children's. However, if an establishment is successful in building sensitive and responsive relationships with children and adults they will usually find it easier to involve the children in the curriculum. Like the playgroup worker with the jelly, the routines will be flexible enough to provide not only developmentally appropriate materials but will also include the following three aspects:

- fun and enjoyment;
- a physical environment which maximizes children's choices;
- activities which focus on the children's interests.

The organization, display and accessibility of equipment, suitable toys and materials

In whatever setting, it is important that there is a wide range of equipment and play materials available, suitable for the number and ages of children who will attend. It is essential that all the materials available – play equipment, books, jigsaws and displays, etc. – follow anti-discriminatory practice and reflect a multicultural environment. Materials need to be carefully checked to ensure that they reflect positive images of gender, racial groups and people with disabilities. Obviously, the way in which the materials are presented to the children is of vital importance and needs to be constantly reviewed.

Not all day care providers will have areas which are solely for the use of the children. Some childminders may have separate playrooms, but the majority use the living areas of the house for childminding. Playgroups frequently use 'shared' premises, which means all equipment must be set out and cleared away at the end of each session. This undoubtedly can create difficulties when planning the curriculum and the range of play activities available to the children. Some services are restricted to the type of play materials they use. For example, they may not be able to use sand and water play activities due to the type of floor covering available. Many playgroups are not allowed to display the children's work, therefore practitioners have to be imaginative and creative in overcoming these obstacles, while still creating a homely, stimulating and practical environment for the children.

Very few childcare facilities ever have enough storage space, but it is crucial to consider what should be stored where and what should be accessible to the children. Very often, shelves are fixed high onto the walls to store play equipment, which means that the children are unable to elect for themselves what they would like to explore and play with. This is especially important for the younger children whose language skills are still immature. Imagine for yourself a scenario where you were unable to communicate or physically reach an object which looked really interesting and you wanted to investigate further. Can you feel the frustration? What can you do about it? How does your frustration show itself? Do you give up? Do you become bored? Do you find something else to do? For example, on a recent nursery visit I spent some time observing the younger children aged from 6 months to 1 year. One child, who had been attending the nursery for some months and was considered well settled, was sitting quietly on the floor. After a period of time I observed this child constantly looking up to a high shelf on the wall. The child gradually made her way by rolling and dragging herself using the play equipment to a position directly under the shelf. Once again she continued to look up at the shelf while also looking around the room at the nursery personnel. It became apparent that she was desperately trying to communicate something and, on drawing the staff's attention to her, they took down her personal bag. The little girl showed her excitement by bouncing up and down. Upon opening the bag, the staff drew out a small blanket which the little girl seized. She then made her way back to some play equipment which she began to explore while at the same time keeping her blanket close by. Once this child had received her blanket her whole demeanour changed and she appeared relaxed and more interested in what was going on around her.

The use of soft furnishings and suitable low level chairs adds aesthetically to the play areas by helping to create a comfortable and homely environment. In addition it is very important that carers have somewhere comfortable to sit while feeding the younger children. All too often I see carers perched on small children's chairs while feeding young babies. Or babies are fed by staff bending over them in their low level bouncy chairs. Apart from the fact that these positions put unnecessary strain on the adults' backs, it does not facilitate the close contact and nurturing which is essential to the well-being of the children.

Labelling equipment and displays help the children with their literacy skills. Using pictures of equipment on storage containers facilitates the children's skills as well as being an aid to self-selection. When labelling it is important to consider the use of different languages in order to develop the children's awareness. Many children in our society are bilingual, and the use of language is recognized as being of crucial importance in developing children's self-esteem, cultural, social, emotional and cognitive development. I look for approaches which demonstrate the ways in which educarers value children's home language.

Attention to health, safety and type of physical environment

Today, childcare facilities can be found in a variety of buildings. Generally there are far more converted premises than there are purpose-built childcare establishments. Whatever building is used it must provide a safe environment for the children. In assessing the suitability of premises the local authority will seek guidance and advice from the Fire, Building Control and Environmental Health departments; providers will be expected to comply with their requirements before registration will be approved.

The Guidance specifies the amount of clear play space (excluding fixtures) that should be available per child. These areas do not include utility areas such as hallways, bathrooms, office/staffroom, etc. Although a facility can be registered without outdoor play areas the local authority would want the provider to demonstrate how they would meet the children's requirements in this area, perhaps by using other community facilities.

In addition to enough space being available it is also important that playrooms have as much natural light as possible and are adequately ventilated. Consideration should also be given to enabling the children to view the world beyond the playroom. Many children spend long periods of time each day in one room and carers need to be imaginative and creative in providing a stimulating play environment. Bathroom/changing facilities should be located as close as possible to the playrooms for ease of use by staff and to support the children's developing independence skills.

For the younger children, I advise carers to install safety mirrors at the children's eye levels in the playrooms and alongside the changing areas. Pictures, mobiles, etc. on or hung from the ceilings can provide interest to the young children who may spend frequent periods of time lying on their backs. Some establishments have decorated their bathroom areas based on themes such as an underworld sea cave and shopping street. Such creativity not only engages the children's interests but indicates staff understanding that a great deal of learning takes place during 'caring' activities, and that care and education cannot be separated.

The outdoor play area is very important and should hopefully provide suitable surfaces to enable outdoor play to take place in all weathers. Consideration needs to be given as to how the youngest children can take advantage of the outdoor environment even though they may not yet be mobile. Although the Guidance does not make any recommendations regarding the amount of external play space per child, under the Education (School Premises) Regulations 1981 a minimum of nine square metres per child is required: this is a useful guide to assist in assessing the suitability of external play areas.

At one nursery I visited they had decided to convert an outdoor building into an additional playroom, but before the room was completed they allowed the children to play in the building and found that it provided a valuable all-weather area. So although it had a roof and sides, the windows were never installed to enable a free flow of air to permeate the building which, therefore, provided a useful shaded area in the warmer weather and a sheltered area when the weather was wet or cold. Another example of child-centred provision!

Safe access to and from the building is also very important. Wherever possible disabled facilities should be provided.

In addition to the physical premises, other aspects of health and safety will need consideration.

Training and professional development

While the Children Act recognizes the need to support day care providers, it gives local authorities a power rather than a duty to provide it (section 3.34 of the Guidance). This means that nationally there is wide variation in the extent and range of support available. For example, some providers will have access to pre-registration training which is either provided or facilitated by the local authority. Others will have no pre-registration training at all. Some local authorities continue to support (either by grants and/or officer involvement) partnership arrangements with local/national early years organizations. It is crucial that if inspection and registration personnel are to be effective they also need access to ongoing training and professional development opportunities.

The range of early years services is very diverse; many aim to keep their costs low in order to make them affordable to parents. However, many early years workers still experience very poor pay and conditions. Without the support of the local authority access to training can be very expensive and difficult to obtain, leading to fragmentation. Where day care facilities are subsidized by employers, pay, conditions and access to ongoing training is generally better than for other services. When a provider has to meet the full costs of running the service through the fees they charge and expenditure must not exceed income, it is very difficult to budget for ongoing training and development while still providing an affordable service. Some local authorities make it a condition of registration that a policy on training and development is required, but by itself this is no guarantee of access to suitable training/professional development.

The introduction of National Vocational Qualifications (or Scottish Vocational Qualifications) was seen as a major step forward and was welcomed as giving experienced practitioners lacking a childcare qualification an opportunity to obtain and progress within their chosen field. Unfortunately, access to courses offering 'underpinning' knowledge and the cost of the assessment procedures has been somewhat prohibitive, despite some excellent attempts to establish cost-effective assessment centres. The Rumbold Report (DES 1990: 24) states:

> We welcome the work of the National Council for Vocational Qualifications (NCVQs) towards establishing agreed standards for childcare workers, including those in educational settings. We believe that, given

adequate resourcing, it could bring about a significant rationalisation in the patterns of training. It should also improve the status of early years workers through recognition of the complex range and high levels of the skills involved, and by opening up prospects for further training and career progression.

Because of the wide diversity of provision the ideologies of the service providers may vary. For example, some playgroups may see themselves as providing social opportunities and play provision for children and can fail to recognize the learning opportunities for the children attending. Child-minders often describe themselves as providing a home-from-home service, but again may fail to recognize the learning opportunities they offer. Nurseries differ tremendously in that some operate on a thematic-based approach similar to primary school practice; others may not plan the curriculum, believing that the children should have the freedom to choose their own play activities. Some prefer to use more structured approaches such as High-Scope, while local authority social services nurseries have traditionally been seen as being health- and care-orientated, with the emphasis being on the physical, emotional and social well-being of the child. I see it as my job to help extend educarers' knowledge and skills and to raise awareness of possible professional development opportunities, while acknowledging and valuing this diversity.

Part 2: Inspection under the Education Act 1992

In Part 1 Shirley has given an overview of the requirements under the Children Act. She has explained the ways in which these inspections look for a broad range of educare issues. I am now going to explore the process of Ofsted inspection, which, although also concerned with broad educare issues, is much more focused on education. It is also a more formal approach involving a team of inspectors.

The Framework for Inspection used by Ofsted, strictly speaking, applies to children who are 4 to 5 but nurseries have always admitted 2- to 3-year-olds; the suitability of provision for them is also being inspected. Of course this raises the usual question about the validity of using watered-down recipes for younger children instead of altogether different ones! However, readers may draw their own conclusions about the process of a section 10 inspection and how it might meet the needs of staff and children under 3.

Despite the demise of the nursery voucher scheme it seems likely that nursery inspections will continue alongside section 10 inspections. Since my major involvement is with section 10, this will be the focus of the following discussion. I am now going to describe the inspection process from both the staff's and the inspector's perspectives in order to draw out the professional development issues.

Getting ready for the inspection

The time available for preparing for the inspection of a nursery is anything from six weeks to one year depending upon when Ofsted inform the nursery school they are being inspected. During the pre-inspection period I will have visited the nursery and met the head teacher, staff and the governing body both to explain the purpose of the inspection and, most importantly, to begin to build a professional relationship with each. For a considerable time before the inspection period, which is usually about three days in the nursery, I will be gathering information about the nursery to enable me to raise some issues for the inspection. These may include hypotheses which need to be tested and questions for which I seek answers while in the nursery. These questions are linked directly to the Framework for Inspection, which lays down exactly the range of information required during the inspection. This may sound very mechanistic and a long way from the children who are the recipients of the nursery education, but let me assure you that it is not like this at all. The easiest analogy I can make is that of being a detective and searching for the evidence to help me reach a series of judgements related directly to the quality of the education received by the children.

I will need to make judgements about the educational standards achieved by the children in the nursery setting and consider the strengths and weaknesses in the teaching and a range of other aspects. Prior to doing any of these, however, I need to establish an effective working relationship with the nursery, be sensitive to their concerns and circumstances and create a climate of mutual understanding in which issues can be shared in a professional manner. To this end, generating a strong sense of partnership between the registered inspector and the head of the nursery is vitally important.

The information required by the inspector prior to the inspection should represent no more than the nursery has in place already. However, the reality tends to be that nurseries get quite a long warning of their intended inspection and use this as a target for getting certain procedures in place. Where the information is available the head teacher usually wishes to give it to the inspection team. However, we all need to remember that it is not the documentation which is being inspected but the impact that this may have on the quality of the education received by the children. A typical list given to the nursery by the registered inspector includes the following:

- a copy of the school brochure;
- a copy of the school development plan;
- a copy of the most recent annual report of the head teacher to the governing body;
- the most recent governing body report to parents, and statements of the governing body's policies;
- copies of any policy statements on matters such as admission, assessment, annual reviews and reassessment for pupils with statements of special education needs;
- attendance, behaviour and discipline and equal opportunities policies;
- copies of curriculum policy statements and long- and medium-term curriculum plans;

- the staff handbook;
- a copy of the routines of the day with timings;
- staff job descriptions;
- the staff development policy, showing how needs are identified and provision made, and details of in-service training undertaken by each member of staff in the past three years;
- information about links with outside agencies.

This information is collected from the nursery and distributed to the inspectors with responsibility for those areas during the week of the inspection to enable a pre-inspection commentary to be completed.

Another important aspect of the inspection is gathering the views of parents from a parental questionnaire and a meeting held just before the inspection. This is an agenda-led meeting covering the following areas: the attainment and progress made by the children, the attitudes and values promoted by the nursery, the information provided by the school for parents, the help and guidance provided to the children by the nursery, the children's behaviour, the part parents are encouraged to play in the life of the school, and the ways in which the nursery deals with parents' suggestions and complaints. As the meeting is only for parents the discussion is usually full and frank and provides an insightful portrayal of the nursery. The views of the parents are shared with the head teacher and the chair of the governing body.

Already you can see that a comprehensive picture of the nursery is emerging. The inspection team will meet prior to the inspection to share their pre-inspection views. This is important for a variety of reasons. Usually at this stage, I (as the registered inspector) am the only person who has had contact with the nursery. I am able to give the team a description of the characteristics of the nursery and raise any issues which the school themselves have identified as important and that they wish the inspection team to investigate further. For example, one nursery school I inspected had prioritized the outdoor environment within their school development plan for that year: they wanted the inspectors to support their evaluation of this area in terms of its contribution to children's learning in all areas of the curriculum, not just physical development.

Undoubtedly getting ready for an inspection may be an intense and stressful time for the head and staff. As one head teacher said, 'It's like getting ready for important visitors. When we do this at home we make sure we put on our very best show': an interesting comparison which very clearly encapsulates part of what the nursery is preparing themselves for. One should remember, though, that the effects of the provision and practice on the quality of education the children receive are the product of much longer-term preparation and the vision of the head teacher and the staff. Nevertheless, staff and head teachers generally set themselves very high expectations for the inspection week, wishing to reveal all their strengths and provide opportunities for the children to demonstrate their capabilities. Staff meetings will be a regular feature of this preparation time as policy statements are revised, rewritten and sometimes written in time for the inspection. The impending inspection may act as a tremendous motivator to complete all those tasks which keep getting further and further down the school's list of priorities.

The inspection week

In a nursery school the inspectors will usually spend about three days in the nursery. During this time they will observe activities, talk with the children about what they are doing and look at the products the children have completed. Very often this is in the form of photographs or it may be collated in a record of achievement or pupil profile. Discussions will be timetabled with staff, the governors (or whoever has overall responsibility for the financial management), and others involved in the work of the nursery. As the manager of the inspection I have to be aware of several key principles which inspectors must adhere to. This is referred to as the Code of Conduct for Inspectors and includes:

- carrying out their work with professionalism, integrity and courtesy;
- evaluating the work of the nursery objectively;
- reporting honestly and fairly;
- communicating clearly and frankly;
- acting in the best interests of the pupils at the school;
- respecting the confidentiality of the personal information received during the inspection.

(Ofsted 1995: 9)

At this point I wish to return to the observation of activities and other aspects going on in the nursery because this is the area in which being an inspector has contributed most significantly to my own professional development. As an early years educator, the observation of children has always been very central to my practice for all sorts of reasons. Observing to help assess what the children are able to do is a fundamental assessment strategy in the early years. As Mary Jane Drummond (1993: 187) concludes, when assessing young children's learning 'we need to describe what there is to see, understand what we see and put that understanding to good use'.

The Ofsted style of observation of young children is not dissimilar. Inspectors complete an observation form for every session or lesson they observe. There are four categories against which evidence is gathered and judgements are made:

- *teaching* – what adults do when interacting with children;
- *response* – made by the children to the activity;
- *attainment* – how well the activity enables the children to meet the desirable outcomes for children's learning (SCAA 1996) and what the children are doing;
- *progress* – what can the children do now that they were unable to do earlier, and are the children progressing in line with what can be expected for children of that age.

Ofsted have provided clear criteria as well as guidance on applying the criteria to inspections. In relation to the education of children under 5 there is additional support provided in the Ofsted *Primary Subject Guidance* (1996).

Teaching

Inspecting and making a judgement on the quality of teaching requires inspectors to:

- observe staff and other adults working with children;
- judge the extent to which the staff have good knowledge and understanding of the needs of younger children as well as the curriculum and learning outcomes;
- observe and take account of the way in which different activities are planned and structured, taking account of the need for children to have some opportunities to initiate activities and take responsibility;
- judge the extent to which the staff and other adults plan and work together;
- judge the extent to which all the adults present sensitively support, reinforce and extend children's responses, using their assessments to enable children to grow in confidence and learn from their mistakes;
- observe how well the available space (in and out of doors), materials and equipment are organized and used to give children a broad and stimulating range of activities.

The above criteria are used in conjunction with those relating to the quality of teaching listed in the *Framework for Inspection* (Ofsted 1995).

There are dangers within the inspection process if inexperienced practitioners are given responsibility for making judgements about the quality of teaching without being able to understand how, for example, high expectations manifest themselves in a teaching situation with young children. Although the criteria are listed and must be followed, it takes a lot of experience both to know that high expectations may be revealed through the questions asked of the children and to understand the nature of the different questions asked. Do these questions challenge the children and encourage them to think, pose questions of their own and solve problems? Are the children encouraged to be independent? Does the adult explain and instruct the children appropriately? Are the resources provided for learning suitable, in that the children are able to use their senses, engage in exploratory play with materials and enter into dialogue with an informed and interested adult? The research findings of Sylva *et al.* (1980), Meadows and Cashdan (1988) and Munn and Schaffer (1993) all highlight the importance of the adult role in children's learning. Understanding the subtleties of that role takes experience and objectivity.

The observation forms constitute a substantial part of the record of evidence in a nursery. They are analysed and overall grades given for teaching, attainment and progress. Response is also analysed; behaviour and personal development are included in the section of the report dealing with pupils' attitudes to learning.

Staff are interviewed and views on their work and roles are considered, along with the head teachers' management and leadership role.

Response

Central to the inspection process is the observation of children. Inspectors are trained to focus on the responses the children make to the experiences provided, by judging the extent to which the children are interested in what they are doing, can sustain concentration, apply themselves to what they are doing and generally are beginning to form constructive relationships with each other and the adults in and around the nursery school. They also observe the way in which children behave in and around the nursery; inspectors also evaluate children's familiarity with the routines of the day which enables them to take some responsibility for their own learning.

Attainment

It is important for inspectors to be familiar with the *Desirable Outcomes for Children's Learning* (SCAA 1996). Indeed, it is necessary to know more than this in order to understand learning outcomes in a nursery environment. For example, the traditional practice of helping children learn their alphabet by repeated drilling is likely to be counterproductive for most young children unless they are led to understand, within a literary context, what the letters represent. An experienced inspector inexperienced in early years could be forgiven for interpreting 'They recognise letters of the alphabet by shape and sound' (SCAA 1996: 3) as children rote learning their alphabet. Thus the knowledge and understanding of the inspector in this area of learning is as crucial as that of the adult educator who enables the children to attain that particular level of competence.

When attempting to make a judgement on the children's attainment, the focus of observation shifts from the contextual features of the learning environment – such as the resourcing, role of the adult and social aspects of the children's development – to a consideration of what the children are demonstrating they know, understand and can do. This requires direct observation of what the children are doing: how well the children listen to and watch each other and adults; their ability to use materials and equipment constructively and imaginatively; how they are able to represent and record their learning by drawing, mark-making, making models or painting; and listening and talking to the children as they work.

Inevitably, the role of the adult has a considerable impact upon the levels which children attain. For instance, when adults engage with the children in role play they will support and encourage the development of imagination and children's oral language; where adults are seen reading with children in small groups and individually – both spontaneously and in a planned way – the children will tend to be more enthusiastic and able to engage with activities.

Progress

This is the final section which inspectors complete as they write an observation form. In order to do this, inspectors need to have found out what knowledge and skills the children have when beginning in the nursery. Baseline assessments carried out by staff when children begin at the nursery are useful for inspectors because they contribute to their own judgements about progress. An example of this comes from my own research in an inner-city nursery unit with a high percentage of children entering the nursery with English as an additional language. A child identified as a focus for my observations was seen on entry to the nursery class to be unable to relate to her peers or communicate (verbally or through gestures) with an adult or peers. She exhibited considerable levels of anxiety. Several weeks into the term the same child has begun to respond to the activities available in a solitary manner. She is now able to relate to one other adult in the nursery (sometimes speaking in Urdu) and copies the English words shared while labelling common objects in a picture book (Rodger 1997).

After the inspection

Within a week the inspection report is completed in a draft form and feedback is provided to the head teacher and governing body (or appropriate authority). Some indication of the outcomes of the inspection may have already been given to some staff and the head teacher of the nursery before the inspection team left the nursery, so there should be no surprises for the nursery at this stage. At this point the professional development opportunities for the staff are identified. The *main findings* of the report are shared with the nursery. They cover:

- A summary of the main inspection judgements on the educational standards achieved by the children. This includes attainment and progress towards the desirable outcomes for children's learning, also the attitudes, behaviour and personal development of the children.
- An evaluation of the nursery's effectiveness in promoting high standards through the quality of education provided, concentrating in particular upon the quality of teaching, and including the spiritual, moral, social and cultural development of the children and the effectiveness with which the school's resources are managed.

Arising from the main findings the *key issues for action* are identified for the nursery to address in constructing their action plan. Often these issues are confirmation of targets within the school development plan and help to support decisions already taken by the nursery. They will tend to be few in number and focus on areas where there is a need for improvement. They need to be practical and achievable by the nursery. The issues will be given in an order of priority which reflects their importance in improving the children's attainment.

The nursery have 40 working days in which to draw up their action plan, which they then allow parents to see. This is an important element in the development of the nursery and provides opportunity for collaboration between all staff and the governors or the local education authority. As an inspector my involvement with the nursery is ended.

Being an inspector has provided me with a welcome professional development opportunity which has enabled me to increase my understanding of the factors which contribute to high quality early years education. Prior to being an inspector most of my thinking about these issues was based on my teaching experiences and interpretations of research, particularly Bruner's (1975) emphasis on the importance of the adult as a scaffolder of children's learning, Meadows and Cashdan's (1988) work on tutorial dialogue, Sylva *et al.*'s Oxford pre-school research (1980) and the work of Hohmann and Weikart (1995) for the HighScope research project.

The most significant factors contributing to quality educare for our younger children now seem to me to include the following:

- an increased understanding of the nature of children's learning and the factors which contribute to this, such as a learning environment which accommodates the need for plenty of space, freedom to move around and make choices both inside and outside;
- the opportunity for children to work closely with adults who encourage, praise, challenge, question and instruct children as they begin to master the range of social, physical, technological and intellectual skills and processes required to function in today's society;
- the role of the head teacher as a team builder, visionary, encourager, trainer, manager and organizer, especially in relation to the wide range of professionals involved in the early years of education.

I believe that inspection helps the nursery staff to appreciate these factors and also brings the benefits of:

- public recognition of the high quality of a lot of the work in nurseries;
- the opportunity to engage in professional debate with outsiders about many of the positive features of the nursery school, and to discuss options for the development and improvement of practices where required;
- time to step back and reflect on practice, review it and possibly consider alternative teaching or management strategies resulting from drawing up an action plan following the inspection.

I am well aware that the period following an inspection can be an anticlimax for the staff and there may follow a period of stability rather than growth. However this period of consolidation is important for reflection and identifying future priorities.

Conclusion

Readers will have realized that both of us regard the process of inspection as something beneficial rather than an event to be feared. We feel that staff may find the inspection criteria useful in considering their own practice and provision, and in identifying staff development needs. Professional development opportunities should not neglect the needs of children under 3. We leave you with a reminder from Chris Athey (1990: 7): 'in the early stages, especially if he/she has to cope with school [a child] must have the mastery of the social skills necessary for engaging in the instructional process'.

References

Abbott, L. and Rodger, R. (1994) *Quality Education in the Early Years*. Buckingham: Open University Press.

Athey, C. (1990) *Extending Thought in Young Children – A Parent–Teacher Partnership*. London: Paul Chapman.

Bruner, J. S. (1975) From communication to language: a psychological perspective, *Cognition*, 3: 255–87.

Department of Education and Science [DES] (1990) *Starting with Quality: the Report of the Committee of Inquiry into the Quality of Educational Experience Offered to 3 and 4-year-olds*. London: HMSO.

Department of Health [DoH] (1989) *The Children Act.*. London: HMSO.

Department of Health (1991) *The Children Act 1989 Guidance and Regulations, Vol. 2: Family Support, Day Care and Educational Provision for Young Children*. London: HMSO.

Drummond, M. J. (1993) *Assessing Children's Learning*. London: David Fulton Publishing.

Hohmann, M. and Weikart, D. (1995) *Educating Young Children*. Ypsilanti, MI: HighScope Press.

Meadows, S. and Cashdan, A. (1988) *Helping Children Learn : Contributions to a Cognitive Curriculum*. London: David Fulton.

Moss, P., Owen, C., Statham, J., Bull, J., Cameron, C. and Candappa, M. (1995) *Survey of Day Care Providers in England and Wales* – A Working Paper from the TCRU Children Act Project, Thomas Coram Research Unit. London: HMSO.

Munn, P. and Schaffer, H. R. (1993) Literacy and numeracy events in social interactive contexts, *International Journal of Early Years Education*, 1(3): 61–79.

Ofsted (1995) *Framework for Inspection of the Educational Provision for Four Year Old Children*. London: HMSO.

Ofsted (1996) *Areas of Learning for the Under Fives in Primary Subject Guidance for Registered Inspectors*. London: HMSO.

Pascal, C. (1994) *Effective Early Learning Research Project*. Worcester College of Higher Education.

Rodger, R. (1997) Using structured play to promote language development in the early years, in R. Halsall (ed.) *Teacher Research and School Improvement*. Buckingham: Open University Press.

School Curriculum and Assessment Authority [SCAA] (1996) *Nursery Education: Desirable Outcomes for Children's Learning on Entering Compulsory Education*. London: DfEE.

Sylva, K., Roy, C. and Painter M. (1980) *Childwatching at Playgroup and Nursery School*. London: Grant McIntyre.

Concluding thoughts – drawing the threads together

Lesley Abbott

In attempting to draw together some of the main points which have emerged from the chapters which make up this book we freely admit that we have attempted to represent a diversity of views. In doing so we have hoped both to highlight and celebrate differences. There is a variety of views expressed in the contributions offered by a range of people from very different backgrounds. We hope that each one has offered a challenge. The perspectives from which the chapters are both written and read will add to the richness and variety which characterizes the early years field.

The question is, then, whether the 'diversity' of the early years field is something to be celebrated. Gillian Shephard, the former Secretary of State for Education, clearly felt so when she said that early childhood services in the UK are 'offering parents a rich range and diversity from which to choose' (Shephard 1995). Our problem with this relates to questions of access to this choice, and also issues of unevenness. Indeed, the overall patchwork quality of early years services means that there are many areas of good quality, as we hope we have shown, but so many parents do not find themselves in a position to take advantage of these, for reasons including location, oversubscription, financial criteria and so on. We therefore understand the feelings of Ball when he calls the levels of provision overall a 'national disgrace' (Ball 1994). The hope must be that by presenting the views of the contributors, all of whom share a commitment to quality care and education for the under-threes, quality services can be developed which meet the needs of more children and their parents.

'Compartmentalization' is another word which has bedevilled the early years field. The National Curriculum has been instrumental in encouraging practitioners to view children's learning under subject headings and to deny the interrelatedness of both learning and development. The introduction of *Desirable Outcomes for Children's Learning on Entering Compulsory Schooling* (SCAA 1996) compounds the problem further and threatens to exert undue pressure on the curriculum experiences of the under-threes. Just as work and play have long been polarized, the roles of early years workers have been separated in ways which have been counter-productive. Training has taken place in different institutions according to the role of the worker and their place in the hierarchy! Funding has been clearly earmarked for one kind of training as distinct from another, thus separating rather than bringing people together.

Fortunately, things are changing, as Chapters 1 and 2 describe. New training initiatives are recognizing and responding to the need to break down barriers and to end the compartmentalization that has prevented real interdisciplinary exchange and development from taking place.

The Rumbold Report *Starting with Quality* (DES 1990) was instrumental in pointing to the need for collaboration and coordination, both of services for young children and their families, and of training opportunities for early years workers:

> We see as essential needs: a closer linkage between the three strands of health, care and education in initial and in-service training. A pattern of vocational training and qualifications for childcare workers which will bridge the gap between the vocational and academic qualifications, safe-guarding both the rigour and relevance of initial training for teachers of the under-fives; and affording improved opportunities of in-service training for childcare workers in educational settings
>
> (DES 1990: 27)

Hazareesingh *et al.* (1989: 8–9) put forward a powerful argument for a holistic approach to education in the early years, at two different but inter-related levels: at the conceptual level of linking the diverse strands of social inequality, and at the practical level of a positive approach to curriculum for early years:

> This philosophy . . . sees the division of human experience into rigidly separated categories as inconsistent with the unity and spontaneity of experience and attributes this fragmentation of experience to social control, which enshrines and legitimizes some forms of knowledge and excludes others . . . In relation to young children, a holistic approach signifies valuing the 'whole' child, i.e. recognising the inter-relatedness of the child's emotional, social, spiritual and cognitive qualities, while also being aware that the harmonious growth of these qualities depends on valuing the child's sense of belonging to a particular family and community.

Throughout this book the focus has been on the adults who work with young children and on the tremendous responsibility which this places upon them. Responsibility to be the 'best' in whatever capacity they are operating – whether as parent, childminder, nursery nurse, teacher, play-group leader, nursery owner, inspector, social worker or support worker.

Responsibility for providing the 'best' in terms of appropriate training and professional support has also been a key aim. Anne-Marie Graham in Chapter 2 highlights ways in which a new training initiative is breaking down barriers and providing access to training previously denied to a large number of women. Collaboration between a local authority and higher education is an important step in providing access to the 'climbing frame' which allows potential to be realized. She presents evidence of students who are 'empowered' and of the effects that access to relevant support and training is having on their lives, at both a personal and professional level.

The report of the RSA Early Learning Inquiry (Ball 1994) asserts that 'a nation's future rests more and more on the quality of children's early learning experiences'. In the same report Sylva (1994: 127) asks, 'Can we afford not to give our children a good start in life?' The answer to this question, which comes forth loud and clear from each chapter in this book, is 'no'. A 'good start' is the entitlement of every child and the responsibility of every adult. Sadly it is not always the view of politicians: there are strong contradictions between policy and practice at both national and local levels and between personal and professional responses to perceived need. Jean Coward highlights some of these responses in her chapter in which she demonstrates a nursery coordinator's very sensitive handling of a professional development programme, which takes staff from a position in which the importance of working with the under-threes is not readily accepted, to the recognition that 'this is what it's all about!'

A sharing of views and perspectives on key issues in the early years field is one of the principal aims of this book. One such issue is the shortage of male workers and the continuing debate about the employment of men to work with very young children. Terry Gould argues that high profile measures should be taken to reduce negative or obstructive policies and practices in order to encourage an increase in male involvement, in what has hitherto been viewed as a female profession. The (British) Labour Party document *Early Excellence – A Head Start for Every Child* (1996: 14) recognizes this as an equal opportunities issue to which they make a strong commitment: 'Labour wishes to encourage more men to work in this field – providing role models and the necessary balance – and this must be reflected in our training, screening and promotional programme.' Exactly how this aim is to be achieved is not clear but it will be interesting to see whether success can be achieved where others have failed.

A similar commitment is made in the Labour Party's early years development plan to meeting the needs of all children. Sylvia Phillips presents interesting case studies of families attempting to cope, in different ways, with the demands of children with special educational needs. The Labour Party document (1996: 14) promises a commitment to the provision of 'effective and efficient services for children with special needs', with specific attention paid to 'the training needs of those who work with these children'.

Communication is the principal aim of this book and the overarching title 'Early interactions' is intended to capture and demonstrate the importance of listening to, valuing and acting upon the views of all those involved in the process of early childhood care and education.

In his chapter on child protection, John Powell emphasizes the importance of 'voice' and of listening, not only to others, but of paying heed to oneself. 'I am listening' is a very powerful message which all early years practitioners should convey not only to children and parents but to colleagues and the wider multi-professional community. It is a theme reiterated by Chris Marsh, as she shares her research findings on ways in which educators develop relationships with parents and children. The adoption of the key worker system is one way in which staff in the centres in which she has been involved sought to ensure that a listening ear was always available. What this chapter demonstrates is the importance of the professional accepting the responsibility to meet other people's needs (i.e. those of the parent) 'by making their expertise available to the parents for their consideration' (Rodd 1994).

Similarly, Jenny Lively and Karen McMahon share expertise, experience and authority with the many adults who accompany young children to the toddler group. Rodd (1994: 153–4), however, raises an important point for the early childhood professional, that of meeting her own needs:

The early childhood professional also meets her own needs by recognising the value of training, experience and philosophy as information sources for making decisions about how, when and where children's development and learning can be facilitated. The leader who effectively creates a partnership with parents in early childhood services possesses the confidence to articulate her philosophy concerning care and early education while simultaneously acknowledging parental rights, information, theories, expectations, problems and pressures. In this way, the perceived complementary expertise of both parent and professional can be brought to meet the needs of the situation in mutually agreed ways.

Sharing expertise and experience is not always the way in which the inspection process is viewed. Both scepticism and criticism have been the more immediate reactions to a process which may generate feelings of both inadequacy and anxiety. However, in sharing their experiences of inspection, as social services and Ofsted inspectors, and now as members of the 'new breed' of nursery inspectors, Rosemary Rodger and Shirley Barnes argue that the benefits to be gained from the inspection process are twofold. First, it provides a clear focus for staff development within centres; second, it is a powerful force in the professional development of the inspector. The mechanistic views of inspection are replaced by those which lean more to issues of quality. An analogy is that of a detective finding evidence to help in reaching decisions about the quality of the education received by the children. Emphasis is placed upon sensitivity, effective working relationships and the 'need to establish a climate of mutual understanding in which issues of professional concern can be shared'.

It has been argued that inspection *should* lead to improvement. One of the strengths of the Ofsted inspections of establishments where there are children under 3 – i.e. nursery schools – is that 'the youngest children receive an entitlement to an inspection process that looks at standards of achievement, quality of education, the efficiency of the school and the children's spiritual, moral, social and cultural development' (Ensing 1996: 11). She does, however, sound a note of caution with regard to the new 'light touch' inspections (DfEE 1995): 'Too light a touch, that is, of minimal requirements, may lead to minimal quality provision and would reduce children's rights' (Ensing 1996: 11). The effects of the inspection process where under-threes are concerned have yet to be experienced. This will be an important area for research.

Throughout this book, quality has been an important concern. In an earlier publication (Abbott and Rodger 1994), many of the authors writing in this book attempted to define 'quality' in terms of the particular work in which they were then engaged. They experienced the same difficulties as many others (Pascal *et al.* 1994; Watt 1994; Williams 1995) in defining what Moss (1994: 6) describes as 'dynamic concept' definitions which 'evolve over time'.

What does emerge in the continuing search for quality in practice and definition is the recognition that, as Moss also points out, definitions of quality are 'values based and relative', and that all 'stakeholders' have a significant voice. One of the problems is ensuring that the voice is heard!

Both of the books under the heading 'Early interactions' have provided a forum for the voices of the stakeholders in early years 'educare' to be heard. We hope that people have listened, and that as a consequence the quality of the lives of young children and the adults who work with them has been enriched.

References

Abbott, L. and Rodger, R. (1994) *Quality Education in the Early Years*. Buckingham: Open University Press.

Ball, C. (1994) *Start Right: The Importance of Early Learning*. London: Royal Society for the Encouragement of the Arts, Manufacture and Commerce.

Department for Education and Employment/Department of Health [DfEE] (1995) *Quality Assurance Regime for Institutions which Redeem Vouchers for Pre-school Education*. London: DfEE.

Department for Education and Science [DES] (1990) *Starting with Quality, the Report of the Committee of Inquiry into the Quality of Educational Experience Offered to 3 and 4-year-olds*. London: HMSO.

Ensing, J. (1996) Inspection of early years in schools, in C. Nutbrown (ed.) *Respectful Educators – Capable Learners – Children's Rights and Early Education*. London: Paul Chapman Publishing.

Hazareesingh, S., Simms, K. and Anderson, P. (1989) *Educating the Whole Child – A Holistic Approach to Education in Early Years*. London: Building Blocks/Save the Children.

Labour Party (1996) *Early Excellence – A Head Start for Every Child*. London: Labour Party.

Moss, P. (1994) Defining quality: values, stakeholders and process, in P. Moss and A. Pence (eds) *Valuing Quality in Early Childhood Services*. London: Paul Chapman Publishing.

Pascal, C., Bertram, A. and Ramsden, F. (1994) *The Effective Early Learning Research Project: The Quality, Evaluation and Development Process*. Worcester College of Higher Education.

Rodd, J. (1994) *Leadership in Early Childhood: The Pathway to Professionalism*. Buckingham: Open University Press.

School Curriculum and Assessment Authority [SCAA] (1996) *Desirable Outcomes for Young Children's Learning on Entering Compulsory Schooling.* London: SCAA.

Shephard, G. (1995) Letter to Sir Ron Dearing, in SCAA, *Desirable Outcomes for Young Children's Learning on Entering Compulsory Schooling.* London: School Curriculum and Assessment Authority.

Sylva, K. (1994) The impact of early learning on children's later development, in C. Ball (ed.) *Start Right – The Importance of Early Learning.* London: Royal Society for the Encouragement of the Arts, Manufacture and Commerce.

Watt, J. (ed.) (1994) *Early Education: The Quality Debate.* Edinburgh: Scottish Academic Press.

Williams, P. (1995) Making Sense of Quality – A Review of Approaches to Quality in Early Childhood Services. London: National Children's Bureau.

Index

abuse
  categories of, 135–6
  protection from, *see* protection from
    abuse
academic training routes, 22
access
  to nursery places, 103–4
  to training, 31–2
accessibility of equipment/materials,
  149–50
accidents/injuries, 123
action plan, 159–60
Adams, J., 68
admission process, 96, 97, 99
Advanced Diploma in Child Care and
  Education (ADCE), 25, 38, 40–1, 47,
  49
adventure, 148
age
  early years provision and, 18–19
  segregation by, 99–100
  staffing ratios, 145
  transition between groups, 102
agenda, 133
'All About Me' book, 56–7
Andersson, B.E., 53
'Anna and Charlotte' (case study), 90–3
assessment
  baseline, 159
  initial for child protection, 134–5
  SEN, 80–2, 85–6
Athey, C., 57, 161

attachment, 100–1, 139
attainment, 156, 158
attendance register, 122
attitudes, 24, 53
  towards SEN, 93
Audit Commision, 17–20, 82
audit of the environment (nursery),
  55–6
autism, 90–3
autonomy, 55, 98

babies, 101, 121
Ball, C., 16, 24, 25, 105, 162, 164
Barcelona Education Institute, 45
Barnes, S., 99, 100
'Barry' (case study), 63–4
baseline assessments, 159
BEd courses, 29
behaviour patterns (schema), 56, 57–8
behaviour problems, 86–7, 90–3
belief systems/values, 133
'bodily dominion', 100–1
book library, 125, 126
books, 121, 122
Bright Sparks project, 44
Broadhead, P., 62
Bruce, T., 54
Bruner, J.S., 160
BTEC, 25
buildings/grounds, 55–6, 66, 151–2
Burgess, G., 9–10

CACHE, 25, 41
career choices, 65
careers officers/teachers, 75
carers: number of, 99
    see also educarers; parents
Carnegie Task Force, 1
case conference process, 138–9
Cashdan, A., 160
central play area, 101–2
Certificate in Child Care and Education
    (CCE), 25
chairs, 150
challenge, 148
Chandler, T., 73
'Charlotte and Anna' (case study), 90–3
child-centred approach, 54–5, 57–8, 144
child development, 85–6, 146
child development team, 79, 80–2
child protection, *see* protection from
    abuse
childcare workers, 15–16, 17–18
    see also educarers
childminders, 15–16, 26, 36, 145
children
    accessing child's voice, 131–3, 138
    interactions between, 144–5
    interactions between adults and, 144
    involvement in planning/choosing
        activities, 149
    observation of responses in Ofsted
        inspection, 156, 158
    parents' behaviour towards, 130, 133
    recognition of developmental needs,
        146
    responses to male educarers, 62–4
    sensitivity to needs of, 55–6, 101
    structuring/supporting children's
        learning, 147–8
    what toddler group offers for, 119
Children Act 1989, 78–9
    child protection, 134, 135, 136
    registration and inspection, 141–53
'Children also Need Men' campaign, 75
'Children Under Three and Their
    Learning' course, 55–6
children's centre, 95–104
City of Salford Social Services and
    Education Departments, 51, 52
Clarke-Hall, Sir William, 136
Code of Conduct for Inspectors, 156
combined nursery centre, 13–14

'Come into Childcare Services You Men'
    campaign, 75
communication, 131–3, 138, 150
Community Insight, 28
community nursery centres, 51–9, 60
compartmentalization, 162–3
construction activities, 121
continuing professional development,
    see professional development
continuity, 97, 103, 103–4, 146
costs of day care/pre-school education,
    18–19
Council for Awards in Children's Care
    and Education (CACHE), 25, 41
counselling, 53
Cowley, L., 97
creative play, 121
curriculum, 149
Curtis, A., 16, 20

day care provision, 18
Denmark, 45–6, 68, 75
    Children's Welfare Commission, 4
Department for Education: *Code of
    Practice*, 79, 81, 84, 85–6
Department of Health: Guidance for
    Children Act, 78, 143–4, 146,
    148–9, 151, 152
development, child, 85–6, 146
developmental plans, 82
developmental play programme, 79
Diploma in Nursery Nursing (DNN), 25
Diploma in Playground Practice, 26
Diploma in Pre-School Practice (DPP),
    26
disadvantage, systemic, 66–7
discrimination, gender, 62, 66–7
'disordered' development, 85
displays, 113, 149–50
diversity of provision, 162
dolls, 122
Dowling, M., 69
Drummond, M.J., 156

Early Childhood Forum, 8, 16, 24
Early Childhood Studies degree, 17, 30,
    37, 38, 39, 49
    Young Europeans Module, 46
Early Years Curriculum Group, 54
early years provision, 18–19, 162
Early Years Trainers Anti-Racist Network,
    28

early years workers, 15–16, 18–19
  see also educarers
educare principle, 2, 17–25, 143
educarers, 15–16, 17–18
  male, *see* male educarers
  meeting own needs, 165
  partnership with parents, 81–2,
    123–4, 146–7, 165
  registration and inspection, 146,
    146–7
  role in child protection, 130–1, 132–3,
    137–8, 138–9
  role and SEN, 84
  role in toddler group, 120, 123–4
Education Act 1981, 79
Education Act 1992, 141, 153–60
Education Act 1993, 79
Education (School Premises) Regulations
    1981, 151
educational qualifications, 53
Elfer, P., 99, 100, 101, 103, 104
Elliot, M., 62
emergency protection order, 136
'Emma' (case study), 130–5, 136–7, 139
emotional abuse, 136
emotional needs, 101
employment/work, 75
Ensing, J., 9, 165–6
entitlements, 4–5
environment, physical, 55–6, 66, 151–2
equal opportunities, 70, 121–2, 148–9
Equal Opportunities Agency, 62
equipment: organization and
    accessibility of, 149–50
European Community/Union (EC/EU),
    8, 38, 39, 45–7, 65
experience, 35–8, 146

Fell, N., 70
friendships, 103, 104, 144–5
funding for training, 31–2

games, 122
gender appropriateness, 65–6
gender discrimination, 62, 66–7
gender-segregated labour market, 75
general developmental delay, 85
general practitioners, 82
Goldschmied, E., 56, 61
government, 75
Griffin, S., 27–8, 101

Gross, J., 81
group size, 145

Hall, D.M.B., 80, 85
Hancock, P., 61, 68
happiness, 103
Hazareesingh, S., 163
health and safety, 122–3, 151–2
health services, 78, 79, 86
health visitors, 118
Hevey, D., 16, 20, 24, 25, 31–2
'high prevalence' SEN, 80
HighScope training, 27
Hodges, M., 101
Hohmann, M., 160
holistic approach, 163
Hollywood Park Combined Nursery,
    107, 108–9
  see also toddler group
home-based support services, 79, 92
home-based teaching, 79, 86
home corner, 121, 122
home/nursery books, 147
Home Office, 133, 134, 135–6
Home Start UK, 28
Honig, A., 100–1
hours: daycare and pre-school provision,
    18–19
Hughes, P., 66
Huttenen, E., 95

identification of SEN, 80–2, 85–6
imagination, 148
induction, 96, 97, 99
infant teacher training course, 13
information
  needed by Ofsted, 154–5
  sharing, 113–15, 125, 126
initial assessment, 134–5
injuries/accidents, 123
inspection, 9–10, 141–61, 165–6
  registration and inspection under the
    Children Act 1989, 141–53
  under Education Act 1992, 153–60
inspection report, 159
interdisciplinary training, 7, 17, 24, 30
investigation, 134–5
Ireland, 45–6
  Northern Ireland, 26

Jackson, S., 56, 61
Jensen, J., 61, 65, 68, 70, 72

Jydsk Paedagog-Seminarium, 45

key worker system, 9, 95–106, 165
    community nursery centre, 51–2,
        56–7
    parental perspective, 95–103
    practical difficulties, 103–4
Kids Club Network, 28
Kirklees Early Years Service (KEYS), 38,
    39, 45
knowledge and understanding, 21

labelling, 150
labour market, 75
Labour Party, 164
layout, 111–12
learning
    foundations for, 116–18
    structuring/supporting, 147–8
learning support teacher, 86
listening, 129, 131
local education authority (LEA), 79, 86,
    141–2
'low prevalence' SEN, 80

Mackeith, R., 83
male educarers, 8, 60–77, 164
Manchester Metropolitan University
    (MMU), 24, 54, 123
    'Pathways to Professionalism' course,
        38, 39, 40, 41, 46, 49
'Marie' (case study), 43–5
'Mark Smith' (case study), 87–90
Marsh, C., 95, 103
materials: organization and accessibility,
    149–50
'Matthew' (case study), 69–70
Meadows, S., 160
meal times, 97–8
medical assessment, 80
men, 116
    see also male educarers
messy play, 121
Miller, L., 101
Montessori training, 26–7
Moss, P., 15, 16, 18–19, 20, 144, 166
multi-professional teams, 2, 37
    assessment of SEN, 79, 80–2, 82–3,
        92–3
    case conferences, 138–9
multi-professional training, 7, 17, 24, 30
multicultural awareness, 121–2, 149

National Childminding Association
    (NCMA), 26
National Children's Homes Action for
    Children Report, 67
National Commission on Education, 17,
    31
National Curriculum, 162
National Play Bus Association, 28
National Toy and Leisure Libraries, 28
National Vocational Qualifications
    (NVQs), 25–6, 152–3
    'Pathways to Professionalism' course,
        37–8, 38, 40–1, 47, 49–50
needs
    recognition of children's
        developmental needs, 146
    sensitivity to children's, 55–6, 101
    toddler group and meeting
        everyone's, 116–18
neglect, 136
New Basic Training Playwork Self-Study
    pack, 26
'New Man', 65
NNEB, 37
Northern Ireland, 26
noticeboards, 113–15, 125, 126
NOW initiative, 38, 39, 45–7
nursery nurses, 14, 15–16, 137–8
Nutbrown, C., 4

observation
    assessment of SEN, 85–6
    Ofsted inspection, 156–9
    of schema, 56, 57–8
Ofsted inspections, 153–60, 165–6
    after the inspection, 159–60
    observation, 156–9
    preparation, 154–6
opportunity playgroups, 86
outdoor play area, 151

parents
    and assessment of SEN, 79, 81–2,
        82–3, 84, 86
    behaviour towards children, 130, 133
    and child protection investigations,
        135, 138–9
    demand for training, 39
    development course, 118
    experience, 35–6
    male educarers' relationships with,
        71–2

and Ofsted inspection, 155
partnership with educarers, 81–2,
  123–4, 146–7, 165
perspectives and key worker, 95–103
Preparing for Nursery Group, 127
and toddler group, 111, 116, 118,
  119–20, 123–4
parents' evening, 147
'Pathways to Professionalism in Early
  Childhood Educare' course, 35–50
  aims and objectives of project, 47–50
  EC funding, 8, 38, 39, 45–7
  need for professional training route,
  35–8
  origins, 38–41
  personal experiences, 41–5
patterns of behaviour, 56, 57–8
Penn, H., 15, 16, 18–19, 20, 104
peripatetic support services, 86, 87, 88–9
PGCE courses, 29–30
philosophy statement, 55
physical environment, 55–6, 66, 151–2
physical injury, 136
planning, 120–2
play, 113, 121, 131, 147, 148
  creative, 121
  messy, 121
  representational, 121
playgroup workers, 15–16
preparation for inspection, 154–5
Preparing for Nursery Group, 127–8
Pre-School Learning Alliance, 26
Pre-School Playgroups Association, 26
pre-school provision, 18–19
primary education, 72
primary educators, 97
Pringle, M.K., 16
professional development, 8, 28–9,
  30–2, 51–9
  child-centred approach, 57–8
  key worker system, 56–7
  registration and inspection, 152–3
  toddler group, 123–4
professionalism, 20
  see also 'Pathways to Professionalism
  in Early Childhood Educare' course
programme of activities, 148
progress, 156, 159
protection from abuse, 9, 67–8, 123,
  129–40, 164–5
  accessing a child's voice, 131–3
  case conference process, 138–9

investigation and initial assessment,
  134–5
procedures and practitioners, 136–8
referral and recognition, 133–4
provision, 18–19
  diversity of, 162
Pugh, G., 16, 31, 131

qualifications, 53
  see also training
quality, 3–4, 10, 166
  child-centred approach, 54
  factors contributing to, 143–4, 160
  qualifications and, 53
  of staff, 103
  see also inspection

'Recruitment of Men for Pedagogic
  Training' campaign, 75
referral, 133–4
reflective-practitioner model, 28–9
register, attendance, 122
registration and inspection, 141–61
  Children Act 1989, 141–53
  see also inspection
representational play, 121
respect, 4
response, 156, 158
restrictions on male educarers, 68, 70–1
rights, 4–5
Rodd, J., 165
Ronanstown Women's Group, 45
Rouse, D., 101
Rouse Selleck, D., 131
routines, children's, 98
RSA Early Learning Inquiry Report, 16,
  24, 25, 105, 162, 164
  see also Start Right
Rumbold Report, 30, 70, 119, 147
  knowledge, skills and attitudes, 20–4
  multi-professional training, 14,
  16–17, 163
  NVQs, 152–3
Ruxton, S., 67

'Sadja' (case study), 41–3
safety, health and, 122–3, 151–2
'Sarah' (case study), 64
Save The Children Fund, 28
SCAA, 158, 162
schemas, 56, 57–8
Scotland, 26

security, 100–1, 139
Selleck, D., 99, 103
sexual abuse, 136
Shephard, G., 162
Sheriff, C., 104
siblings, 84, 102–3
significant harm, 134, 136
Simeonsson, R.J., 81–2
Siraj-Blatchford, I., 4, 69, 97, 105
skills, 21–4
Smedley, J., 70
social services departments, 78, 79
social workers, 131–2, 134–5, 136
Spain, 45–6
special educational needs (SEN), 9,
    78–94, 164
  and children under three, 78–9
  identification in nursery, 85–6
  identifying SEN of under-threes, 80–2
  implications for educarers, 84
  parents' perspectives, 79, 81–2, 82–3,
    84, 86
  special educational provision case
    studies, 86–93
speech therapy, 87
stability of staff, 103, 104
staff development time, 55
staffing ratios, 145
Start Right Report, 16, 24, 25, 105, 162,
    164
  see also RSA
statements, 86
statutory assessment, 86
Stearman, K., 65
stereotypes, challenging, 69–71
storage, 150
study community, 39–40
Sweden, 75
Sylva, K., 160, 164
systematic disadvantage, 66–7

teacher education, 29–30
Teaching Certificate, 13
teaching: Ofsted inspection and, 156,
    157–8
Thompson, R.A., 139
timetable of events, 125, 126
toddler group, 9, 107–28

toy library, 124–5
toys: organization and accessibility of,
    149–50
training, 13–34, 163–4
  access and funding, 31–2
  childminders, 26
  continuing professional development,
    see professional development
  'educare' concept, 17–25
  HighScope training, 27
  key issues, 28–9
  models of, 20, 22–3
  Montessori training, 26–7
  multi-professional, 7, 17, 24, 30
  NVQs, 25–6
  other training providers, 27–8
  qualifications and quality of educare,
    53
  registration and inspection, 146,
    152–3
  teacher education, 29–30
  useful contacts, 32–3
  see also 'Pathways to Professionalism
    in Early Childhood Educare' course
training institutions, 74–5
transition between (age) groups/rooms,
    102

UN Convention on the Rights of the
    Child, 5, 9
under-twos unit, 96, 97, 98, 99–100, 102
understanding, knowledge and, 21

values/belief systems, 133
Van der Gaag, N., 65
visual impairment, 87–90
voice: accessing child's, 131–3, 138
voucher scheme, 153

Wales, 26
Webb, L., 32
Weikart, D., 160
welcome, 116
Windle, K., 16
Woodhead, M., 4, 10
work-based training, 23

Young Europeans module, 46

QUALITY EDUCATION IN THE EARLY YEARS

Lesley Abbott and Rosemary Rodger (eds)

Lesley Abbott and her team of contributors identify and explore high quality work (and what shapes it) in early years education. They show us children and adults variously working and playing, talking and communicating, learning and laughing, caring and sharing in a rich tapestry of case studies which highlight quality experiences and interactions. Every chapter is based around a particular case study, each one tackling a different issue: the curriculum, play, assessment, roles and relationships, special needs, partnerships with parents, and equal opportunities.

All the writers work together in early years education on a day-to-day basis enabling them to pool their different expertise to create a balanced but challenging approach. They give inspiring examples of, and outline underlying principles for, quality work and ask important questions of all those involved in the education and care of young children.

Contents
Introduction: The search for quality in the early years – A quality curriculum in the early years: Raising some questions – 'Play is fun, but it's hard work too': The search for quality play in the early years – 'Why involve me?' Encouraging children and their parents to participate in the assessment process – 'It's nice here now': Managing young children's behaviour – 'She'll have a go at anything': Towards an equal opportunities policy – 'We only speak English here, don't we?' Supporting language development in a multilingual context – 'People matter': The role of adults in providing a quality learning environment for the early years – 'You feel like you belong': Establishing partnerships between parents and educators – 'Look at me – I'm only two': Educare for the under threes: The importance of early experience – Looking to the future: Concluding comments – Bibliography – Index.

Contributors
Lesley Abbott, Janet Ackers, Janice Adams, Caroline Barratt-Pugh, Brenda Griffin, Chris Marsh, Sylvia Phillips, Rosemary Rodger, Helen Strahan.

224pp 0 335 19230 0 (Paperback) 0 335 19231 9 (Hardback)

STARTING FROM THE CHILD?
TEACHING AND LEARNING FROM 4 TO 8

Julie Fisher

Early years practitioners currently face a number of dilemmas when planning an education for young children. The imposition of an external curriculum seems to work in opposition to the principles of planning experiences which start from the child. Does this mean that the notion of a curriculum centred on the needs and interests of children is now more rhetoric than reality?

In a practical and realistic way *Starting from the Child?* examines a range of theories about young children as learners and the implications of these theories for classroom practice. Julie Fisher acknowledges the competence of young children when they arrive at school, the importance of building on their early successes and the critical role of adults who understand the individual and idiosyncratic ways of young learners. The book addresses the key issues of planning and assessment, explores the place of talk and play in the classroom and examines the role of the teacher in keeping a balance between the demands of the curriculum and the learning needs of the child.

This is essential reading, not only for early years practitioners, but for all those who manage and make decisions about early learning.

Contents
Competent young learners – Conversations and observations – Planning for learning – The role of the teacher – Encouraging independence – Collaboration and cooperation – The place of play – The negotiated classroom – Planning, doing and reviewing – Evaluation and assessment – References – Index.

192pp   0 335 19556 3 (Paperback)   0 335 19557 1 (Hardback)

THE EXCELLENCE OF PLAY

Janet R. Moyles (ed.)

Child: When I play with my friends we have lots of fun . . . do lots of things . . . think about stuff . . . and . . . well . . .

Adult: Do you think you learn anything?

Child: Heaps and heaps – not like about sums and books and things . . . um . . . like . . . well . . . like *real* things.

Anyone who has observed play for any length of time will recognize that, for young children, play is a tool for learning. Professionals who understand, acknowledge, and appreciate this can, through provision, interaction and intervention in children's play, ensure progression, differentiation and relevance in the curriculum.

The Excellence of Play gathers together authoritative contributors to provide a wide-ranging and key source text reflecting both up-to-date research and current classroom practice. It tackles how we conceptualize play, how we 'place' it in the classroom, how we relate it to the curriculum, and how we evaluate its role in learning in the early years. It will stimulate and inform debate through its powerful argument that 'a curriculum which sanctions and utilizes play is more likely to provide well-balanced citizens of the future as well as happier children in the present'.

Contents
Introduction – Part 1: The culture of play and childhood – Play and the uses of play – Play in different cultures and different childhoods – Sex-differentiated play experiences and children's choices – Play, the playground and the culture of childhood – Part 2: Play, schooling and responsibilities – Play and legislated curriculum. Back to basics: an alternative view – 'Play is ace!' Developing play in schools and classrooms – Fantasy play: a case for adult intervention – Making play work in the classroom – Part 3: Play and the early years curriculum – Play, literacy and the role of the teacher – Experiential learning in play and art – Bulbs, buzzers and batteries: play and science – Mathematics and play – Part 4: Assessing and evaluating play – Evaluating and improving the quality of play – Observing play in early childhood – Play, the universe and everything! – Afterword – References – Index.

Contributors
Lesley Abbott, Angela Anning, Tony Bertram, David Brown, Tina Bruce, Audrey Curtis, Rose Griffiths, Nigel Hall, Peter Heaslip, Jane Hislam, Victoria Hurst, Neil Kitson, Janet R. Moyles, Christine Pascal, Roy Prentice, Jeni Riley, Jane Savage, Peter K. Smith.

240pp 0 335 19068 5 (Paperback)